Black Cilicia

A Study of the Plain of Issus during the Roman and Late Roman Periods

Jennifer Tobin

BAR International Series 1275
2004

Published in 2016 by
BAR Publishing, Oxford

BAR International Series 1275

Black Cilicia

ISBN 978 1 84171 375 5

© J Tobin and the Publisher 2004

Volume Editor: John W Hedges

BAR Publishing is the trading name of British Archaeological Reports (Oxford) Ltd.
British Archaeological Reports was first incorporated in 1974 to publish the BAR
Series, International and British. In 1992 Hadrian Books Ltd became part of the BAR
group. This volume was originally published by John and Erica Hedges Ltd. in
conjunction with British Archaeological Reports (Oxford) Ltd / Hadrian Books Ltd,
the Series principal publisher, in 2004. This present volume is published by BAR
Publishing, 2016.

Printed in England

BAR
PUBLISHING

BAR titles are available from:

BAR Publishing
122 Banbury Rd, Oxford, OX2 7BP, UK
EMAIL   info@barpublishing.com
PHONE   +44 (0)1865 310431
FAX   +44 (0)1865 316916
www.barpublishing.com

TABLE OF CONTENTS

LIST OF ILLUSTRATIONS

The author has created all drawings, maps and photographs, with the exception of Figs. 10, 17 and 47.
All images pertain to Küçük Burnaz unless otherwise noted.

ACKNOWLEDGEMENTS

Many individuals and institutions have helped in the creation of this publication. I am indebted to Marie-Henriette Gates and Ilknur Özgen, for bringing the ruins at Küçük Burnaz to my attention and encouraging me to study them. My thanks to the Turkish Ministry of Monuments and Museums and the staff at the Hatay Museum, Antakya, for permitting and facilitating my fieldwork. My deepest gratitude goes to those who suffered the heat, humidity and various insect and animal life during the 1994-95 seasons: Ümmühan Eker, Ebru Tanır (students of Bilkent University), Nurhan Turan (representative from the Ministry of Culture), and architects Andrew Fletcher and Steven Beverly. Without their help I could never have conducted this study. I also thank Bilkent University for funding the 1994 field season and Toros Gübre ve Kimye Endüstresi A.S., who generously hosted the 1994-95 project.

The subsequent study seasons, conducted on the premises of the Kinet Hüyük Excavation House, were made possible through the generosity of Marie-Henriette Gates. I am grateful to her and her staff, especially Charles Gates, Roz Schneider, Scott Redford, Salima Ikrem and Fran Cole, for their helpful advice and lively interest in my project. I also greatly benefited from observations made by scholars visiting Kinet Hüyük, who took the time to examine my material and offer useful comments: Christopher Lightfoot, Nicholas Rauh, Kenneth Harl and Andrew Goldman. I also extend my thanks to the Humanities Institute of the University of Illinois, Chicago, who funded the 2000 study season.

I am grateful to Vera Shearon-Ball at Io Design for her patience, expertise, generosity and humor. She made the final stages of book production a pleasure. I also thank my colleagues in the Department of Classics and Mediterranean Studies at the University of Illinois, Chicago, for granting me a semester's leave of absence in order to concentrate on this manuscript. Finally, several scholars took the time to read portions of this work or discuss certain issues it addresses: James Russell, Marcello Spanu, Kathleen Warner Slane, Jane DeRose Evans, Scott Redford, Sandra Knudsen and especially Andrew Goldman and Marie-Henriette Gates. I have taken to heart their comments with gratitude; any errors remaining in this manuscript are my own.

This work is dedicated to Toni Cross, who was among the first to see the ruins at Küçük Burnaz, and whose love for Turkey, both modern and ancient, has served as an inspiration.

INTRODUCTION

In 1838, in a report to the Royal Geographic Society, the topographer William Ainsworth described his travels in a rarely visited part of Turkey, the area around the Gulf of Iskenderun (maps 1-3). Lured to the region by the possibility of determining the site where Alexander the Great defeated Darius III of Persia in 333 B.C., Ainsworth not only examined the possible battlefield located on the eastern side of the gulf, but also the desolate area to the north:

The plain here is covered by a sand-flood, and is not above two miles in width, being bounded to the north by a range of low sandstone hills. Ruined arches are seen peeping in two or three places out of the sands. They are constructed of tile-bricks. The hilly country is soon united with the sea by loftier mounds of Plutonic rocks, and the direction of the shore changes to the southwest. In this place, thus enclosed between hills and the sea, are many ruins of former times: a little brook runs through its centre....[1]

At the beginning of the 20th century, Prussian Alexander Janke visited the same region, also in hopes of establishing the location of the famous battle. In his 1904 publication he related his impressions of the area seen by Ainsworth some 65 years earlier and recorded the following:

Nach eingehendem Besuche verliessen wir das Ruinenfeld von Gösene gegen 11 Uhr vorm. Das vegetationslose schwarze Gestein setzte sich an den Bergen im Westen fort. Die Massen von basaltischen Mandelsteinen, Doleriten, Wacken und Trapptuff stellen ein entscheiden vulkanisches Gelände dar. Wir kamen nach einer Stunde über bebautes Land zu dem ärmlichen Dorfe Burnaz und nach 25 Minuten zu dem hochgelegenen Dorfe Turuschlu, wo ein grosser guterhaltener Befestigungsturm und andere Ruinen der Wasserleitung sich vorfinden....[2]

On the heels of Janke's survey, Gertrude Bell visited the same region in 1905 and reported:

The plain of Issus, over which we were passing, is exceedingly fertile; the villages are set in gardens of fruit trees and of vines, but the climate is abominable, and even at that season of the year we were conscious of a damp and stuffy heat which, in the summer, renders the strip of land between the mountains and the sea almost uninhabitable. .... we took a track almost due north which led us across a grassy plain scattered with shafts of columns, some plain and some voluted, with capitals and with dressed stones of black basalt, possibly the ruins of a colonnade which extended from Geuzenne to the sea.[3]

These accounts depict a plain nestled between the mountains and the sea - barren and sand-filled near the coast and surprising fertile inland. Although possessing a climate that renders the region "almost uninhabitable," the mention all the authors make to ruins testifies to a thriving population in antiquity. Characteristic of the plain is the presence of black basalt, which comprises the hills to the north and west and served as a chief building material in antiquity. Because of the presence of this stone, unique to this region, the area has been recently referred to as Black Cilicia. [4]

The present work is a study of the Plain of Issus, or Black Cilicia, in antiquity. The research was catalyzed by the discovery of a Roman settlement at the coastal site of Küçük Burnaz, located in the heart of the region described by the authors quoted above (map 3). The remains of the settlement, probably identical with those seen by Ainsworth "peeping" out of sand dunes, came to light as a result of illegal bulldozing. In the course of assessing those remains it became clear that they could be only understandable when viewed within their historical and regional context. Since no study of the region exists, it was a logical choice to include one with the examination of the ruins at Küçük Burnaz. Therefore, this study is divided into two parts. The first provides an overview of the region, its geography, history and antiquities, while the second is an assessment of the architecture and finds from Küçük Burnaz.

---

[1] Ainsworth 1838, 188-89.
[2] Janke 1904, 15.
[3] Bell 1906, 3.
[4] See Spanu (2003, 21) who coined the name and provides a plan (fig. 5) that delineates the parameters of Black Cilicia.

Geography

Black Cilicia, an area roughly equivalent to the Plain of Issus, occupies the easternmost portion of ancient Cilicia, a region that extended along the south coast of present day Turkey from Alexandria ad Issum (modern Iskenderun) in the east to Coracesium (modern Alanya) in the west (map 1).[1] Ancient Cilicia comprised two discretely different regions, "Rough" Cilicia, Cilicia Tracheia to the west, which as the name implies is mountainous and "Smooth" Cilicia, Cilicia Pedias to the east, a plain where the mountains recede from the sea. The point of division between the two was the Lamus River (the modern Lamas Çayı), located east of Elaeussa.[2] The settlement patterns of these two regions differed according to the terrain - Rough Cilicia was sparsely populated and a notorious holdout for bandits and pirates, while Smooth Cilicia had a long history of urbanism.

Smooth Cilicia is bordered on the north by the Taurus Mountains, on the east by the Amanus Mountains and on the south by the Mediterranean (map 2). While rugged terrain separated this region from the rest of Asia Minor and from Syria, major passes, among them most notably the great Cilician Gates, allowed transit through the region. Thus throughout its history, Smooth Cilicia was a crossroads for populations moving east/west between the Anatolian Plateau and Mesopotamia, and north/south between Anatolia and the Levant.

Smooth Cilicia is essentially a vast flood plain created by three major rivers, the Cydnus (Tarsus Çayı), the Sarus (Seyhan) and the Pyramus (Ceyhan). The first two originate in the Taurus Mountains, while the last emerges from the Amanus Range. The plain, known as the Aleian Plain in antiquity and today as the Çukurova, consists of a rich loamy soil that makes the region extremely fertile. In antiquity, numerous crops were cultivated, including cereals, rice, figs, dates, vines and flax.[3] Today the region is one of the most productive in Turkey, cultivating fruits and vegetables, cotton, wheat and sesame.[4] The climate is hot and humid in the summer and mild in the winter. In the past the Çukurova had been thinly settled due to the marshy nature of the region, which often flooded in the winter and in the summer bred malaria-bearing mosquitoes. Since 1950 attempts to alleviate the problems through the construction of dams and insect control has created a healthier environment.[5] Today the cities of Mersin, Tarsus and Adana are among the most densely populated in Turkey.

At the easternmost end of Smooth Cilicia is the Plain of Issus, separated from the Aleian Plain by a low range of mountains, the Djebel Misis. To the east the plain is bordered by the Amanus Mountains. These two ranges are united at the northwest by low volcanic hills, the most distinctive of these being Hama Tepe. Ancient lava flows in the region have left behind basalt beds that were quarried by builders in antiquity, and, as mentioned, have given cause for the region's nick-name, Black Cilicia. Although there is no threat of volcanic activity at present, the Plain of Issus is located along several fault lines and is plagued by earthquakes.[6] One of the most recent, occurring in June 1998, claimed over one hundred lives in the town of Ceyhan and its environs.

The Plain of Issus is separated into two parts by a spur of the Amanus Mountains, with the larger northern section of the plain oriented to the northeast, running between the Amanus and the Djebel Misis. The narrow southern portion of the plain is located between the Amanus and the sea. Like the Aleian Plain, both sections of the Plain of Issus are alluvial fans created by a number of small streams issuing from the Amanus Mountains, including the Payas Çayı, the Deli Çayı, the Karabasdan Suyu, the Burnaz Suyu and the Küçük Burnaz Suyu. Marshes have been created where the streams meet the coast and these, combined with the sand and sediment brought down from the mountains, have caused the sea to recede as much as 1 km from the ancient shoreline. Much of the coast of the Plain of Issus is occupied by the Karabasamak coastal dunes, which begin at the northwestern edge of the Gulf of Issus and extend southeast along the edge of the shore for ca. 12 km. The width of the dune fields varies between 1-3 km and the height of the individual sand hills can measure from 4-12 m. The dunes demonstrate evidence for two periods of development. The older formations are gray in color and stable, serving as soils for the cotton fields in the region. The newer formations are pale in color and are constantly shifting.[7]

The marshy quality of much of the Plain of Issus made this region a malarial zone until recent times. Consequently, while large towns, such as Dörtyol and Payas exist in the southern section of the plain, only small villages such as Burnaz, Turunçlu and Gözene occupy the heart of the plain. In the past twenty years, however, industrialization has spread across the coastal strip. The area is now home to several industrial plants: a fertilizer and cement factory (Toros Gübre ve Kimye Endüstresi A.S.), a gas bottling facility (Delta Petrol Ürünleri Ticaret, A.S.) and Botaş, a company that oversees the gas pipeline from Iraq. Within the last ten years a superhighway (the TEM) has been built across the plain with one branch (the E-90) leading to Gaziantep and another (the E-91) to Iskenderun. This increased industrialization has brought to light ancient remains, but often damaging them in the process.

Ancient Passes and Roads

In antiquity, as today, the Plain of Issus was fairly sheltered from neighboring regions since it only could be entered easily via three defensible passes. The southern entrance to the plain was through the Syrian-Cilician Gates (map 2), located 11 km north of Alexandria ad Issum (Iskenderun) and today the site of two wall fragments constructed from white marble ashlars. Traditionally known as the Pillars of Jonah, they may be the remains of a triumphal arch built by Septimius Severus in honor of his victory over Pescennius Niger in A.D. 194.[8] Beyond this defense point lay the Syrian Gates, today known as the Beylan Pass, which guarded a pass through the Amanus Mountains to Syria.[9] The northern entrance to the Plain of Issus is a defile where the Amanus Mountains meet the Djebel Misis. The pass, called the Amanus Gates by Arrian, today is associated with Toprakkale, an Armenian fort rebuilt in the Mamluk period.[10] The western entrance to the Plain of Issus is a pass that follows a stream through the Djebel Misis. Strabo refers to this pass as the Amanus Gates.[11]   A ruined arch and well-preserved walls of basalt-faced mortar and rubble masonry give the ruins its modern name, Karanlıkkapı, the Black Gate (map 3).

The pass guarded by Karanlıkkapı was part of the so-called Pilgrim's Road, one of the major arteries of Asia Minor by which one could travel from Constantinople to Jerusalem (map 1). Although the road appears to have been laid out chiefly under the Flavians, it became increasingly important in the 4th c. and later, as newly converted Christians desired to make the difficult journey to the Holy Land.[12] These pilgrims include pious ladies such as Paula, Fabiola, Marcella and Melania, as well as Egeria who documented her passage through Cilicia.[13]

The route through Asia Minor has been elucidated by David French's study of milestones, literary testimonia and archaeological remains. According to French, the section of the road between Tarsus and Antioch marched through the pass of Karanlıkkapı and then ran eastward along the curve of the

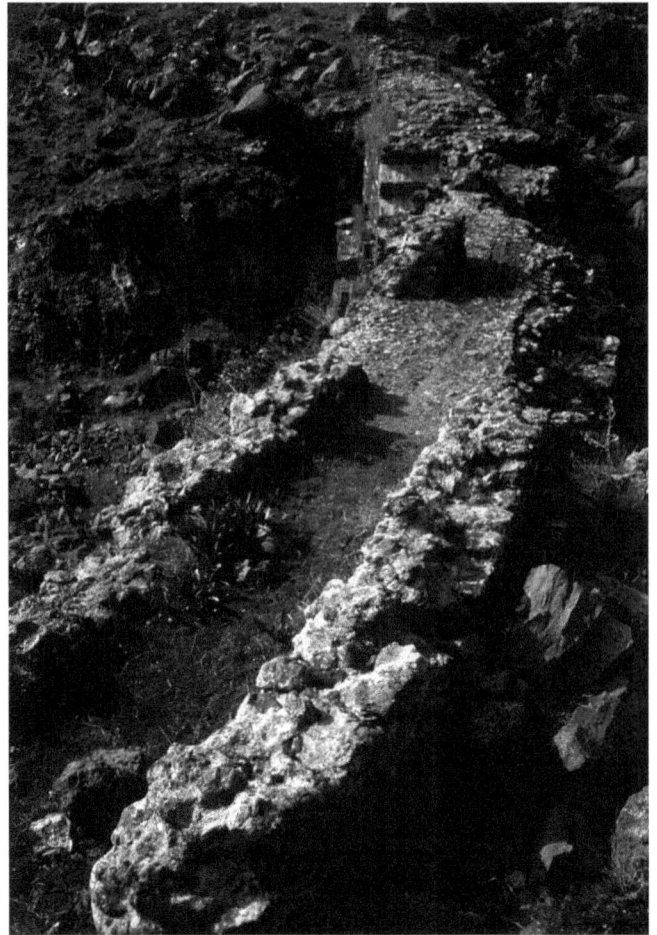

Figure 1. Aqueduct over the Incırlısuyu, top view

Figure 2. Aqueduct over the Incırlısuyu, from the east

Gulf of Issus. A section of this road has recently been excavated near Kinet Hüyük, ancient Issus, on the eastern side of the gulf.[14]

Traces of other roads have been recorded in the Plain of Issus, including one running N/S past the city of Epiphaneia. Seen by Janke in the early 20th century, the road probably led from the sea to the pass at Toprakkale.[15] Sections of another road can be seen running parallel to the western shore of the Gulf of Issus for 3 km. It is paved with cobblestones of black basalt and has a water channel on its western side. It may have originally connected to an aqueduct bridge that crosses the Incırlısuyu, some 8 km to the southwest (figs. 1 and 2).[16] The road probably extended south, at least as far as Kızlarsuyu (where a milestone was found) and beyond to Aegeae.[17]

The well-watered, rich farmlands of the Plain of Issus, protected by mountains and the sea, should have assured a thriving, stable population in ancient times. Its role as a crossroads, between north and south, east and west, however, predicated a different fate, as will be demonstrated in the following chapter.

---

[1] Strabo 14.5.2. For a discussion of Cilicia and a gazetteer of sites with particular emphasis on Late Antiquity see Hild and Hellenkemper (1990). For recent bibliography on Cilicia see Equini Schneider (1999, 391-439). A useful travel guide to the region is Freely (1998, 107-273).

[2] Strabo 14.5.8.

[3] Jones 1983, 20; Plin. *NH* 13.48, 16.113, 18.81.

[4] Kiray 1974, 184; Dewdney 1971, 180. Accounts of the region in the 19th c. can be found in Cuinet (1891, 13-15) and Barker (1853, 110-27).

[5] Kiray 1974, 185; Dewdney 1971, 180.

[6] Özgen and Gates 1992a, 388; Bingöl 1985; Brinkmann 1976, 97-100.

[7] Ozaner, Gates and Özgen 1993, 357-59.

[8] For a recent discussion of the pass see Hammond (1994); for descriptions and images of the architecture see Hellenkemper and Hild (1986, 108-11, fig. 17), Heberdey and Wilhelm (1896, 19, fig. 2.), Janke (1904, 17-24, fig. 1) and Ainsworth (1838, 186). See Hild and Hellenkemper (1990, 302) and Taeuber (1991, 202-04) for the identification of the Pillars of Jonah as the arch of Severus.

[9] Hild and Hellenkemper 1990, 212; Janke 1904, 32-7; Marmier 1884.

[10] Arr. *Anab.* 2.7.1; Sinclair 1990, 326-28; Janke 1904, 37-44.

[11] Strabo 14.5.18.

[12] This route had less military significance than the one that passed eastward from Ancyra to serve the eastern limes. French 1981, 13. For the pilgrimage route and conditions of the journey see Maraval (1985, 163-182), Hunt (1982, 50-82) and Wilkinson (1981, 27-30).

[13] Hunt 1982, 50; Cameron 1993, 68.

[14] French 1981, 13-14, map 7; Sayar 2002, 452-64. Marie-Henriette Gates, personal communication.

[15] Janke 1904, 14. The road is recorded on the Peutinger Map, section X.4, and in Islamic itineraries.

[16] Özgen and Gates 1992a, 390; 1992b, 5; Hellenkemper and Hild 1986, 127, fig. 196.

[17] French 1981, 94-95; Heberdey and Wilhelm 1896, 16.

A detailed history of the Plain of Issus at this stage is impossible, owing to a lack of historical sources and in-depth archaeological study in the region. The account presented here, whose scope runs from the 15th c. B.C. to the 14th c. A.D., relies on an examination of events occurring in the larger region of Smooth Cilicia. Although the combined annals of Rough and Smooth Cilicia have been the subject of several scholarly works, the disparate regions often experienced very different histories. Therefore since the work presented below concentrates on Smooth Cilicia alone, it is free to focus on events essential to the region of the Plain of Issus. Likewise, previous studies have been concerned with specific historical periods - Hittite, Persian, Seleucid and Roman. The following, however, provides a diachronic narrative of events pertaining to Smooth Cilicia, from its absorption into the Hittite Empire to the Mamluk conquest. Because the date of the archaeological remains found in the Plain of Issus, including those at Küçük Burnaz, appear to fall chiefly between the Hellenistic and late Roman periods, this era will be examined in greater depth. Fortunately, it is also the case that rich documentation survives for this epoch.

Throughout its history, Smooth Cilicia functioned as a border between east and west, serving as a land bridge between Central Anatolia and the Near East. As such, the region not only hosted scores of troops marching east or west, but also on occasion provided the battleground upon which these armies clashed. Its strategic importance determined that Smooth Cilicia was a goal of conquest, while at the same time the relative isolation of the fertile Cilician plain, bordered by the sea and by mountains on three sides, allowed for brief periods of political independence.

Smooth Cilicia as a Crossroads: 1500-333 B.C.

Understanding of this long period relies chiefly on the occasional reference in Near Eastern and Greco-Roman texts and on a few inscriptions found in Smooth Cilicia. Consequently, the series of events during this time cannot be fully fleshed out. During the 2nd millennium B.C. Smooth Cilicia was occupied by Luwian and Hurrian populations and was known as Kizzuwatna.[1] Originally an independent kingdom, Kizzuwatna became incorporated into the Hittite Empire as a vassal state at the end of the 15th c. B.C. and remained under Hittite control for the next two centuries.[2] With the fall of the Hittite Empire at the end of the 13th c. B.C. it is likely that Kizzuwatna fragmented into several small principalities under the control of a local ruler.[3] This was certainly the political situation when the Assyrian King Shalmaneser III raided the region in 839 B.C. The Assyrian Royal Annals refer to the area as Que, which, like Kizzuwatna, comprised the Cilician plain and the mountains to the north, but also extended northward into Cappadocia.[4] The annals also mention Hilakku to the west of Que, a region that more or less conformed to the later Rough Cilicia.[5] Over the next century Assyrian rulers continued to raid Que, exacting tribute from its local rulers. During the reign of Sargon II (722-705 B.C.), Que became a

province of Assyria. Although the local rulers still appear to have had a modicum of direct control over their homeland, the absorption into the empire seems to have included some deportation of the populace, since there are records of people of Que and Hilakku serving as laborers for Sargon's palace at Nineveh.

It is possible that after the death of Sargon Que enjoyed a brief period of independence. From this time comes the bilingual inscription of Karatepe, located in the hills north of the Plain of Issus. The text glorifies, in the Phoenician alphabet and in Luwian hieroglyphs, Azatiwata, a local prince who answered to a king ruling from Adana.[6] In the 7th c. B.C., however, Que once again came under Assyrian rule, and although it gained its independence following the destruction of Nineveh in 612 B.C., it was increasingly threatened by another power from the east, Babylon. It is unclear whether the Neo-Babylonians actually conquered Cilicia, but texts from the reign of Nebuchadnezzer (605-562 B.C.) mention prisoners from Hume (the Babylonian name for Que) and Neo-Babylonian princes seem to have been active in the region from the 590's onward.[7] As was the case under Assyrian rule, local rulers maintained some autonomy in Hume and in the area to the west, Pirindu (the Assyrian name for the Hilakku region). The most important of these rulers bore the title of Syennesis.[8]

According to Xenophon, when Cyrus the Great arrived in the region, sometime between 546 and 539 B.C., the inhabitants entered into an alliance with the Persians which allowed them to exist as an independent vassal state under a line of local dynasts. These kings continued to hold the title of Syennesis and ruled from Tarsus.[9] In 401 B.C., as a result of one of these kings submitting to Cyrus the Younger, Artaxerxes placed the region directly under a Persian satrap.[10]

Smooth Cilicia in Hellenistic Times: 333-64 B.C.

In 333 B.C. Alexander the Great brought an end to Persian rule in the region with his decisive victory over Darius III at a battle on the Pinarus River near Issus, a settlement located at the southeastern extremity of the Plain of Issus, recently identified with Kinet Hüyük.[11] After Alexander's death the region first fell to Perdiccas and then to Antipater, but eventually, Smooth Cilicia became part of the great Seleucid Empire.[12] During the Hellenistic period, valuable information about the region can be gained from coinage, which is especially helpful in the realm of city foundation. By the 1st c. B.C., when Smooth Cilicia becomes a focus of interest to the Romans, literary sources, particularly Strabo and Plutarch are also useful.

Throughout the Hellenistic period, although Rough Cilicia was often disputed territory between the Seleucids and the Ptolemies, Smooth Cilicia stayed for the most part firmly in the hands of the former.[13] At this time several cities in Smooth Cilicia became intellectual hubs, with important centers of philosophy at Soloi, Tarsus and Mallus.[14] During the early

3rd c. B.C. it is probable that Seleucus Nicator reinforced his claim over the region with the re-founding of old cities, renaming Tarsus as Antioch on the Cydnus and Magarsus as Antioch on the Pyramus.[15] He also probably founded the new cities of Aegeae (named for the Macedonian capital) and Alexandria ad Issum (commemorating Alexander's great battle) which would serve to control the Gulf of Issus.[16] A century later, perhaps to compensate for the loss of Seleucid territory following the Peace of Apamea in 188 B.C., Antiochus IV Epiphanes reasserted Seleucid control over Smooth Cilicia by following the policy of re-foundation set by Seleucus I.[17] Thus in the 2nd c. B.C. the ancient city of Adana became known as Antioch on the Sarus, Mopsuestia became Seleucia on the Pyramus, Castabala became Hierapolis on the Pyramus and Oiniandos was renamed Epiphaneia.[18] During the reign of Antiochus IV the cities of Smooth Cilicia were accorded certain freedoms, including the minting of municipal coinage which bore the royal portrait on the obverse and the city name on the reverse.[19]

After the death of Antiochus IV, continuing dynastic wars allowed Seleucid control over Smooth Cilicia to slip. Many of the cities that had been given royal titles reverted to their original names and began to mint coins featuring their own civic symbols. The lack of Seleucid domination, however, ultimately served to destabilize the region, and the latter half of the 2nd c. saw the rise of local chieftains as well as a growing threat from piracy and banditry. Eventually the pirate menace proved to be a threat to Roman interests and precipitated the first Roman incursion in Cilicia. This came in the form of the command of the *provincia Cilicia*, held by Marcus Antonius in 102 B.C. In spite of the term Cilicia, the base of command was actually Pamphylia and the territorial limits included Lycia, the Milyas region and parts of Phrygia, not actually Cilicia itself.[20] The object of the command was the suppression of piracy in Cilicia. Until the 60's B.C. the command was taken up sporadically when needed, either in order to defend against piracy or to deal with other matters relating to the peace in Asia Minor.[21] Even with the new Roman intervention, during this period the cities of Smooth Cilicia suffered both from commercial disruptions caused by piracy as well as outright pirate raids, which regularly seized inhabitants for the slave trade.[22] The greatest blow, however, occurred in 83 B.C. when King Tigranes of Armenia conquered Northern Syria and Smooth Cilicia, carrying away the inhabitants of twelve cities in order to swell the population of his new city of Tigranocerta.[23]

Tigranes held Smooth Cilicia for nearly 15 years, until L. Licinius Lucullus defeated him near Tigranocerta in 69 B.C. The Roman general forced the king to retreat to Armenia and give up all claims to the region. Lucullus then reinstated the Seleucid king, Antiochus XIII, and set him once again to rule over Northern Syria and Smooth Cilicia. Shortly thereafter in 67 B.C. Pompey the Great's expedition against the pirates further stabilized Smooth Cilicia. Having vanquished the pirates at Coracesium in Rough Cilicia, Pompey installed the more amenable ones in three underpopulated cities of Smooth Cilicia, Adana, Mallus and Epiphaneia.[24] As a result, these cities, like many others in the region, counted their era from

67 B.C.[25] Pompey also repatriated the people of Soloi, who had been in exile in Tigranocerta; thereafter the city was known as Pompeiopolis.[26]

The First Province of Cilicia: 64 B. C.-A.D. 72

During this period good documentation survives for the history of Smooth Cilicia and the Plain of Issus, since many events occurring there pertained to the Roman Civil Wars and the fall of the Republic and have been chronicled by Plutarch, Appian, Dio Cassius and others. In 64 B.C. after Pompey's annexation of the kingdom of the Seleucids, Smooth Cilicia was finally added to what Syme describes as the "motley and composite" province of Cilicia.[27] The new province stretched along the seacoast from Cape Gelidonia to the Gulf of Issus, including Pamphylia, the Milyas territory, Pisidia and, after 58 B.C., the island of Cyprus. The province also reached inland as far north as Bithynia, including the three dioceses of Phrygia, Laodiceia, Apameia and Synnada. In the east it abutted against the kingdoms of Galatia, Cappadocia and Commagene and in the west it ran against Lycia and the province of Asia. The province of Cilicia served as a buffer zone between Asia and the non-Roman world, while it controlled the important road system between Asia and Syria.[28] Within this sprawling province Smooth Cilicia was of particular importance, both because it controlled the southern reaches of the great pass at the Cilician Gates, and also because it backed against non-Roman territory to the north. As a reflection of the importance Smooth Cilicia held within the province of Cilicia as a whole, the capital of the new province was now located at Tarsus.

Smooth Cilicia's nearest foreign neighbor was the small domain of Castabalis, whose first ruler, Tarcondimotus son of Strato, made his capital at Castabala Hierapolis, located in the foothills north of the Issus plain.[29] The precise parameters of the kingdom are not known; it comprised the two inland cities of Castabala and Anazarbus and likely the hinterland tribal districts of Bryclice, Lacanitis and Characene.[30] The kingdom may also have encompassed coastal cities, perhaps Aegeae and the western settlements of Corycus and Elaeussa.[31]

Certainly the most famous governor of the new province of Cilicia was Cicero, who took office in 51 B.C.[32] Through lively letters to friends and relatives, Cicero provides a wealth of information concerning the Plain of Issus. The ruinous administration of his predecessor, Appius Claudius Pulcher, coupled with a wide-spread harvest failure in 51 B.C., had left the province financially exhausted.[33] After six months of fair and humane dealings, however, Cicero earned acclaim throughout the province.[34] One month after arriving in the region, Cicero learned of a Parthian army poised to cross the Euphrates and invade Roman territory. Just two years after Crassus' defeat at Carrhae, it is surprising to learn that the Roman military presence in Cilicia was relatively weak, consisting of two undermanned legions and 2600 horse.[35] Cicero and his troops, bolstered by enlisted local Roman citizens and some natives, planned to muster at Cybistra in Cappadocia, whose position, north of the Taurus Mountains near the

Cilician Gates, would allow Cicero time to strike whether the Parthians marched through Armenia or through Syria. As he was approaching Cybistra, however, Cicero received word from Tarcondimotus that the Parthians were invading Syria.[36] Since Cappadocia was no longer threatened, Cicero and his troops marched through the Cilician Gates into Smooth Cilicia. Fortunately, the brunt of the army had been checked at Antioch and the Parthian invasion never reached as far as Cilicia, although a cohort garrisoned at Epiphaneia killed some Parthian out riders.[37]

Although the Parthian threat proved inconsequential to Smooth Cilicia, the events served to stir up certain inhabitants of the neighboring region. Shortly after learning of the Parthian defeat, Cicero mounted a campaign against rebellious tribes in the Amanus Mountains, resulting in the destruction of several mountain strongholds and the capture of prisoners. For this victory Cicero was proclaimed "Imperator" by the army while encamped near Alexander's battlefield of Issus.[38] Soon thereafter, Cicero moved against another group of tribesmen known as the "Free Cilicians,"[39] a truculent people who had never recognized Seleucid rule nor the imperium of Pompey, and had long been practicing banditry throughout the region. Cicero and his troops besieged Pindenissus, a fortress town in the mountains, for 56 days before taking it. Even with these victories, Cicero considered the region barely pacified.[40]

In the years following, the civil war between Caesar and Pompey had repercussions on Smooth Cilicia. Like much of the East, the region sided with Pompey at the battle of Pharsalus in 48 B.C. Tarcondimotus, toparch of Castabalis sent him ships.[41] After the battle, the victorious Caesar treated the vanquished partisans of Pompey with clemency. On route from Egypt to Asia Minor in 47 B.C., Caesar stopped in Tarsus, having requested representatives from various communities to meet him there.[42] Among the pardoned was Tarcondimotus, to whom he may have granted citizenship.[43] As a result of this visit Caesar may well have begun planning to reorganize the cumbersome province of Cilicia, since shortly after his death in 44 B.C., Smooth Cilicia was attached to the province of Syria.[44]

In the aftermath of Caesar's assassination Smooth Cilicia was visited with dark days. After fleeing Rome, the conspirator Gaius Cassius occupied the province of Syria and against their will, forced the people of Tarsus as well as Tarcondimotus to become allies with him. When the Tarsiotes later attempted to rebel, Cassius punished them with fines so exorbitant that people were sold into slavery to make their payments.[45] In 41 B.C., after the defeat of Brutus and Cassius at Philippi, Marcus Antonius visited Tarsus and recompensed the Tarsiotes for their suffering under Cassius, exempting them from taxation and liberating those sold into slavery. It may have been at this time that Antonius developed his friendship with Tarcondimotus, perhaps granting him the title of king, since he is called King Tarcondimotus Philantonius in coinage from the period.[46] It is at Tarsus that Antony received the fateful visit from Cleopatra and shortly thereafter followed

her to Alexandria, leaving Tarsus in the clutches of his favorite Boethius.[47] The following year Cilicia was invaded by a troop of Parthians led by Quintus Labienus, a follower of Cassius and Brutus, who had been sent to Parthia to gain assistance for Caesar's murderers. Although too late to help at the battle of Philippi, Labienus convinced the Parthians to march against Rome. The invaders managed to invest the south coast of Asia before a Roman army under Publius Ventidius Bassus engaged the Parthians near the Cilician Gates. Driven into the Cilician plain, the invaders were routed and Labienus killed.[48]

During the following decade, while certain territories of the old province of Cilicia were given to rulers loyal to Antony, Smooth Cilicia remained in Roman hands, still attached to Syria.[49] At the Battle of Actium in 31 B.C., these eastern rulers held true to Antony. King Tarcondimotus demonstrated his loyalty by personally leading a fleet, and losing his life during a skirmish shortly before the battle.[50] Like Caesar before him, the victorious Octavian treated the vanquished with leniency, allowing most of the eastern dynasts to retain their kingdoms. A notable exception was the treatment of the kingdom of Castabalis. Since King Tarcondimotus had died in battle, his son Tarcondimotus Philopater had expected to succeed to the throne. Perhaps suspecting lingering loyalty to surviving factions of Antony, Octavian delayed the succession for ten years.[51] When, in 20 B.C., Tarcondimotus Philopater was allowed to take up his kingdom, the city of Anazarbus (which was probably still part of the kingdom of the Tarcondimotids) adopted a new era and assumed the name Caesareia in honor of the event.[52]

Tarcondimotus Philopater ruled as king of Castabalis from 20 B.C. until his death in A.D. 17, at which time Tiberius disbanded the kingdom. The region of Bryclice in the west is thought to have come under Roman control, since the colony of Augusta (named for Livia) was established there in A.D. 20.[53] The eastern territories of Characene and Lacanatis eventually came into the hands of Antiochus of Commagene when his kingdom was reinstated in A.D. 38.[54] In A.D. 52, in honor of Claudius' adoption of Nero, the colony of Neronias was founded in the hills northeast of the Plain of Issus.[55]

The Second Province of Cilicia: A.D. 72 to the end of the 3rd c.

In A.D. 72, upon the annexation of the Kingdom of Commagene, Vespasian united the region of Rough Cilicia with Smooth Cilicia, the latter having been detached from Syria.[56] The western border of the new province lay between the cities of Syedra and Iotape, while the eastern and northern borders were formed by the natural boundaries of the Amanus and Taurus ranges respectively. At this time the region of Castabalis, formerly ruled by the Tarcondimotid dynasty was added to the province. In the northeast the colony of Flaviopolis was founded in A.D. 74[57] and the neighboring city of Neronias was given the new name of Irenopolis.[58] Tarsus remained the provincial capital.[59]

The history of the province of Cilicia for the next hundred years is fairly uneventful, and knowledge depends chiefly upon coinage and inscriptions. Vivid documentation pertaining to civic life, however, can be found in two orations of Dio Chrysostom, who relates the bickering between Tarsus and her neighbors, Aegeae, Mallus, Soloi and Adana.[60] Trajan took an interest in Smooth Cilicia, no doubt for its strategic position controlling routes south to Syria and east to Parthia. During his reign the city of Epiphaneia was given the name of Trajanopolis.[61] Castabala Hierapolis to the north set up a statue to the Emperor, perhaps between 114 and 117 in connection with Trajan's Parthian campaign.[62] The Emperor Hadrian likewise received numerous honors indicating that he may have passed through Smooth Cilicia en route from Asia to Syria in A.D. 129.[63] Adana, Aegeae and Mopsuestia assumed the name of Hadriana, while the western city of Zephyrium became Hadrianopolis. A festival called the Hadrianeia was instituted in Tarsus,[64] and a statue was dedicated to Hadrian at Anazarbus.[65] He is credited with building a bridge over the Sarus River at Adana.[66] On his return from the Parthian Wars in A.D. 175/6, Marcus Aurelius passed through Smooth Cilicia, stopping in Tarsus to hear the 15-year old Sophist Hermogenes declaim.[67] Soon thereafter, the Empress Faustina the Younger died just north of the Cilician Gates at the village of Halala, which Marcus Aurelius renamed Faustinopolis.[68]

Late in the 2nd c. A.D., Smooth Cilicia was once again swept into the center of conflict when Septimius Severus and Pescennius Niger struggled for control of the Eastern Empire. In A.D. 194 Severus' army under the command of Cornelius Anullinus won a decisive battle against Niger at Issus.[69] Severus himself arrived in the region soon after the battle and received tribute from the Cilician cities. Adana, Aegeae and Tarsus took the name Severiana and Tarsus created the "Severan Olympics." A triumphal arch with a quadriga was set up near the battle site.[70]

Caracalla passed through Smooth Cilicia on route to Parthia in A.D. 215. At Tarsus he presented the city with grain and was awarded the honorary title of *demiurge*. Tarsus also assumed the title of Antoniana Severiana and of Antoninopolis,[71] as did the city of Mopsuestia,[72] and a statue was set up in the emperor's honor at Castabala Hierapolis.[73] After Caracalla's murder by Macrinus in A.D. 217, Tarsus, with well considered alacrity, shifted her name to Macrianiana and Aegeae became Macrinoupolis. The brief reign of Macrinus was terminated when Julia Maesa, an aunt of Caracalla, along with her grandson Elagabalus attacked Macrinus at his headquarters at Antioch. Macrinus fled to Aegeae and then to Asia Minor, where he was eventually captured and killed. During his short rule, Macrinus' successor Elagabalus (A.D. 218-222) received honors from the cities of Smooth Cilicia. Games were founded in his honor at Anazarbus, and Adana took the name Antoninopolis.[74] The cousin and successor to Elagabalus, Alexander Severus was similarly honored. Tarsus once again changed its name, this time to Alexandriana, perhaps in gratitude for a reduction in taxes,[75] and a statue was set up for Alexander Severus at Anazarbus.[76]

Milestones from Smooth Cilicia bearing the names of Caracalla, Macrinus, Elagabalus and especially Alexander Severus attest to repairs to the roads leading from the Cilician Gates east towards Parthia and south into Syria.[77] This critical passage for the Roman army would see much traffic over the next fifty years. Also during this time there is evidence for troops from various parts of the empire passing through Smooth Cilicia on their way to the eastern wars. Several tombstones with Latin or bilingual texts commemorating *equites singulares* have been found at Anazarbus. They date to A.D. 215/216 and thus probably belonged to soldiers in Caracalla's army.[78]

With the death of Alexander Severus in A.D. 235, the Roman Empire was thrust into a half century of unstable succession, spiraling inflation and invasion. This turmoil was keenly felt within Smooth Cilicia since the region was particularly threatened by the new Sassanid dynasty that had recently seized the Persian throne. In A.D. 242 King Shapur I marched to the Euphrates, threatening Syria. The young Roman emperor Gordian III advancing his legions across Asia Minor, through the Cilician Gates to Syria, drove the Sassanid army back to Ctesiphon.[79] Evidence for Gordian III's passage though Smooth Cilicia can be seen in a statue base honoring the emperor from Castabala Hierapolis, and an altar for him from Aegeae.[80] The emperor also renewed the roads in the region.[81] Ten years later Shapur I's army invaded again, reaching as far as Antioch.[82] In A.D. 260 Shapur invaded a third time, this time taking Antioch and subsequently capturing the Roman Emperor Valerian. Shapur then proceeded westward into Smooth Cilicia. His route has been recorded in the *Res Gestae Divi Sapporis*.[83] After ravaging Alexandria ad Issum he moved around the Gulf of Issus, subjugating Catabolos, Aegeae, Mopsuestia, and Mallus before turning north to Adana and Tarsus. He also took the coastal town of Zephyrium in Smooth Cilicia, as well as Elaeussa and Corycus in Rough Cilicia. Shapur then despoiled the inland cities of Smooth Cilicia, including Castabala Hierapolis, Irenopolis (Neronias), Flaviopolis and Epiphaneia before marching into Cappadocia. Two officers, Callistus (or Ballistus) and Macrianus managed to rally the remnants of Valerian's army and drive the invaders back beyond the Euphrates.[84] In the aftermath of Shapur's invasion, Smooth Cilicia continued to be visited with upheaval, suffering the invasion of Palmyrene troops in A.D. 269, the subsequent recovery of the region by Aurelian in A.D. 272 and the murder of the Emperor Florian in Tarsus in A.D. 276.[85]

The Third Province of Cilicia and Cilicia I and II: end of the 3rd c. A.D. to A.D. 636

Evidence for this period relies on a few inscriptions and a limited number of authors: Ammianus Marcelinus, Theophanis, Eusebius, Procopius and John Malalas. At the end of the 3rd c. Smooth Cilicia, like the rest of the Roman world, was finally stabilized by Diocletian. In his reorganization of the empire Diocletian subdivided the province of Cilicia, creating the smaller provinces of Isauria (corresponding to the region of Rough Cilicia) and Cilicia (the region of Smooth Cilicia). Both regions were part of the Oriens diocese.[86] Upon Diocletian's retirement in A.D. 305 Maximinus Daia was appointed Caesar over the Asiatic provinces and Egypt. Eight years later, however, in his struggle with Licinius for supremacy in the east, Maximinus died in Tarsus.[87] During the subsequent joint rule of Licinius and Constantine a milestone found in the Cilician Gates attests to some road repairs.[88]

In A.D. 333, Smooth Cilicia along with Syria was visited by famine. The shortage of food may have been exasperated by the presence of troops in the region preparing for war against Persia.[89] The Persian Wars of the 4th c. A.D., however, had little direct impact on Smooth Cilicia, except that the region lay on the main route from Constantinople to Antioch.[90] In A.D. 362, the Emperor Julian passed through the region, visiting Aegeae where he restored the columns of the Temple of Asclepius, which had by then been converted into a church.[91] Apparently he was so favorably impressed with Tarsus that he planned to transfer the imperial residence there from Antioch. Although this goal was never realized, he did achieve his desire to be buried in Tarsus after he was killed in war against the Persians in A.D. 363.[92]

At the end of the 4th c. A.D. Smooth Cilicia was beset by raids by the Tzannoi (a Black Sea tribe), the Huns and the Isaurian Balbinas, who burned the cities of Anazarbus, Irenopolis (Neronias) and Castabala Hierapolis.[93] Soon thereafter, in A.D. 408 during the reign of Theodosius II, Diocletian's province of Cilicia was subdivided into two smaller provinces, Cilicia I in the west, with its metropolis at Tarsus, and Cilicia II in the east, whose metropolis was Anazarbus. Cilicia Prima included the cities of Elaeussa, Corycus, Pompeiopolis (Soloi), Adana, Augusta, Mallus and Zephyrium, while Cilicia Secunda contained the cities of Mopsuestia, Aegeae, Epiphaneia, Alexandria ad Issum, Rossos, Irenopolis, Flaviopolis and Castabala Hierapolis.[94]

During the 5th c., the Isaurean regime ushered in by the eastern Roman emperor Zeno sparked bloody conflict throughout the Eastern Empire. With the death of Zeno in A.D. 491 and the eventual quelling of the Isaureans, Cilicia entered a period of prosperity reflected by the number of churches constructed in the late 5th and early 6th c.[95] This prosperity was cut short, however, by a combination of natural and man-made disasters. Earthquakes rumbled through Anazarbus in A.D. 525 and 561 and devastated Antioch in A.D. 526 and 528. The Emperor Justinian sent relief to both cities.[96] Other natural disasters occurred as well, most notably the flooding of the Cydnus River, which damaged Tarsus. In response to the flood Justinian rebuilt two bridges, one at Adana and the other at Mopsuestia.[97] In A.D. 531 Huns, in alliance with the Persians, invaded Cilicia Secunda and in A.D. 540 the Persians themselves came close to the region, capturing and burning Antioch before returning to their homeland.[98] Two years later plague struck the Eastern Mediterranean, rising the following year and again in A.D. 561.[99] The region also suffered a cattle plague in A.D. 553 and earthquakes hit Antioch in 551, 557 and 558.[100] Finally, during this time there were

violent clashes among chariot factions at Tarsus.[101]

Throughout the late 6th and early 7th c. A.D. Smooth Cilicia once again saw the passage of troops marching against Persia. In A.D. 613, having lost Antioch, the Emperor Heraclius fell back to Cilicia and was besieged at the Cilician Gates. The Persians conquered Tarsus along with the rest of Smooth Cilicia and held the region until Heraclius recovered it in A.D. 627. The area would remain in Roman hands for less than a decade, however. After the defeat of the Roman army by the Arabs at Yarmuk in A.D. 636 Heraclius abandoned the territory south of the Taurus Mountains. Garrisons were evacuated and the populations of Mopsuestia, Anazarbus, Adana, and Tarsus fled into Asia Minor. For a time Smooth Cilicia became a no-man's land, a frontier between the Romans and Arabs.[102]

Smooth Cilicia under Arab, Byzantine and Armenian Rule: 8th-14th c. A.D.

During the 8th c. the Arabs fortified Smooth Cilicia, beginning with the rebuilding of Mopsuestia by Caliph Omar II (A.D. 717-720). By this time the Cilician plain was only sparsely inhabited. In A.D. 787-788 Harun al Rashid rebuilt Tarsus and in subsequent years fortified Adana, Mopsuestia, Anazarbus, Irenopolis (Neronias) and Epiphaneia.[103] Although the Byzantines made several attempts to regain Smooth Cilicia from the Arabs throughout the 9th and early 10th c., it was not until A.D. 965, thanks to the efforts of Emperor Nicephorus, that the region once again came under Byzantine control.[104] In the mid-11th c. the Byzantines repopulated Smooth Cilicia with Armenians resettled from their kingdom in the north. During the latter part of the 11th and throughout the 12th c., Armenians, Byzantines, Crusaders and Turks all vied for control of the region. Finally in 1198 Smooth Cilicia was unified under Armenian rule and was recognized by the Europeans as the Kingdom of Cilicia. This ushered in a period of relative peace and prosperity interrupted first by Mongol raids and finally brought to an end by the Mamluk conquest of the 14th c. The last Armenian king was carried off in captivity to Egypt in A.D. 1375.[105]

This historical overview provides a framework in which to place the settlements in the Plain of Issus, which are discussed in the next chapter. As shall be seen in Part 2, it also helps explain the presence of the ancient remains at Küçük Burnaz.

---

[1] Jean 1999, 32-33. The parameters of Kizzuwatna were fairly flexible over time, but chiefly consisted of the Cilician plain as well as the mountains to the north and northeast.
[2] Freu 2001, 25-31; Desideri and Jasink 1990, 51-109; Gurney 1990, 19; Garstang and Gurney 1959, 50-62. According to Yakar (2001, 41-43) this annexation resulted in a 70% rise in settlements in the region of the Ceyhan River (ancient Pyramus) and the area to the east (the Plain of Issus). Yakar interprets this expansion as a state initiated settlement policy.
[3] Jasink 1991, 255. Jones (1983, 191-93) suggested that during this time Cilicia was colonized by Greek refugees, the Kelekesh of the Sea Peoples, perhaps to be identified with the

Cilicians of the Troad mentioned in *Iliad* 6.397 and 415. In support of this theory are the numerous foundation myths from various Cilician cities. For these myths see Mutafian (1988, 29-109). Recently, however, Jean (1999) has presented convincing arguments to the contrary, and suggests that any Greek activity in Cilicia would have been limited to traders in transit to Syria and Egypt.

[4] For the following see Jasink (1991, 256-59) and Desideri and Jasink (1990, 111-63).

[5] The name was eventually adopted by the Greeks as "Kilikia" and came to stand for both regions.

[6] Jasink 1995, 117-24, Desideri and Jasink 1990, 151-63. It is during this time that Greeks may have tried to gain a foothold in Cilicia, since there is mention of "Ionians" being repulsed by Sennacherib in 696 B.C. It has been suggested by Jones (1983, 193-94) that during the same period several Greek settlements were established on the coast of Rough Cilicia, as well as a single colony at the western end of Smooth Cilicia at Soloi.

[7] Earlier commercial texts from the reigns of Nabopolassar through Nabonidus (626-539 B.C.) also mention the region of Hume. Desideri and Jasink 1990, 165-75.

[8] Herodotus (1.74) records that Syennesis the Cilician and Labynetos the Babylonian acted as mediators between the Lydians and the Medes in 585 B.C. Houwink ten Cate (1961, 28-29) interprets this to mean that the Cilician and the Babylonian must have been of equal stature and suggests that Syennesis ruled Pirindu (Hilakku/Rough Cilicia) while the Babylonian Labynetos controlled Hume (Que/Smooth Cilicia).

[9] Desideri and Jasink 1990, 177-202.

[10] Xen. *An.* 1.2.22-27; Olmstead 1948, 376. Casabonne (1999) argues that the imposition of a satrap did not mark the end of local rule.

[11] For a discussion of the logistics of the battle see Bauer (1899), Janke (1904, 49-74) and Hammond (1980, 94-110). For the identification of the mound of Kinet Hüyük with Issus see Hellenkemper (1984). Although Janke and other scholars have identified the Pinarus River with the Deli Çayı, Hammond and now Ozaner and Çalık (1995) give compelling reasons why the Payas River is the better candidate for the Pinarus. For reports on the recent excavations at Kinet Hüyük (Issus) see Gates 1994a, 1994b, 1995, 1996, 1997, 1999, 2000, 2001, 2002, 2003.

[12] Diod. Sic. 18.3.1, 18.39.6; Curt. 10.10.

[13] An exception occurred during the mid-3rd c. B.C., when Ptolemy III took Soloi, Zephyrium and Mallus. Antiochus III regained these cities in 197 B.C. After the Peace of Apamea the lands south of the Taurus Mountains, i.e. Cilicia, were left to Antiochus, indicating that this region was a basic component of the Seleucid kingdom. See Cohen (1995, 362).

[14] Strabo 14.5.8, 14.13-16; Desideri 1991a, 147-52.

[15] Cohen 1995, 55-56.

[16] Desideri 1991a, 144. Jones (1983, 197-98) suggests that Aegeae was a military colony of Macedonians and that Alexandria ad Issum may have been a synoecism of Myriandus and Issus, two neighboring cities that lost importance in the Hellenistic period. For more on these cities see Cohen 1995, 355-57 (Aegeae), 358-60 (Antioch on the

Cydnus/Tarsus), 360-62 (Antioch on the Pyramus/Magarsus).

[17] So Magie (1950, 280-81), but see Cohen (1995, 56) and Mørkholm (1966, 116-18) who admit the likelihood that Antiochus IV was responsible for these foundations, but point out that there is no direct evidence for associating the cities' name changes with the king.

[18] Cohen 1995, 362-63 (Antioch on the Sarus/Adana), 365-66 (Epiphaneia/Oeniandus), 366-69 (Hierapolis/Castabala), 371-72 (Seleucia on the Pyramus/Mopsuestia).

[19] Meyer 2001; Jones 1983, 199-200. Although certain Cilician cities minted coins under Persian rule local coinage had ceased with the Macedonian conquest, with the exception of the city of Soloi.

[20] Jones 1983, 201.

[21] The basic discussions of the *provincia Cilicia* between 102 and 67 B.C. can be found in Syme (1939), Liebmann-Frankfort (1969), Levick (1967, 21-25), Sherwin-White (1976, 1984, 97-101) and Freeman (1986). Although it has been suggested that Cilicia was annexed when the *provincia Cilicia* was established, most scholars agree that this did not occur until the time of Pompey.

[22] Jones 1983, 201.

[23] Plut. *Vit. Luc.* 14.5, 22.5, 26.1, 29.4. It is known that the city of Soloi in Smooth Cilicia was depopulated by Tigranes and it has been suggested that among the other eleven cities were those which later were given pirate populations, namely Adana, Mallus and Epiphaneia. Magie 1950, 296 n. 36.

[24] Strabo 14.665, 671; Plut., *Vit. Pomp.* 28.4; App. *Mith.* 96,115; Dio Cass. 36.37.6; Flor. 1.41.14, Vell. Pat. 2.32.5; Pomp. 1.71, Livy, *Per.* 99.

[25] Magie 1950, 298-300. For Pompey's installation of the pirates see Leach (1978, 73), Seager (1979, 37-38) and Greenhalgh (1980, 96). For the eras of cities in Smooth Cilicia see Ziegler (1993).

[26] Strabo 8.75, 14.3.3, 14.5.8. For the date of its era see Boyce (1969); for the remains of the harbor of Soloi Pompeiopolis see Vann (1995).

[27] Syme 1939, 305.

[28] Syme 1939, 302-305; Magie 1950, 383-84, n. 18; Levick 1967, 24.

[29] For Tarcondimotus see Sullivan (1990, 187-92), Hoben (1969, 195-211), Syme (1995, 161-65), Calder (1912) and more recently Sayar (2001, 373-80) and Tobin (2001, 381-87). It is assumed that Tarcondimotus was installed by Pompey around 64 B.C., although the earliest reference to him does not appear until 51 B.C. when he is mentioned by Cicero (see below). Cicero calls him a toparch, as does an inscribed statue base from Castabala Hierapolis (Heberdey and Wilhelm [1896] 28, #63). Later the title of king is bestowed on him, either by Caesar or more likely, Antony (see below).

[30] Jones 1983, 204. For Castabala see Heberdey and Wilhelm (1896, 25-31), Verzone (1957, 54-57), Dupont-Sommer and Robert (1964), Krinzinger and Reiter (1993), Sayar, Siewert and Taueber (1989), and Syme (1995, 153-60). For Anazarbus see Heberdey and Wilhelm (1896, 34-38), Gough (1952), Verzone (1957, 9-25), and Sayar (2000).

[31] Tarcondimotus must have had access to the sea, since he sent ships to fight both at Pharsalus and Actium (see below).

Since Aegeae began a new era in 47 B.C., it is thought that Tarcondimotus may have been stripped of that city after Pharsalus. In 20 B.C. Augustus, who had formerly removed the Tarcondimotid dynasty from power, reinstated the kingdom. According to Dio, however, he did not return their coastal holdings but gave them to Archelaus of Cappadocia (Dio. LIV.9). Although the coastal regions are not mentioned by name, it is known that Cappadocia received Corycus and Elaeussa at that time. See Jones (1983, 205) and Magie (1950, 377, n. 53). Both Jones and Magie agree that the dynasty should have had a port closer to hand, somewhere on the Gulf of Issus. At one time the author suggested that the port could have been that at Küçük Burnaz. See Tobin (2001, 385-86).

[32] Magie 1950, 390-401; Sherwin-White 1984, 290-97.

[33] For Pulcher's governorship, see Magie (1950, 387-90).

[34] Cic., *Att.* 6.2.4.

[35] Cic., *Att.* 5.15.1, 5.18.1, 5.20, 5.21.2; Cic., *Fam.* 8.10, 15; Plut., *Vit. Cic.* 36.

[36] Cicero (*Fam.* 15.1.2) praises Tarcondimotus as the most faithful ally beyond the Taurus and the most friendly to the Roman people.

[37] Cic., *Fam.* 15.4.7.

[38] Cic., *Att.* 5.20; Plut., *Vit. Cic.* 36.5.

[39] For a discussion of the Cicero's campaign against the "Free Cilicians" see Shaw (1990, 223-26).

[40] A few years later Metellus Scipio also earned the title of Imperator from a victory against tribesmen in the Amanus. Caes., *B. Civ.* 3.31; Magie 1950, 403.

[41] Dio Cass. 41.63; Flor, 2.13.6; Magie 1950, 402-404.

[42] Caes., *B. Afr.* 66.

[43] Dio Cass. 41.62; Magie 1950, 410. Although the terms of Caesar's pardon are not known, it is significant that a daughter born to Tarcondimotus around this time was named Julia, who later bore a son named Gaius Julius Strato. It has been suggested that Julia was named after the victor of Pharsalus, but it may well be that Caesar had conferred Roman citizenship on Tarcondimotus. However, if Tarcondimotus had indeed been in possession of Aegeae at this time, it is possible that Caesar took the port city from him, since it celebrated its era in 47 B.C.

[44] Dio Cass. 49.22.3. The dismemberment of Cilicia began earlier, however. In 49 B.C. the three Phrygian dioceses were transferred to Asia. Likewise by 43 B.C. Cyprus was in Egyptian hands, probably given to either Arsinoe or Cleopatra by Caesar. Also by 43 B.C. Pamphylia had been transferred to the province of Asia, although this could have occurred previously, perhaps at the time of the transferal of the Phrygian dioceses. See Syme (1939, 324-28).

[45] Dio Cass. 47.26.1-2; Appian, *BC* 4.64; Magie 1950, 419-21.

[46] Strabo 14.5.18, in a chronologically vague passage, says that Tarcondimotus was given the title of king by the Romans during his (Strabo's) time. For the coinage and portrait of Tarcondimotus, see Tobin (2001, 383-85).

[47] Dio Cass. 48.24.2; Appian, *BC* 5.8 and 5.11; Plut., *Vit. Ant.* 25.

[48] Dio Cass. 48.24, 3 and 39; Frontin., *Str.* 11.5.36, Appian, *BC* 4.63, 5.65; Livy, *Per.* 127; Strabo 14.660; Vell. Pat. 2.78.1; Just., *Epit.* 42.4.7; Plut., *Vit. Ant.* 28.1, 30.1, 33.1, 4; Flor.

2.19.3; Magie 1950, 430-32.

[49] Syme 1939, 326. Amyntas of Galatia received Pisidia, while Polemo of Laodicea was given territory called "Cilicia," probably Lycaonia. Rough Cilicia was transferred to Cleopatra.

[50] Plut., *Vit. Ant.* 61.1; Dio Cass. 50.14.

[51] Dio Cass. 54.9.2; Magie 1950, 443-45. Upon the restoration of the monarchy, whatever coastal possessions that had been attached to the previous kingdom were given to Archelaus of Cappadocia. Magie 1950, 475.

[52] Pliny, *NH* 5.93; Jones 1983, 204.

[53] Jones 1983, 205; Gough 1952, 93-94. For Augusta see Gough (1956) and Hild and Hellenkemper (1990, 201-202). The city of Anazarbus came under Roman rule no later than the reign of Claudius, see Gough (1952, 94).

[54] Jones 1983, 205; Magie 1950, 512-14. In A.D. 17, upon the death of King Antiochus III, Tiberius had annexed Commagene.

[55] Hild and Hellenkemper 1990, 245-248; Gough 1952, 94; Hild 1993, 222. The city was later renamed Irenopolis, see Hild (1993) and (Honigman) 1950.

[56] Suet.,*Vesp.* 8.4.

[57] Modern Kadirli, see Hild and Hellenkemper (1990, 378-79), Jones (1983, 204-05), and Gough (1952, 94).

[58] See above, note 55.

[59] Hild and Hellenkemper 1990, 33; Magie 1950, 576.

[60] Dio Chrys. *Or.* 33 and 34; Desideri 2001; Jones 1983, 206-207; Magie 1950, 599-600; Broughton 1938, 791-92.

[61] Attested on a few coins, see Cohen (1995, 366), Gough (1976), and Magie (1950, 595).

[62] Sayar 1993, 323.

[63] Halfmann 1986, 193.

[64] Magie 1950, 620-21.

[65] Set up by the guild of linen workers in A.D. 136. Gough 1952, 96; Hicks 1890, 240-41.

[66] Sayar 2002, 458.

[67] Philostr., *VS* 2.71; Halfmann 1986, 48, 213.

[68] SHA *M. Ant.* 26.4.9; Ballance 1964, 140-42.

[69] SHA *Sev.* 9.5; Magie 1950, 669-71; Birley 1999, 112.

[70] Hdn. 3.6.9. Probably to be identified with the Pillars of Jonah. See above, p. 2.

[71] Magie 1950, 685; Halfmann 1986, 224. Levick (1969) suggested that Caracalla's route to the east followed that of Alexander the Great. Her use of the archaeological record (coins, inscriptions) to chronicle the places where Caracalla stopped en route has been fine-tuned by Johnston (1983) who removes a number of Levick's entries as insecurely associated with Caracalla.

[72] Johnston (1983, 73), contra Levick (1969, 436) who associates the name change with Elagabalus.

[73] Sayar, Siewert and Taeuber 1989, 10-12.

[74] For the games, Levick (1969, 435) and Johnston (1983, 72). For the name change of Adana, Johnston (1983, 73) *contra* Levick (1969, 435) who assigns the name change to the reign of Caracalla.

[75] SHA *Sev. Alex.* 39.6; Magie 1950, 690.

[76] Sayar 1993, 320 n. 10; Dagron and Feissel 1987, 161, no. 101.

[77] For a discussion of Roman roads in modern day Turkey with

a catalogue of milestones, see French (1981). Milestones of Caracalla: nos. 6, 26; Macrinus: no. 5; Elagabalus: nos. 1, 16, 24; Alexander Severus: nos. 3, 15, 27, 30, 31. For a recent discovery of another milestone of Alexander Severus see Sayar (1993, 320). Alexander Severus was also responsible for building a bridge over the Pyramus River at Mopsuestia, and Caracalla widened the path leading through the Cilician Gates, Sayar (2002, 454).

[78] Russell 1991, 287; Sayar 1993, 319-20.

[79] Magie 1950, 697-98; Kettenhofen 1982, 23-37.

[80] Halfmann 1986, 233-34; Sayar, Siewert and Taeuber 1989, 12; Weiss 1982, 202.

[81] Two milestones of Gordian III are in the Adana Museum. French 1981, nos. 11 and 21.

[82] Kettenhofen 1982, 38-96.

[83] Maricq 1958, 313, lines 27-30; Kettenhofen 1982, 106-13.

[84] Magie 1950, 708-709.

[85] Hild and Hellenkemper 1990, 34.

[86] Barnes 1982, 201, 206.

[87] Hild and Hellenkemper 1990, 34-35.

[88] French 1981, 10, no. 26.

[89] Theophanis *Chronographia* (ed. de Boor) 5824, p. 29.13-23; Hild and Hellenkemper 1990, 34; Downey 1961, 354.

[90] On returning from the wars in A.D. 361, the Emperor Constantius II died in Mopsucrene while traveling through the Cilician Gates. Amm. Marc. 21.15.1-3; Hild and Hellenkemper 1990, 36.

[91] According to Euseb., *Vit Const.* 3.56., Constantine had attacked the temple.

[92] Amm. Marc. 22, 23.2.4-5, 25.9.12-13; Hild and Hellenkemper 1990, 36-37.

[93] Ioannis Malalae *Chronographia* (ed. Dindorf) 345-47.

[94] Hild and Hellenkemper 1990, 38-39; *Notitia Dignitatum* (ed. Seeck), Or. 1.62, Or. 22 (Cilicia) and 30 (Cilicia Secunda); Ioannis Malalae *Chronographia* (ed. Dindorf) 365.

[95] Hild and Hellenkemper 1990, 40-42.

[96] Ioannis Malalae *Chronographia* (ed. Dindorf) 419.5-422.8; Procop., *Hist. Sec.* 18.42. In gratitude, Anazarbus first called herself Justinopolis and then Justiniapolis. Gough 1952, 98. Both Justinian and Theodora helped rebuild Antioch. Downey 1961, 519-29.

[97] Procop., *Aed.* 5.5.17-20; *Hist. Sec.* 18.40.

[98] Ioannis Malalae *Chronographia* (ed. Dindorf) 472; Downey 1961, 533-46; Hild and Hellenkemper 1990, 42.

[99] Theophanis *Chronographia* (ed. de Boor) 6053 p. 235; Downey 1961, 553-57.

[100] Downey 1961, 558.

[101] Procop. *Hist. Sec.* 17.2-4; Hild and Hellenkemper 1990, 42-43; Dagron 1980.

[102] Honigmann 1987, 521; Kaegi 1992, 237-40; Bowersock, Brown and Grabar 1999, 377; Hild and Hellenkemper 1990, 43-44.

[103] Hild and Hellenkemper 1990, 47-48.

[104] For a discussion of these events as well as the sources, Hild and Hellenkemper (1990, 43-59) and Ostrogorsky (1980, 290).

[105] For the history of the Armenians in Cilicia see Ghazarian (2000), Hild and Hellenkemper (1990, 63-84), Edwards (1987, 3-10), and Boase (1978, 1-33).

Early Travelers

As has been recently pointed out, before the 20th century Cilicia received many fewer European visitors than the rest of Turkey, because of the remoteness of the region, its often unhealthy climate, and the prevalence of bandits.[1] Fortunately, some doughty travelers did visit the Plain of Issus and recorded what they saw there. Because of the recent industrialization of the plain, their testimonia is particularly valuable since many of the monuments they describe no longer exist.

One of the earliest visitors was Pierre Belon du Mans, who journeyed from Alexandretta (Iskenderun) to Adana in the 16th c. His narrative comments chiefly on the rich wildlife and plant life abounding in the region, paying special attention to a small variety of wolf native to the plain.[2] More useful is Richard Pococke's travelogue of 1745 in which he related the testimonia of "some English gentlemen" who describe what they call the "Iron Gates" (Karanlıkkapı).[3] Early in the 19th c. Sir John MacDonald Kinneir describes his passage through the Karanlıkkapı and along the sandy and marshy shore of the Gulf of Issus, while traveling from Misis (Mopsuestia) to Payas (Baeae).[4] More informative are the writings of William F. Ainsworth, who made several visits to the Plain of Issus in the 19th c. and provides good descriptions of the ruins at Karanlıkkapı and those at the neighboring mound of Muttalip Hüyük. He also mentions seeing a gate buried in sand, located in the dunes east of Muttalip Hüyük. This ruin, probably to be identified with the Eastern Arch of Küçük Burnaz (Building 6), is the only part of the site mentioned by any early traveler.

Shortly after Ainsworth's visit to the region Victor Langlois also reported briefly on passing through what he called the "Gates of Timur or the Iron Gates" (Karanlıkkapı), on his route from Misis to Payas.[5] Late in the 19th c. Rudolf Heberdey and Adolf Wilhelm, as part of their masterly survey of Cilicia, visited the Plain of Issus and provide a good discussion of the ruins at Karanlıkkapı, including a plan of the gateway.[6] Probably the most valuable description of the area comes from Alexander Janke, who conducted a lengthy study of the remains in and around the Plain of Issus early in the 20th c.[7] One year after Janke's work was published, Gertrude Bell passed through the region, visiting Epiphaneia.

Modern Studies in the Plain of Issus and Survey of Sites

The few modern studies conducted in this region have been surveys, although one excavation is currently taking place. In the 1950's Michael and Mary Gough visited Epiphaneia after completing their survey of Anazarbus and Castabala Hierapolis to the north. They camped at the site for several weeks in order to survey the remains. Although disappointed by the poor preservation of the ruins and the lack of inscriptions, the Goughs undertook some detailed measurements of some of the buildings. Unfortunately they did not create a

plan of the site, and their results were never completely published.[8] In 1951 Veronica Seton-Williams surveyed a large tract extending from Mersin to Payas and as far north as Kozan in the foothills of the Taurus Mountains. Her focus was primarily on Bronze Age sites, and she did not include the swampy and sandy shoreline of the Gulf of Issus.[9] More recently Hansgerd Hellenkemper and Friedrich Hild have produced two valuable works concerned with the topography and monuments of both Smooth and Rough Cilicia.[10] Although their works concentrates on Late Antiquity and embrace a large area, their research is of immense value for the study of the Plain of Issus in all periods.

In 1991, Ilknur Özgen and Marie-Henriette Gates of Bilkent University, Ankara conducted a survey of the coastal regions of the Gulf of Issus, from Yumurtalık to Payas, concentrating on the regions not surveyed by Seton-Williams.[11] The results of the survey, as yet published only as a preliminary report, are of great importance to the present work, since they provide the only systematic study of the region directly fronting the Gulf of Issus. Upon the completion of the survey, Gates began the excavation of a large mound located on the eastern side of the Gulf of Issus, Kinet Hüyük (ancient Issus). The on-going excavations have produced evidence of settlement from the Neolithic through the Hellenistic periods, and after a gap, medieval.[12]

It was also in the course of the Özgen/Gates survey that the site at Küçük Burnaz was first identified. In 1994 the author studied these remains, the results from this project are presented in the second part of this work. As mentioned above, however, the key to understanding this site lies in recognizing its relationship with its neighboring settlements. Thus the following few pages summarize the evidence for the ancient remains in the northern Plain of Issus, those found near the shoreline within a 12-km distance from Küçük Burnaz (map 3). This overview is based on the testimony of early travelers, previous scholarship and personal observation. The value of this survey is twofold. First it gives context for the remains at Küçük Burnaz, and second, it provides documentation for sites that at present are imperiled by the current industrialization of the region.

Epiphaneia[13]

The most important site in the plain was Epiphaneia, almost certainly to be associated with the ruins at Gözene, situated 7 km west of modern Erzin and 12 km northeast of Küçük Burnaz.[14] The city is located in the center of the Plain of Issus along an ancient road that connected the pass at Toprakkale to Baeae. The Burnaz Suyu runs along the eastern edge of the ruins. The original name of Epiphaneia was Oiniandos, which may actually have been a Hellenized version of the Hittite name Winowanda.[15] The name change occurred some time in the Hellenistic period when the city was apparently re-founded, either by Antiochus IV Epiphanes or one of his descendants.[16] In 67 B.C. Epiphaneia, which may have been depopulated by the Armenian king Tigranes earlier in the century, received a settlement of pirates from Pompey; during Cicero's governorship of 51 B.C. a garrison was stationed there; in A.D. 260 Epiphaneia was one of the cities sacked by Shapur I. The city appears to have converted to Christianity early on, becoming the seat of a bishopric by the 4th c., with the bishops participating in various synods and councils over the next three hundred years. As was the case with the rest of the plain, the region was abandoned to the Arabs in the wake of Arab invasions of the 630's but in A.D. 806 Epiphaneia was rebuilt and fortified by Harun al-Rashid. The city, under the name of al-Kanisa, was featured in several Arabic itineraries, which listed it as a stage on the road between al Haruniya (Irenopolis) to the north and Bayyas (Baeae) to the south.

In a recent conference on Cilicia, Epiphaneia was characterized as the least studied city in the region.[17] No plan of the site exists, although Epiphaneia was featured in Seton-Williams' Cilician survey, where she collected material dating to the Roman, Late Roman, Byzantine and Islamic periods.[18] In recent times the remains have suffered from the increased agriculture and industry in the region, and today the ruins have been given over to the cultivation of wheat and vegetables. Lately the ruins have been further damaged by the construction of the E-90, a highway that cuts through the western quarter of the site. In the absence of a modern study and in light of the recent damage to the site, it is important to review both the testimonia left behind by early travelers as well as the few modern commentaries that exist. Also, the author has visited the site annually from 1993-2000 and can offer some observations.

Today the substantial ruins, which stretch over 150 ha., are dominated by an acropolis whose natural formation is enhanced by habitation debris, perhaps from a pre-Roman settlement.[19] The structure that most impresses the visitor to Epiphaneia is the aqueduct, whose arcades approach the city from the east, flanking the dirt road leading to the site (fig. 3). The aqueduct was seen by Heberdey and Wilhelm, as well as by Janke, who recorded that the channel was supported on

Figure 4. Aqueduct pier, Epiphaneia

116 arched piers. Today, many fewer piers exist. They are constructed of mortar and rubble with a facing of black basalt ashlars (fig. 4), and terminate at the southeastern slope of the acropolis in a semicircular structure, perhaps a nymphaeum.

Northeast of the terminus of the aqueduct is a low hill whose southern face contained a theater. Mentioned by Heberdey and Wilhelm, Janke and Bell, the theater was measured by Michael and Mary Gough, who determined its diameter of 87 m, making it the largest theater in Cilicia.[20] Although today the scene building and seats of the theater have been robbed

Figure 3. Aqueduct arcade, Epiphaneia

Figure 5. Theater, Epiphaneia

out, much of the upper wall of the cavea has survived. The eastern wall of the theater is particularly well preserved, built of mortar and rubble with a facing of irregularly shaped basalt stones laid in rough courses. Semi-circular buttresses help support the wall (fig. 5).

South of the theater are the remains of a round structure, perhaps an odeion, and in the field below are the stumps of marble columns, still in situ, forming three sides of a colonnaded court or agora. These can probably be associated with a colonnaded street commented on by all the early travelers, and seen by the Goughs. West of this is a large structure of mortar and rubble, whose wall facings have been robbed out. Recent

looting within the building has exposed hypocaust tiles, indicating that the structure was a bath (fig. 6). In this same area Bell mentioned a structure she identified as a gymnasium, and it is likely that she was referring to the same building. The fields closest to the bath are filled with pottery; some of Roman date but also much sgraffiato ware of the 13th c. A.D. Since many fragments of kiln furniture are found in the fields as well, it is likely that Epiphaneia was a pottery-manufacturing center in the medieval period (color plate 1), and below.

The sketchy remains of two temples and two churches can be seen at Epiphaneia. Directly south of the terminus of the aqueduct is a broad terrace constructed of mortar and rubble; in

Figure 6. Hypocaust tiles, Epiphaneia

Reproduction of Color Plate 1. Pottery scatter, Epiphaneia, found on page 95.

places molded orthostate blocks are still in situ. This may be the remains of a temple platform. Along the edge of the field south of the colonnaded court is a jumbled pile of massive limestone blocks, which preserve moldings, anatharosis and cuttings for clamps (figs. 7, 8). In the field east of the blocks are terracotta tiles with crosses in relief. These represent the

Figure 7. Temple block, Epiphaneia

remains of a building, which, according to Hellenkemper and Hild, had been bulldozed in 1983 in the course of clearing fields for farming.[21] The structure, seen by all the early travelers, and identified by Heberdey and Wilhelm as a church and by Janke as a temple, was studied by Gough who determined that it was a church dating to the 5th or 6th c. A.D., which incorporated spolia from an Imperial temple.[22] Gough identified a second church from the same period, although he

Figure 8. Temple blocks, Epiphaneia

did not indicate where in the city it was located. It may be identified with a structure lying north of the bath, just below the theater, originally roofed with a groin-vault. Bell identified this building as a church.

Originally, a city wall with projecting towers surrounded Epiphaneia. Measured at 2 m thick by Gough in 1950, by 1969 when Hellenkemper and Hild visited the site there was no longer any trace of the wall. To the west of the city can still be seen a series of graves cut into the basalt bedrock, presumably located out of the city limits.

Several Greek inscriptions have been found at Epiphaneia. Heberdey and Wilhelm transcribed a dedication set up by the boule and demos honoring one Caecilius son of Heliodoros, and Hellenkemper and Hild recorded an inscription from the 3rd c. A.D. in which the demos honored a leading woman in the community, Pakovia.[23] Another inscription, discovered in Epiphaneia in the late 1950's, also honored a woman, Praxia, for whom the boule and demos erected a statue.[24]

Karahüyük (Tell Araklı)[25]

This small (15-m high) steep-sided mound is located 9 km southwest of Epiphaneia and approximately 8 km west of Küçük Burnaz. Its ancient name is not known. Although today it stands 4 km from the sea, it appears to have been directly on the shoreline in antiquity. In her survey of the site, Seton-Williams reported the presence of Bronze Age and Iron Age pottery but no ceramics of later date. She attributed walls visible on the mound to the Hittite Period. During the 1991 survey conducted by Özgen and Gates, however, Roman and medieval ceramics were collected, but no earlier material was found.[26] The walls on the mound, constructed of fist-sized basalt stones facing a stone and mortar core with the occasional decorative band of brick, appear to be late Roman in date.

A Greek inscription dating to the 1st or 2nd c. A.D. discovered 50 m south of the mound attests to further Roman activity in the region. The inscription records the dedication of a grain market by one Dionysios son of Alexander, in fulfillment of a promise made by his father when he served as *demiurge* for the second time. Dionysios also paid for the purchase of the houses that encroached upon the building site.[27] The inscription is noteworthy for being one of the few inscriptions found in the Plain of Issus. The dedicant appears to have been a member of a family of *euergetes*, since he not only paid for a market, but his father had served twice as *demiurge*, an eponymous magistrate in the cities of Cilicia. The name of the city in which the market was built is not mentioned, and it has been suggested that the inscription originally came from Epiphaneia.

Karanlıkkapı (The Black Gate)[28]

The remains known as Karanlıkkapı (the Black Gate), Demir/Temir Kapı (the Iron Gate), or the Gate of Tamarlane, are located 5 km northwest of Küçük Burnaz. They stand at the end of a narrow defile created by a stream, which runs for 3.5 km through the Djebel Misis. This pass, which Strabo called the Amanus Gates, lies along the roadway from Misis (Mopsuestia) to the Plain of Issus, and was a main artery used from antiquity up to recent times. Many western travelers passed through the pass and commented on the ancient remains. The ancient route is now bypassed by a superhighway running from Adana to Gaziantep, which cuts through the Djebel Misis to the north.

The Black Gate itself was located at the eastern end of the pass. A 17th c. itinerary describing the route from Constantinople to Mecca comments on the "Timur Kapı," a stone arch standing in a wooded and dangerous region.[29] In 1707 Paul Lucas passed under the arch noting a quantity of executed Turks hanging from it.[30] The arch was constructed of mortar and rubble with a facing of tightly fitted basalt ashlar blocks. It was noted by Ainsworth and an etching of the gate, dating to 1838, depicts the appearance of the gate around the time of his visit.[31] At the end of the 19th c. Heberdey and Wilhelm visited the gate and were reportedly unimpressed, believing that it could not have been very ancient. They created a plan, however, and supplied measurements for the structure.[32] Janke, who mapped the entire pass through the Djebel Misis and carefully described the ruins, published a photograph of the arch, which was still standing at the time of his visit in the early 20th century. When Hellenkemper and Hild visited the pass in 1983, however, the arch had collapsed.

The 1838 etching also shows that the road leading up to the arch was flanked on one side by a wall constructed of small polygonal stones and on the other by a construction of white (?) limestone blocks. Heberdey and Wilhelm saw the limestone remains and identified them as a second arch whose vault had collapsed. They suggested that this was the predecessor to the one in black basalt.[33] Hellenkemper and Hild located the remnants of the limestone structure seen by Heberdey and Wilhelm and proposed that the building may have been a side gate. Hellenkemper and Hild also report that

east of the arch they found traces of the original Roman road and to the north, on the hill above the arch, they observed the ruins of a Roman bath, perhaps from a *mansio*.

When the present author visited the gate in 1994 there was no trace of the limestone structure and most of the basalt arch had disappeared. The only well-preserved feature was a basalt wall located on the northwest side of the arch (fig. 9). This wall, described by Ainsworth, Janke and Heberdey and Wilhelm, and depicted in the 1838 etching, was constructed of mortar and rubble faced with polygonal-shaped basalt stones, divided at intervals with stringcourses of tufa.

A second visit to the site in 1997 revealed that the fieldroad leading to Karanlıkkapı had been bulldozed. The present state of the ruins is unknown.

Muttalip Hüyük[34]

This mound is located on the sea at the confluence of the Karanlıkkapı and Boğazdere streams, and is 4 km west of Küçük Burnaz. Today it stands within the confines of the Toros Gübre ve Kimya factory (fig. 10). The 18-m high mound is ovoid with a N/S axis, measuring 170 m N/S and 130 m E/W. The profile of the mound is steep, except at the south where it slopes gently towards the sea. Several early travelers record walls ringing the mound, as well as the remains of towers and arches.[35] In the survey conducted by

Figure 9. Karanlıkkapı

Figure 10. Muttalip Hüyük

Özgen and Gates, walls were found on the top of the mound, chiefly on its western and northwestern sides. Constructed of a mortar and rubble core with a black basalt facing, occasionally interrupted with stringcourses of brick, the walls are of late Roman date. At the southern foot of the mound is a wall of large basalt blocks, identified by the Özgen/Gates team as a possible harbor wall. The pottery collected on the mound dates from the Hellenistic through the medieval period, including many Islamic-period ceramics. Further evidence of Roman activity at the mound comes from an unfinished marble sarcophagus (fig. 11), decorated with swags, bucrania and an uninscribed *tabula ansata*, probably dating to the 2nd or 3rd c. A.D.[36]

Figure 11. Sarcophagus from Muttalip Hüyük

Earlier pottery was identified immediately north of Muttalip Hüyük, where the mound had been bulldozed for a large parking lot. Although all that remained was a thin deposit of burnt soil and burnt clay bricks, the pottery scatter dated to the Chalcolithic Period, thus giving evidence for occupation during the late 5th-4th millennium B.C.

Hellenkemper and Hild have identified the mound as Mutlubakke, whose modern name Mutallip seems to be linguistically related. The city is first documented in A.D. 431 when it sent their bishop Valentinos to the Council at Ephesus.[37] Although the reference does not firmly establish the location of Mutlubakke, the *Acta Conciliorum Oecumenicorum* lists it directly after Castabala Hierapolis, thus placing it somewhere in the Plain of Issus. Hellenkemper and Hild associate the site with al-Mutaqqab, a fortified coastal settlement mentioned in Arabic sources, located in the vicinity of al-Massisa (Mopsuestia) and al-Kanisa (Epiphaneia). Since the Özgen/Gates survey collected many Islamic-period ceramics from the site, Hellenkemper and Hild's identification appears likely. The Arabic name seems to be a variation on Mutlubakke.[38] It is interesting to note that the name Mutlubakke does not appear to be Greek or Latin, and may be the indigenous name for the mound. The first part of the word "mutlu" is reminiscent of the Anatolian/Luwian stem *muwa*- meaning "strength" or "vigor."[39] Thus the mound may have borne the name long before the Greco-Roman occupation of the site.

Figure 12. Tower, Turunçlu

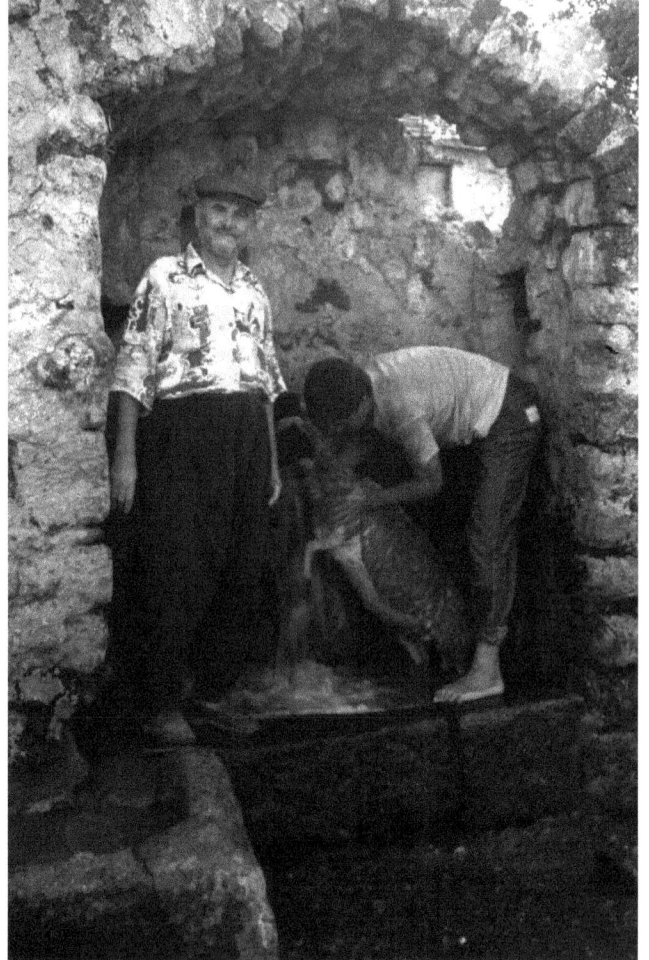

Figure 13. Rebuilt aqueduct, Turunçlu

Figure 14. Aqueduct system, west of Turunçlu

Figure 15. Aqueduct system, west of Turunçlu

Turunçlu and neighboring aqueducts[40]

The village of Turunçlu, a producer of oranges (as its name implies) lies 4.5 km north of Küçük Burnaz. The ancient remains there include a (Byzantine?) tower built from black basalt blocks (fig. 12) and a section of ancient water channel, still in use today, which has been greatly modified over time (fig. 13). This waterway appears to connect to an aqueduct system running SW along the foothills of Hama Tepe, where long sections of a water channel rest on the ground (fig. 14). The channel is built of rubble and mortar with a facing of basalt polygonal stones and brick string courses. In certain cases where the channel turns a corner, the facing is of brick (fig. 15). The channel is lined with waterproof cement. Near this aqueduct system was found an inscribed statue base honoring Demetrios Tullianos, a philosopher. Its discovery so far from a city center is surprising, but it may have come from a rural villa.[41] Traces of a different (?) aqueduct system have been noticed on the slopes of a hill southwest of Turunçlu, 1 km north of Muttalip Hüyük, which probably brought water to that site.[42] Another section of aqueduct southwest of Muttalip Hüyük may also have served the settlement (figs. 1, 2).[43]

The history and appearance of the monuments that ring the northern end of the Gulf of Issus give testimony to occupation in Black Cilicia from the Chalcolithic period to Mamluk times. At least two roads and, by Roman and late Roman times, several aqueduct systems formed the infrastructure for a region that included a city, Epiphaneia, and other settle-

ments whose ancient identities are as yet unknown (Turunçlu, Karahüyük). Certainly a port would have serviced the region, perhaps located at Mutlubakke (Muttalip Hüyük). Most of the monuments discussed above have been known from the 19th c., the remainder of this work, however, will examine the recently discovered site at Küçük Burnaz.

---

[1] Borgia 2003, 41.
[2] Belon du Mans 1554, 163-64.
[3] Pococke 1745, 175.
[4] Kinneir 1818.
[5] Langlois 1861, 468.
[6] Heberdey and Wilhelm 1896, 17.
[7] Janke 1904, 44-49.
[8] Information on Epiphaneia is recorded in a memoir by Mary Gough (1954, 135-52) and in a short encyclopedia entry by Michael Gough (1976, 315).
[9] Seton-Williams 1954.
[10] Hild and Hellenkemper 1990; Hellenkemper and Hild 1986.
[11] Özgen and Gates 1992a; 1992b.
[12] For the identification of the site as Issus and a bibliography of the excavations, see Chapter 2, page 9, n. 11.
[13] For a full discussion of the history of this site and an overview of its remains see Hild and Hellenkemper 1990, 249-51; Hellenkemper and Hild 1986, 102-04, 127-28. Pertinent early travelers reports: Heberdey and Wilhelm 1896, 18; Janke 1904, 14-15; Bell 1906, 3-4.
[14] Although several inscriptions have come to light from

Gözene, none mention the place name. Ancient literary testimonia make the position of Epiphaneia at Gözene likely.

[15] Trémouille 2001, 64, n. 53.

[16] Mørkholm (1966, 117) suggests the possibility that the city could have been founded by Antiochus VIII (121-96) who also used the epithet Epiphanes.

[17] Spanu 2001, 449.

[18] Seton-Williams 1954, 155.

[19] Although Seton-Williams found no pre-Roman material during her survey, other visitors including the author have found what appear to be Iron Age sherds, and sherds perhaps from the Bronze Age (Prof. Marie-Henriette Gates, personal communication). This is to be expected if the association of Oiniandos with Hittite Winowanda is valid.

[20] Spanu 2001, 449-50.

[21] For a plan of the church, reproduced from one made by Heberdey and Wilhelm, see Hild and Hellenkemper (1984, 194, fig. 3).

[22] Gough 1955, 202-04.

[23] Heberdey and Wilhelm 1896, 18. The Pakovia inscription has been recently republished by Dagron and Feissel 1987, 210, n. 3.

[24] Doblhofer 1961-1963, 14-18.

[25] Özgen and Gates 1992a, 392; Özgen and Gates 1992b, 10; Hild and Hellenkemper 1990, 440; Seton-Williams 1954, 159; Janke 1904, 15.

[26] Özgen and Gates (1992a, 392) suggest that alluviation may have obscured the lower and earlier levels of the mound.

[27] Dagron and Feissel 1987, 209-11.

[28] Hild and Hellenkemper 1990, 174; Hellenkemper and Hild 1986, 101-02; Ainsworth 1838, 189; Heberdey and Wilhelm 1896, 17; Janke 1904, 44-49.

[29] The account is found in Mutafian 1988, 325-26.

[30] Lucas 1714, 283-4.

[31] Reproduced in Mutafian (1988, fig. 32.1) and Alishan (1899, 475).

[32] Width of the arched passageway: 3.30 m., length of the arched passageway: 5.40 m., length of the entire gateway including walls flanking the passage through the arch: 18.20 m.

[33] Heberdey and Wilhelm 1896, 17.

[34] Özgen and Gates 1992a, 390; Özgen and Gates 1992b, 4-5; Hild and Hellenkemper1990, 361-62.

[35] Ainsworth (1842, 90-91 and 1838, 188) and Janke (1904, 15-16) call the mound Kara Kaya and Heberdey and Wilhelm (1896, 17) refer to it as a tumulus.

[36] The sarcophagus was removed from Muttalip Hüyük in 1949 and now rests in the courtyard of the mosque of Sarımazıköyü, a village 6.5 km north of the mound.

[37] *Acta Conciliorum Oecumenicorum*, 1.1.3.25.

[38] According to Tomaschek (1891, 71). Medieval European naval charts list a site on the Gulf of Issus, alternatively called Montecaybo, Caybo Mons, Monte Gabo or Monte Gaibo, whose names seem to stem back to the Arabic.

[39] Houwink ten Cate 1961, 166-69. I am grateful to Theo P.J. van den Hout of the Oriental Institute for his discussing this issue with me.

[40] Hild and Heberdey 1990, 452; Janke 1904, 14.

[41] Dagron and Feissel 1987, 211.

[42] Özgen and Gates 1992a, 390; Özgen and Gates 1992b, 5; Hellenkemper and Hild 1986, 102; Janke 1904, 15; Heberdey and Wilhelm 1896, 18.

[43] Hild and Hellenkemper 1990, 362; Hellenkemper and Hild 1986, 127.

During the course of the 1991 Özgen/Gates survey, the remains of an ancient settlement featuring several large and well preserved Roman-period structures, were first documented. The ruins, designated in the survey report as Site 11, lay 4 km east of Muttalip Hüyük, 500 m inland from the coast and along a small stream, the Küçük Burnaz.[1] The site presented an undulating vista of rolling sand dunes punctuated by occasional plants: fig trees, oleander bushes and snake grass (fig. 16). The ruins emerged from the dunes sporadically, some having been exposed by bulldozer, while others only appear when the gently drifting sand dunes shift. The settlement was first brought to light in 1987, when several local factories began bulldozing the area for sand. Enticed by the broad dunes, which promised the easy collection of sand, the factory workers soon discovered that the dunes actually comprised a thin layer of sand over ancient structures. Nevertheless, bulldozing continued for the next seven years.

The Özgen/Gates team spent one day at the site, collecting pottery and sketching and describing the architecture. A geomorphological study of the site was also conducted, which concluded that it originally stood directly on the seashore. Over the centuries the accumulation of sand and silt brought down from the hills by various streams had caused the sea to recede, leaving the ruins at Küçük Burnaz approximately half a kilometer from the seashore. Özgen and Gates suggested that the site had been a port in antiquity; a marsh lying just south of the ruins probably indicated the position of the original harbor.[2] The team identified at least five structures, all standing at an impressive height, at or near ceiling level. The pottery collected indi-

cated three phases of occupation: early Imperial Roman, middle-late Roman and Medieval.

In a report made to the Turkish Ministry of Culture, Özgen and Gates stressed the danger Site 11 faced from illicit digging for sand. They reported that in August 1991 trucks were being driven up to various buildings, removing the sand and weakening the support for the structures, and noted that the arcade of an aqueduct was on the verge of collapse. They concluded their report with a plea for the protection for the site and the need for it to be carefully surveyed and planned.[3]

From 1991 to 1994 the dunes covering the site were periodically bulldozed. Although the staff at the Hatay Museum in Antakya, within whose district the ruins fell, visited the site and voiced concern about its potential destruction, their distance from the site and limited resources made it difficult to protect it from further damage. In 1994, at the invitation of Özgen and Gates, the author agreed to undertake a detailed study of Küçük Burnaz, both in the hopes of stopping the bulldozing and in order to understand the date and function of the ruins.

In the summer of 1994 with the help of two Bilkent University students and architect Andrew Fletcher of Bilkent University, the author conducted a two-week survey under a permit issued by the Turkish Ministry of Culture. The permit allowed the pick-up of artifacts and the measuring of buildings, but not the clearing of sand or soil to further expose the structures. This was a conscious choice on the part of the author, because it was clear that the high degree of preservation of the structures was thanks to the protecting mantle of sand. Once the sand sur-

Figure 16. Küçük Burnaz, general view

Figure 17. Aqueduct in 1991

Figure 18. Aqueduct in 1995

rounding the structures was removed, the structures were in danger of collapse. This can be clearly demonstrated in the case of the aqueduct that runs through the site.

A photograph taken by the Özgen/Gates team in 1991 documents how a bulldozer had exposed the eastern face of the aqueduct's arcade, leaving the sand piled against its western side (fig. 17). By 1994, the sand had eroded away from the aqueduct's western face, and by 1995 one of the piers had collapsed (fig. 18). For the sake of the integrity of the structures, no more sand was removed during the 1994 investigation.

Since the goal was to collect as much data as possible in order to understand the site, all fragments of ceramic and glass and all other finds were gathered for study. Only the areas of the site disturbed by bulldozing yielded finds - the areas that still lay under the layer of sand were sterile. Thus the collection was biased towards gathering objects from the most damaged areas of the site, areas selected at random by the bulldozer. In order to maintain control over the data, the survey team made initial collections over the whole site, walking from north to south in 5-meter wide passes. The first pass, Pass 1, was located at the western banks of the Küçük Burnaz stream, and the final pass, Pass 11, was located over 500 m to the west.[4]

Figure 19. Building 12

Thereafter the team collected all visible materials from the bulldozed regions, noting at which building or area the collection took place.

The remains of eighteen buildings were studied and planned during the 1994 and 1995 seasons at Küçük Burnaz. For the purposes of the study a "building" was defined as having at least two walls joining or in close proximity with one another. During the 1994 season the team began creating a plan of the ruins, compiled from points plotted with an electronic distance measurer (EDM), along with stone by stone drawings of the buildings using hand tapes. The plan was completed in a short season the following year.

The constant motion of the sand created interesting problems for mapping. The present plan, created in July of 1995 depicts all the walls visible at that time (map 4). In subsequent visits to the site (from 1996-2000), however, walls previously plotted have become buried in sand and new walls have appeared. Other unexposed walls can be inferred by observing the position of plants at the site. Since the plants only grow where their roots can gain purchase, they tend to collect on top of walls. Building 12, for example, which has a long N/S-running wall, clearly extends further north than the visible masonry, indicated by a line of snake grass extending due north from the end of the wall for several meters (fig. 19). Such observations help to add information concerning the extent of the structures at Küçük Burnaz, but because of the impressionistic nature of the evidence, the positions of walls indicated through plant growth alone have not been included in the plan.

As can be seen by the site plan, the structures share the same orientation, all of them lying approximately four degrees east of north. The site appears to have been laid out on a grid. Although no actual streets were found, we can infer the position of a few of them. The most obvious is a street running westward from the Eastern Arch (Building 6) to the Central Arch (Building 19). Running perpendicular to this is another road, which skirts the western face of Building 12. A long N/S-running declivity in this region may reflect a roadway. Other streets must have run parallel to these.

One important result of the 1994-95 seasons of fieldwork at Küçük Burnaz was that the Turkish Ministry of Culture successfully put a halt to the damage to the site by compelling Toros Gubre, the company chiefly responsible for bulldozing the site, to erect a fence around the ruins. Another was the rich data set, well-preserved architecture, pottery, glass and coins, analyzed in the remainder of this work.

---

[1] Özgen and Gates 1992b, 2.
[2] Özgen and Gates 1992a, 391; Ozanar, Gates and Özgen 1993.
[3] Özgen and Gates 1992b, 7, 11-2, 1992a, 391.
[4] Cursory investigation also took place on the eastern side of the Küçük Burnaz stream, as well as in the area west of Pass 11. Neither area presented ceramic remains or traces of architecture. Since their terrain was comprised of undisturbed sand dunes, however, buildings and artifacts could have been sealed beneath the sand.

CHAPTER 5. THE ARCHITECTURE

MATERIALS AND TECHNIQUES

All the buildings identified at Küçük Burnaz are constructed with a very fine textured mortar. It is bright white in color, apparently lime-based. Although the site is in a volcanic region, the color of the mortar indicates that it does not comprise volcanic sand. The mortar is used in two ways, as a bond between bricks or as a core mixed with rubble and faced with stone or brick. In the latter case the mortar is quite dense with no evident voids, but it is also very friable. It is mixed with flecks of colored gravel and fist-sized lumps of basalt, but the proportion of stone to mortar is very low. These qualities lend the material a rather unique character compared to that used elsewhere in Asia Minor, where there are usually a great many stones used within the mortar, and the mortar itself has frequent gaps.[1] Although the mortar found at Küçük Burnaz approaches the quality of true Roman *opus caementicium*, it is technically more correct to refer to it as mortared rubble, mainly because it does not appear to have the strength or chemical make-up of the Italian material. It has often been stated that the architecture of Cilicia, unlike that of other provinces in Asia Minor, uses true Italo-Roman techniques in concrete, both because of a strong Roman presence in the region, and due to the volcanic nature of the local sand. Whether these statements are true for the architecture at Küçük Burnaz will be discussed below.

Six varieties of construction techniques are found at Küçük Burnaz, several within a single building. The first four types utilize a stone facing, while the final two types are brick constructions, where brick is used as a facing and as a solid wall material. They have been classified by facing material (stone preceding brick) and by degree of construction effort.

Type 1: Ashlar facing over a mortar and rubble core

Three buildings use ashlars as facings: the two arches (Buildings 6 [fig. 67] and 19), which are faced with large fine grained basalt ashlars and Building 5 (fig. 64), which has an ashlar facing of white limestone. All three buildings use a mortar and basalt rubble core as described above.

Type 2: Carefully shaped polygonal facing over a mortar and rubble core

This construction type can be found in many buildings at Küçük Burnaz: in the reservoir of Building 2 (fig. 21), in the aqueduct (Buildings 15 and 18 [fig. 29]), in Building 1 (the exterior of the northern and eastern walls [figs. 56, 63]), in Building 3 (a section of wall abutting its southwestern corner) and probably in Buildings 4, 12, 8 and 7 (fig. 78). It is characterized by having the dense mortar and rubble core described above, faced with basalt stones whose outer faces have been carefully flattened. Although their edges are occasionally worked to form rough rectangles, more often they are polygonal. The stones average 30 x 30 cm in size and are laid in rough

courses. Occasionally small stones are fitted into the interstices between the larger ones, and in some cases a line of narrow stones form a sort of leveling course within the facing. The joints between the stones are of the same white mortar as used in the core, and are often quite thick, in places measuring up to 10 cm between the stones. This first kind of polygonal facing often has a stringcourse of brick bands, which do not penetrate through the core (figs. 56, 58). These serve as a stabilizer for the facing, in the manner of *opus mixtum*, a technique common in Imperial Roman masonry of the west, but uncommon in Asia Minor, where the bricks typically run through the core.

Type 3: Roughly shaped polygonal facing over a mortar and rubble core

This second type of polygonal facing is much rougher than that of Type 2. It tends to be found on narrower walls, with two faces sandwiching a meager core of white mortar. The mortar joints around the blocks are thinner than in Type 2, and the outer faces of the stones themselves are less well finished. No brick bands are associated with these walls. Examples of this type of masonry occur in Building 2 (in the north exterior wall of Room C [fig. 41], the north wall of Room A [fig. 32], and the eastern extension wall of the reservoir). It is also found in Building 1 (in the eastern wall of the reservoir), in Building 3 (figs. 70, 71), and probably in Building 13.

Type 4: Polygonal facing over a mortar and rubble core with the occasional brick fragment

A third type of polygonal facing can be found within the scanty remains of Buildings 10 and 14. It distinguishes itself from the previous two masonry types by the inclusion of bits of brick intermixed haphazardly within the core and the facing. A few walls built in this type of masonry also include limestone blocks, perhaps spolia (fig. 79). Thus Type 4 walls may reflect the latest phase of construction on the site.

Type 5: Brick facing over a mortar and rubble core

In addition to basalt facings, brick facing is quite common at Küçük Burnaz. The core is identical to that used with the stone facings. Brick facing is found in Building 1 (the reservoir [fig. 47], the inner walls Rooms A, B and C), in Building 2 (Room B, parts of Rooms A, and C [fig. 34]) and in Building 18. Throughout the site the brickwork is fairly consistent. The bricks are usually square, measuring 30 to 35 cm per side, although occasionally rectangular bricks are used (which have a longer side of around 45 cm). The bricks have an average thickness of 3.5 cm, and the mortar joints are of the same height. The top faces of some of the bricks have incised lines creating an X division of four triangles, while others have incised lines that bisect the brick into two triangular regions (fig. 36). The bricks, however, do not seem to have been intentionally broken along these lines.

Type 6: Solid mortared brick

Walls of mortared brick are also found at Küçük Burnaz, usually utilized in apses, seen most readily in the apse of Room A in Building 1 (figs. 59, 60). Solid brickwork also is found lining certain walls (as in the water chamber of the reservoir of Building 2).

As will be seen, the various masonry techniques often occur within the same building, sometimes within a single room. Although at first glance this appears to reflect different phases to the building, or possibly repairs or modifications, it is more likely that in most cases the different masonries are contemporaneous and reflect a specific structural need within a section of a building.

THE BUILDINGS

During the 1991 survey of Küçük Burnaz, five buildings were identified and given consecutive numbers. The 1994 survey recognized thirteen more buildings, which were numbered in the order in which they were found, beginning where the earlier numbering system left off. Because most of the finds are correlated to the original field numbers of the buildings, it has been decided to maintain the original numbering system, even though this often means that the numerical order of the structures does not relate to their relative positions. Many of the buildings, however, can be securely or tentatively identified by function. Thus the buildings whose functions are known or can be guessed will be listed below by title, followed by their field number. Instead of arranging the buildings in the rather random order of field number, or examining them from a given direction, say from north to south, the buildings with known or suspected functions will be discussed first, followed by buildings of unknown use. For clarification of the position of each building, see the site plan (map 4).

The Smaller Baths (Building 2) and Aqueduct (Buildings 13 and 15)

Building 2 lies at the heart of Küçük Burnaz and, of all the structures of the site, has been the most extensively exposed by bulldozing and the subsequent erosion of sand (fig. 20). Its identification as a bath building is fairly secure; it had an aqueduct that provided a steady source of water, it possessed intersecting rooms of unusual shape (some of which contained pipes in their walls) and it presented evidence of ornate decoration. The finds associated with the building are also consistent with a bath: hypocaust tiles, pipes, plaster, marble revetment and window glass.[2] It is referred to as the Smaller Baths, because another larger bath building (Building 1), has been identified to the west. The Smaller Baths is a complex of buildings including a reservoir, aqueduct and a block of rooms to the south.

Figure 20. Building 2, general view with Building 19 at upper left

Figure 21. Building 2, north wall of reservoir

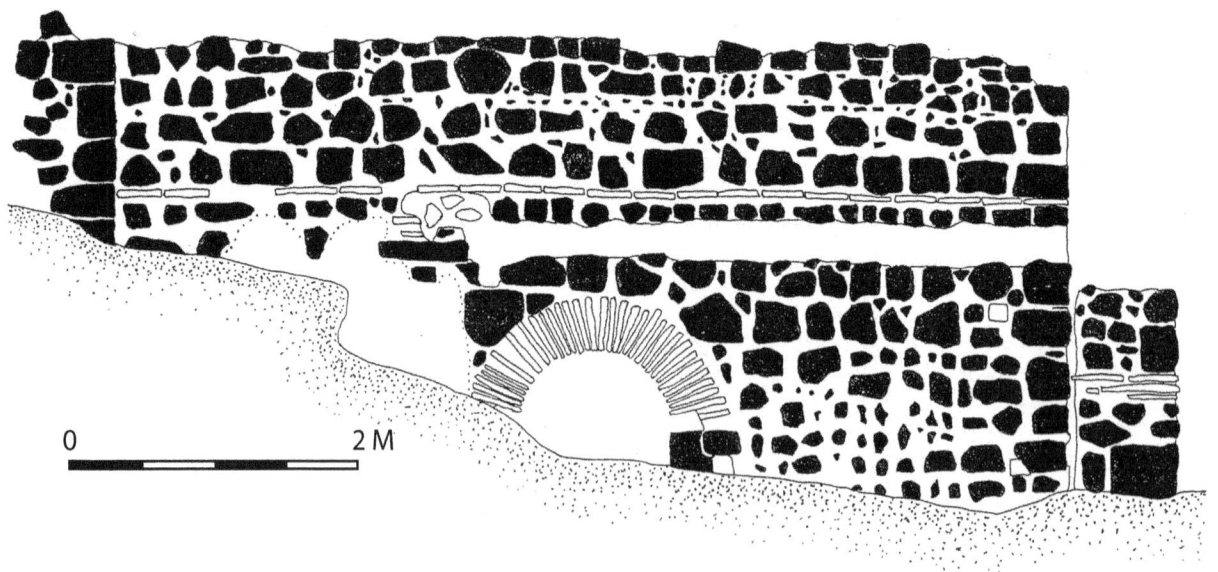

Figure 22. Building 2, drawing of north wall of reservoir

The Reservoir and Aqueduct

The best-preserved portion of the complex is the reservoir. It received water directly from an aqueduct and stands 1 m north of the main bath building. It is rectangular, measuring 6.52 m E/W and 4.70 m N/S, and consists of a lower vaulted room that supports two water basins on its roof. Today it stands at a height of 3 m above the sand, but since its foundations are not visible the original height of the building cannot be determined. It is constructed of Type 2 masonry.

The north wall of the reservoir was clearly the main side of the building (figs. 21, 22). Set into the middle of the wall is an arched doorway of brick, measuring 1 m in width. Above the line of the door a band of bricks, one brick high, runs the length of the wall and above this the wall is recessed by 12 cm. The line of bricks and the setback in the wall may reflect the position of the bottom of the rooftop basins. This wall exhibits evidence for some later modifications. A long trough located just above the line of bricks runs from the western edge of the wall to just beyond the eastern edge of the doorway. It is not part of the original design, since it was created by removing stones, exposing the mortar and rubble core. The trough probably served as the bedding for a roof and perhaps dates to the 13th c. A.D., when it is clear that this building was reoccupied.[3] Similarly, slots cut into the doorway probably reflect modifications in medieval times.

The west wall of the reservoir, partially obscured by sand, does not have the brick band or wall inset seen in the north (figs. 23, 24). A curious feature found here is a square pillar, built in Type 2 masonry which stands *c.* 5 cm from the wall. The function of this pillar is not clear. A similar feature is built into the west wall of the reservoir of the Larger Baths (Building 1). These both may have had something to do with the movement of water.

Both the north and west walls originally were coated in plaster. This is particularly evident on the lower reaches of the building, regions that have been protected by the sand for the longest period of time. Many of the exposed buildings at Küçük Burnaz were so decorated.

The southern and the eastern walls of the reservoir are abutted by a wall which runs along these sides to a point 20 cm beyond the north face of the reservoir and then turns eastward, where it extends for some 8 m before disappearing in the sand (figs. 20, 25). The wall is of Type 3 masonry. At its western end where it abuts the northeastern corner of the reservoir, large quadratic blocks were used. Numerous scaffolding holes are in the wall and its eastern face (that flanking the eastern side of the reservoir) was stuccoed.

At first glance this appears to be a later wall, both because it uses a different type of masonry and because at no place does it bond with the reservoir. However, its function seems to be integral to the basic design of the reservoir, in that it serves as a strong support wall for the southern and eastern water chambers on the top of the building. Also, the N/S-running section

Figure 23. Building 2, west wall of reservoir

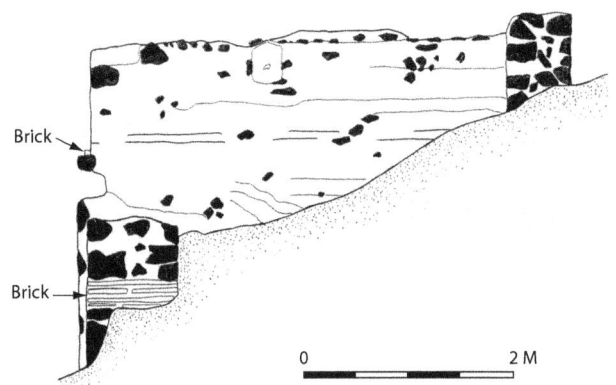

Figure 24. Building 2, drawing of west wall of reservoir

of the wall is on line with the eastern wall of Room D to the south. Thus this wall may be contemporary or closely contemporary with the reservoir.

The top of the reservoir is divided into two nearly square basins (figs. 25-27). The northern limit of the basins is formed by the upper reaches of the north wall of the reservoir. Similarly, on the west the upper reaches of the west wall bound the chamber, but here the inner face of the wall is lined with bricks. The eastern and southern walls are also of rectangular bricks (measuring 44 x 36 cm and 3 cm high) which form a double wall with the Type 3 masonry wall discussed above. The wall dividing the two chambers is constructed of square bricks. All the walls were lined with waterproof cement. Since the interiors of the basins were filled with sand their depths could not be determined but it is possible that the brick band and the inset wall seen on the north face of the reservoir mark the bottom of the basins. The two basins must have communicated with one another, since water from the aqueduct only spilled directly into the eastern basin. The basins were probably open to the air.

Below the basins within the lower portion of the reservoir was a vaulted chamber accessed via the doorway in the north wall and through a short barrel-vaulted passage (fig. 27). The walls of the chamber are in Type 2 masonry while the vault is of brick. The bricks are laid radially in the lower sections of

Reservoir

N

A
B

D

A

B

C

5 M

0

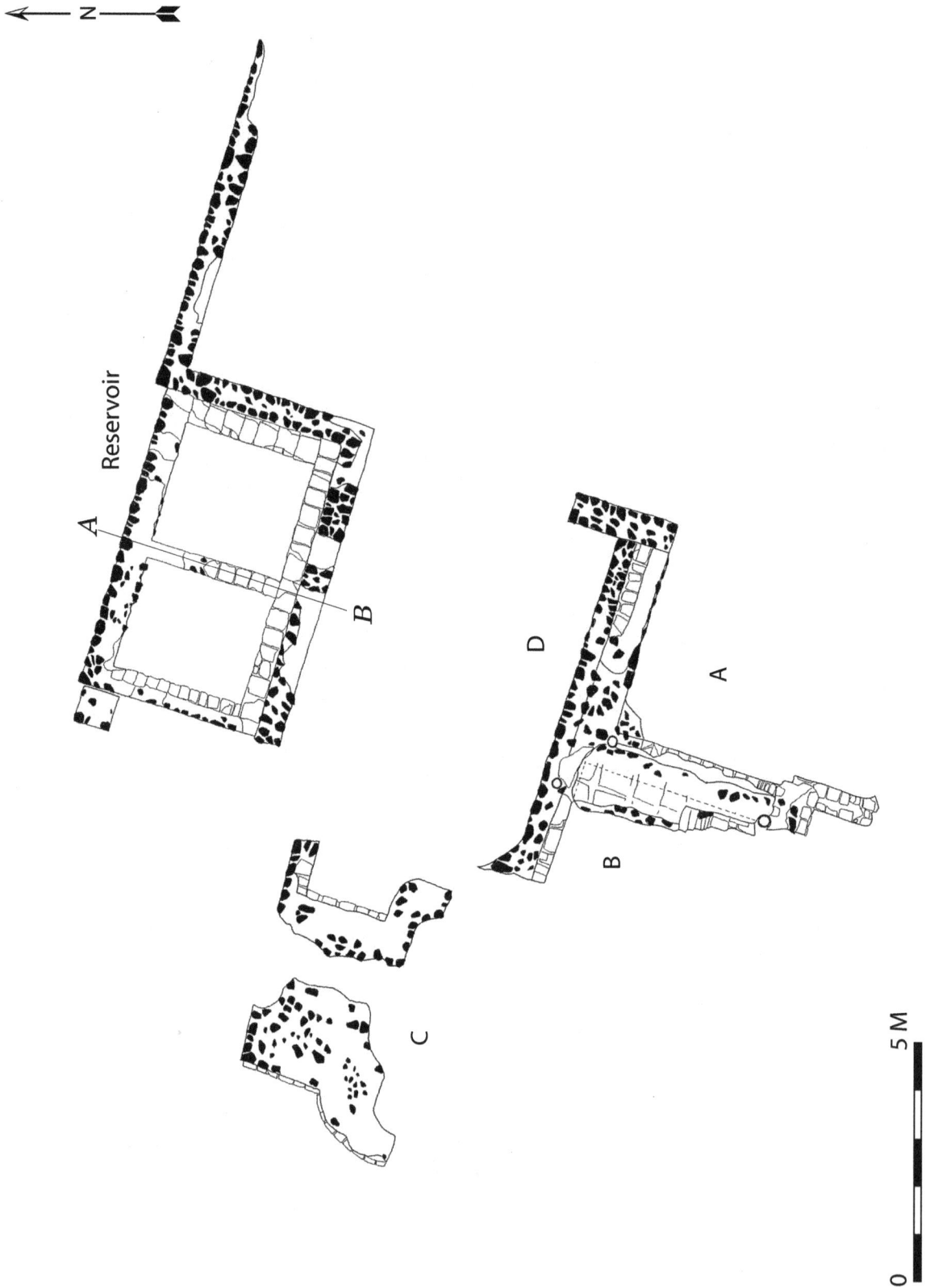

Figure 25. Building 2, state plan

Figure 26. Building 2, top of reservoir

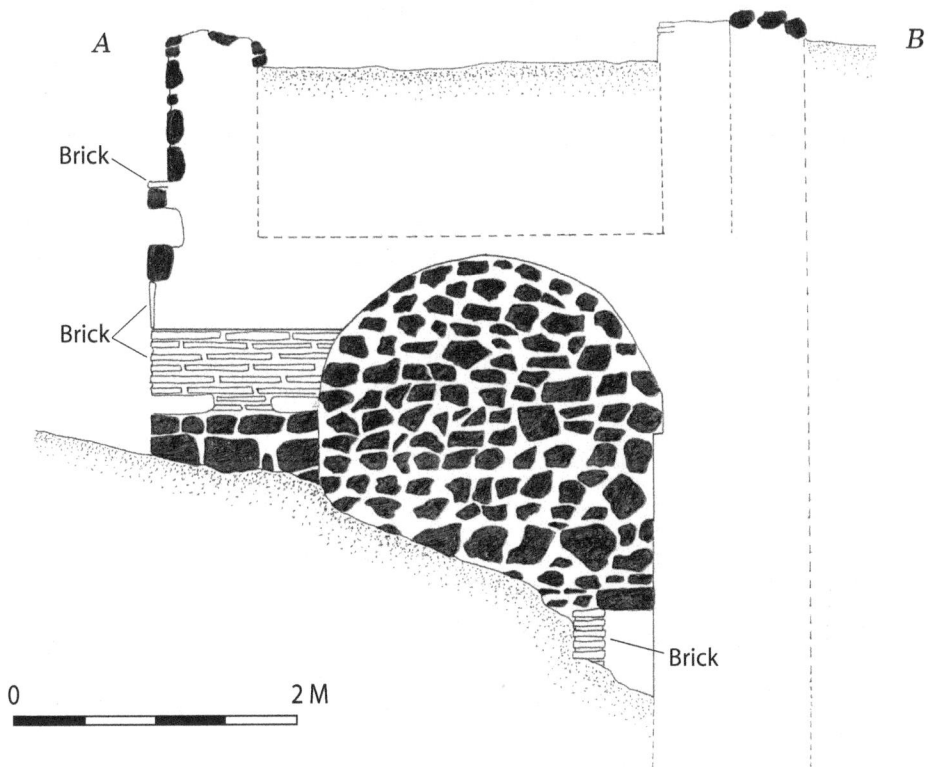

Figure 27. Building 2, section drawing of reservoir

Figure 28. Building 2, aqueduct

the vault but then are pitched to form its upper section, identical to the arrangement found in the vaulted chambers of the reservoir of the Larger Baths (Building 1), discussed below. Today the chamber is partially filled with sand, with the result that its floor is not visible. In the southeast corner, however, a rectangular brick-lined opening is visible, perhaps some sort of conduit. No waterproofing was found on the walls, giving the impression that this chamber may have been used for storing bath equipment or for some other maintenance function.

An aqueduct, whose piers approach in a gently arcing path from the northwest, fed the reservoir (figs. 20, 28, map 4). Twenty piers survive, each spaced approximately 1.50 m from

Figure 29. Building 2, aqueduct, detail of piers

one another. Because the sand level covers their foundations, it is impossible to calculate their exact height. The piers are square (measuring 1.10 m on each side) and are in Type 2 masonry; surviving sections indicate that the arches were also in Type 2 masonry and their outer faces were lined with radially set brick (fig. 29). The *specus*, or water channel, which would have sat atop the arches, has not survived.

The aqueduct disappears into the cotton fields to the northwest after a run of approximately 25 m (fig. 28, map 4). Over 150 m north of the final preserved pier is Building 15, the northernmost building identified in our survey. It is roughly wedge-shaped and constructed in Type 2 masonry. These scanty remains may have had some connection with the aqueduct, since they share the same orientation and construction technique.

Beyond Building 15 the aqueduct cannot be traced. As mentioned in Chapter 1, the region is well-watered and several aqueducts have been identified within the landscape. The city of Epiphaneia was served by an aqueduct fed from a spring near the modern city of Erzin. The same aqueduct apparently ran west of Epiphaneia and can be traced in the low hills north of Küçük Burnaz. This may have connected with a portion of aqueduct identified near Muttalip Hüyük which may in turn have extended as far as Aegeae.[4] While the aqueduct attached to Building 2 is clearly independent of this, it is interesting to note that it was not unique in the immediate vicinity.

The aqueduct was designed to serve the reservoir. Typically an aqueduct terminates in the *castellum divisorum*, a tank which collects the water from the aqueduct and then disburses it into different regions of a settlement.[5] According to the standard variation described by Vitruvius (8.6), there should be a triple basin arrangement in which each basin governed water destined for a different purpose in the city: public fountains, baths and houses. The two best known examples, from Pompeii and Nimes demonstrate a complicated division of water. Although the terminus of the aqueduct at Küçük Burnaz appears to lack the sophisticated arrangements just described, nevertheless, the reservoir may be considered a *castellum*. Rather than serving the entire settlement, it is possible that the two basins allowed water to be fed to different sections of the neighboring baths.

The combination of a rectangular reservoir adjacent to a major building (usually a bath) is a repeating feature in Cilicia.[6] It is found in the Larger Baths (Building 1) at Küçük Burnaz, although there it is not fed directly by a raised aqueduct. At Selinus in Rough Cilicia a reservoir with three vaulted rooms and an open-air rooftop basin stands at the north side of the baths.[7] In Smooth Cilicia two large brick buildings from Augusta, one of which was a bath, have rectangular reservoirs on their eastern sides.[8]

The Bath Building

One m south of the reservoir lie four contiguous sand-filled rooms (fig. 25). To the southeast is Room A, which is nearly square, measuring roughly 4 m on each side (figs. 30, 31). The northern wall of Room A is constructed in Type 3 masonry and is 75 cm wide (figs. 32, 33). It abuts the south wall of Room D and the thickness of the combined walls allowed space for a deep brick barrel vaulted niche that occupies one third of the wall. West of the niche and at a much lower elevation is another arched opening, barely emerging from the sand. The lintel is of brick and flatter than the curve of the adjacent niche. Although it was not possible to investigate

Figure 31. Building 2, Room A

this archway due of the level of sand, it appears to be a doorway between Rooms A and D.

The west wall of Room A is constructed in Type 5 masonry, brick facing over a mortar and rubble core (figs. 34, 35). A doorway at the northern end of the wall communicates with Room B. The actual passageway is below the sand level but can be recognized from a relieving arch built into the wall above the doorway. It is likely that the lintel of the doorway stood at the same height as the top of the doorway in the adjacent wall.

None of the east wall of Room A is still standing. Its point of attachment to the north wall can be seen, however, and fallen masonry lies around the region where the wall once stood (fig. 31). From the debris it is clear that this wall, like its counterpart in the west, was of Type 5 masonry. An apse, inset from the west wall (figs. 30, 36) occupied the southern wall of Room A. The apse was constructed in Type 5 masonry; the bricks here have incised grooves running from corner to corner.

Room A was covered with a groin vault. The intersecting edges of the brick barrel vaults are visible in the three surviving corners of the room as well as in the fallen east wall (figs. 31-35).

The room preserves evidence for its decoration. Numerous fragments of marble revetment were collected here, and metal pins and plaster reflect the means of their attachment (fig. 33).[9] There is also clear evidence that the room had painted plaster decoration. On the upper reaches of the west wall near the relieving arch bright red plaster still adheres to the wall. More red plaster is found in the lower corners of the groin vaults (color plate 2). The painted decoration was not monochromatic, however, since fragments of green, yellow and white plaster, in addition to the red were recovered from the room. It is likely the lower walls were decorated with marble revetment, while the upper walls and vaulting were painted.[10]

West of Room A is Room B (fig. 30), whose east wall, part of its north wall, and the beginning of its south wall are still

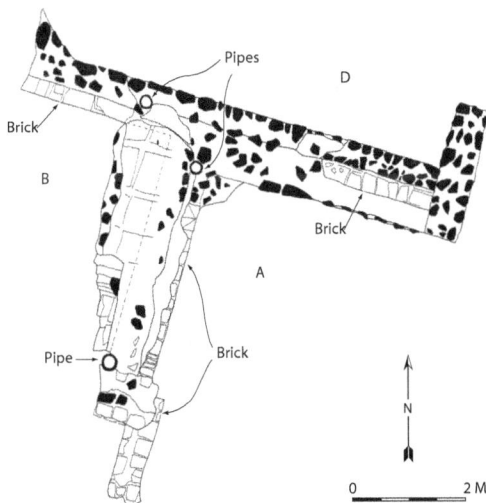

Figure 30. Building 2, state plan of Rooms A, B, D

Figure 32. Building 2, Room A, north wall

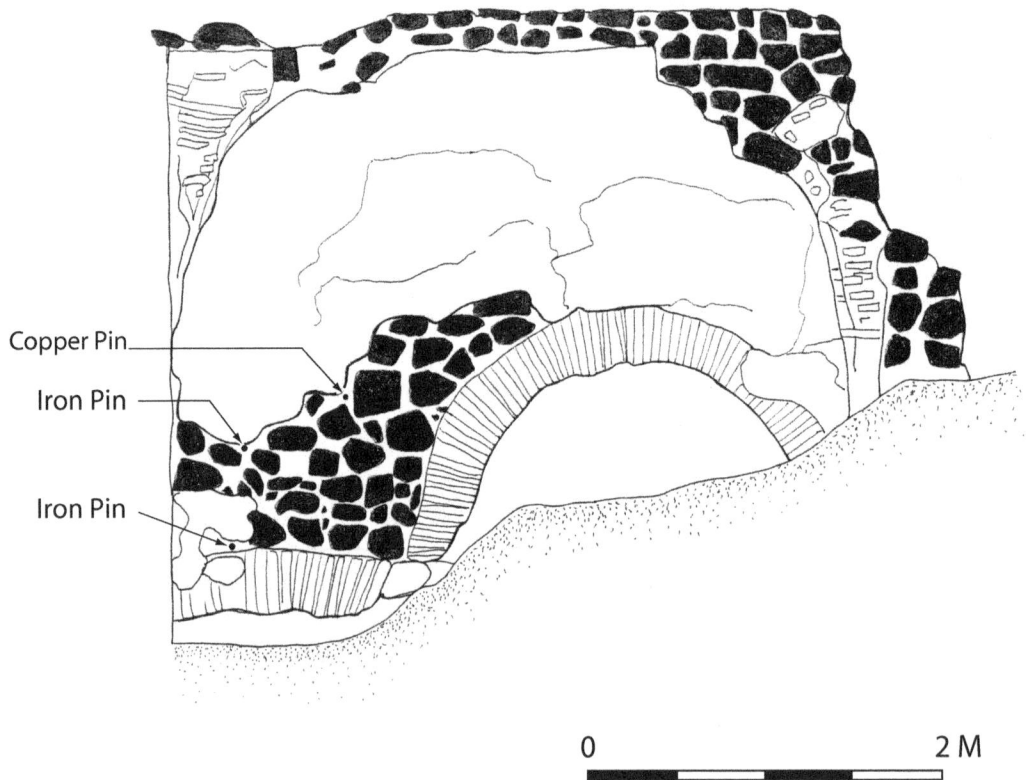

Copper Pin

Iron Pin

Iron Pin

0   2 M

Figure 33. Building 2, drawing of north wall of Room A

Figure 34. Building 2, Room A, west wall

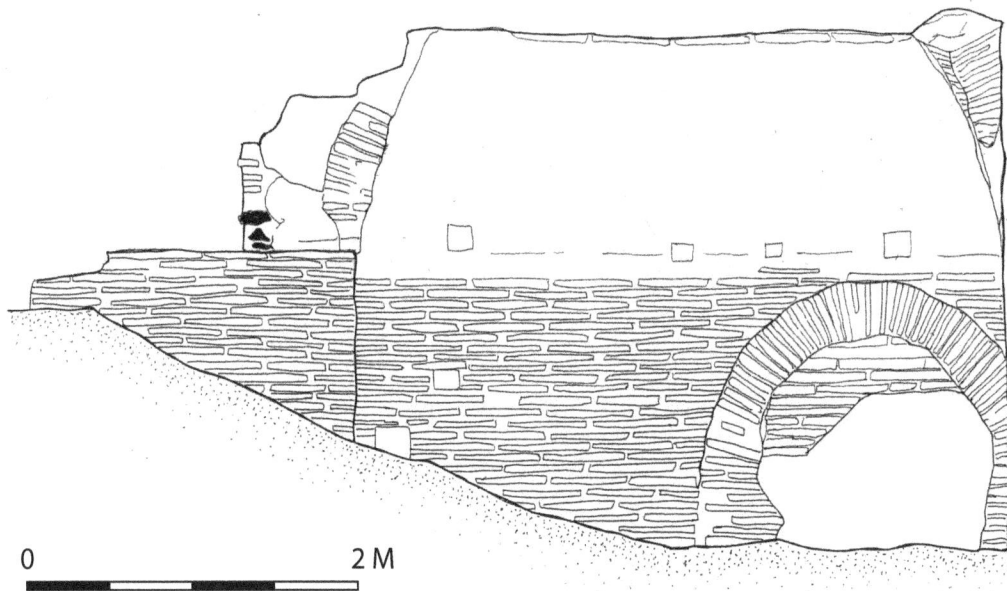

0   2 M

Figure 35. Building 2, drawing of west wall of Room A

Figure 36. Building 2, Room A, apse

standing and constructed of Type 5 masonry. The north wall appears to share its mortar core with the south wall of Room D, which has a basalt facing. Embedded in this core is a terracotta pipe, which most likely served as a flue to usher out heat and fumes from the heating system of the baths (figs. 37, 38).[11] Several flues are also found embedded in the east wall (fig. 39).

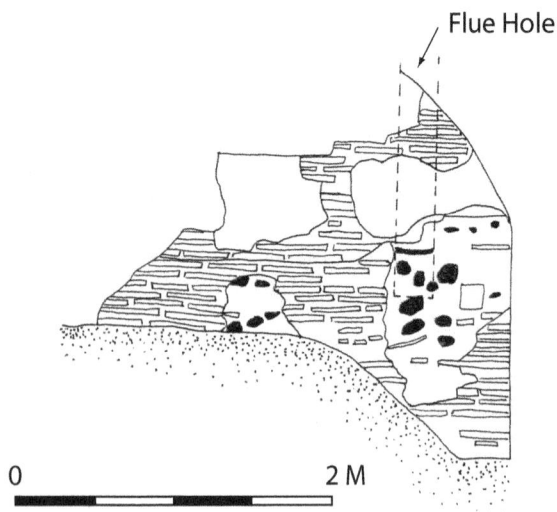

Figure 37. Building 2, drawing of north wall of Room B

Figure 38. Building 2, Room B, flue hole, from top

The east wall preserves traces of the barrel vault that originally roofed Room B (fig. 40). Here it is clear that the lower sections of the vault were of brick, but the very top appears to have been of mortar and rubble. By extrapolating the curve of the vault we can estimate that the room measured 3.12 m E/W.

Room B was also decorated with revetment, since plates of marble were found within this room and numerous iron pins still project from the eastern wall (fig. 39). Plaster adheres to the barrel vault, but no trace of color survives. Nevertheless it is likely that the decoration scheme found in Room A, of painted plaster on the upper reaches of the room and marble revetment below, was repeated in Room B.

Located northwest of Room B is Room C, a particularly difficult area to understand since sand virtually fills it up to roof level and the growth of oleander, fig and snake grass obscures the tops of the walls (fig. 25). Its northern wall is constructed in Type 3 masonry (fig. 41). Extending south from this wall are two cross walls which form a small square chamber originally covered by a barrel vault, whose curved inner lining of brick can just be seen in the sand. The exterior of the vault is flat and consists of a casing of basalt rubble and mortar. Similar "cladding" can be found at the Bath-Gymnasium Complex at Sardis and Building G at Augusta.[12]

An arched opening, barely emerging from the sand, pierces the north wall of Room C. Given its height in relationship to the reservoir (it stands at the level of the basins, that is, at the top of the reservoir), the opening probably should be interpreted as a window. It is possible that a doorway stood below the window, and if this were the case then the barrel-vaulted section of Room C would have served as a passageway.

Beyond the barrel-vaulted region Room C broadens by means of two symmetrical apses preserved to roof level. Traces of brick vaulting indicate the apsidal region was covered in a half dome, whose exterior still preserves the same kind of flat mortar and rubble cladding described above (fig. 42). On the west, part of the wall of the apse has been exposed to show that at least its upper wall was of mortared brick, Type 6 masonry (fig. 43). At its southern extremity where the wall

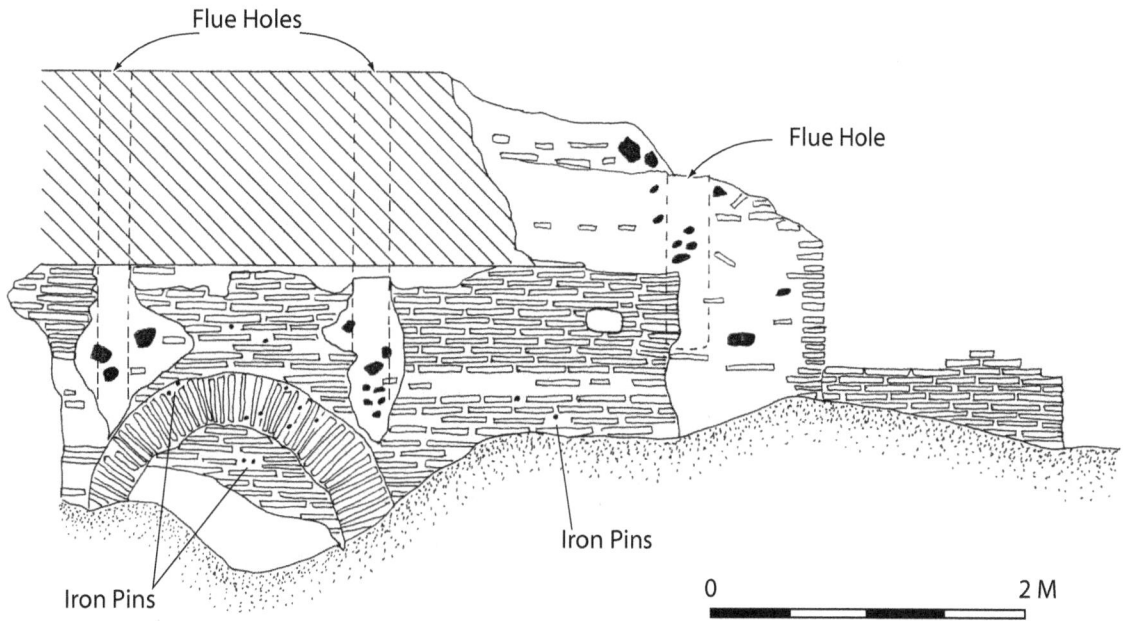

Figure 39. Building 2, drawing of east wall of Room B

Figure 40. Building 2, Room B, north wall

Figure 41. Building 2, Room C, from north

Figure 42. Building 2, Room C, view of vaulting

has collapsed traces of an arched opening can be seen, probably remnants of a window. Other bits of fallen vaulting lie to the south. Unfortunately it is unclear what shape this room took. Figure 44 offers a possible reconstruction.

To the east of Room C is Room D, which, like the other sections of Building 2, is filled with sand (fig. 25). The entire length of its southern wall is preserved and is quite thin (40 cm). The northern wall of Room A abuts the eastern section of its southern face, making the wall appear thicker, but it is in fact a double wall. All walls are in Type 3 masonry.

On the western side of Room D are the remains of an apse (fig. 30) and by extrapolating its curve the dimensions of the room can be obtained: 8.0 x 3.8 m (fig. 44). A fortuitous aspect of the reconstruction is that the projected north wall of Room D is in line with the north wall of Room C. A less happy consequence of the reconstruction is the awkward space created between the two rooms at the northwestern side of the apse. However, a doorway or passageway connecting the two rooms could have occupied this space. No trace of the roofing system was found in Room D. Since the thin walls and lack of brickwork preclude the possibility of the room being vaulted, it may have had a tiled wooden roof. Certainly many rooftiles were recovered in the area (see below).

Although much of Building 2 remains buried in sand, enough has been exposed to allow the creation of a restored plan, which helps recover the function of the rooms and the path of

Figure 43. Building 2, Room C, view of vaulting from the west

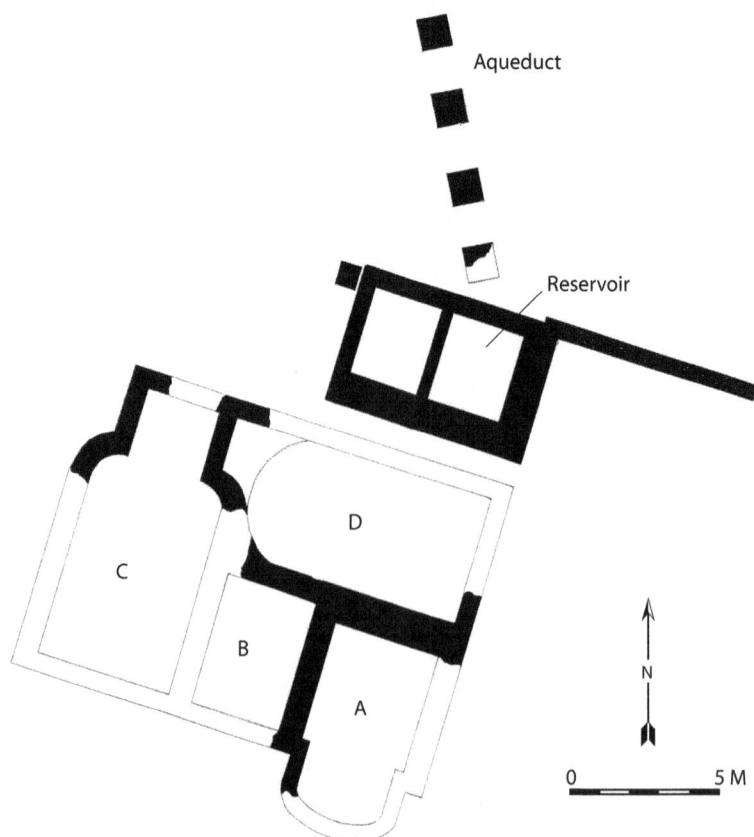

Figure 44. Restored plan of Building 2

circulation (fig. 44). It is possible that Room D, perhaps with a doorway in its eastern wall, served both as the entrance to the complex, and as the apodyterium. Room A communicated with Room D through a doorway in its northwestern corner. None of the surviving walls of Room A show evidence of having been heated, a typical feature of Roman baths from the 1st c. B.C. onwards,[13] thus Room A may have served as the frigidarium.[14] The walls of the neighboring Room B also lack evidence for having been heated, but the flues embedded within them indicate that Room B was located fairly close to the furnace. This room may have been the tepidarium. This leaves Room C as the caldarium, perhaps accessed from Room B through a doorway in a party wall (now lost).[15] Since only the tops of the walls of Room C are visible, it cannot be determined whether the walls were fitted with heating devices. Three hypocaust tiles found in the region just west of Room C, however, lend strength to the suggestion that Room C was the hot room of the baths. It is likely that the bather would have followed a retractive path, by which he progressed through the rooms from cold to hot and then retraced his steps. Alternately, Room C may have also connected with Room D, allowing for an annular circulation.[16]

Even though the designations of the specific rooms are speculative, the general plan of the baths is in keeping with that of many small asymmetrical baths from Lycia, Pamphylia and Rough Cilicia during the Roman and late Roman periods.[17] There, a preponderance of baths have a row of three parallel rooms with a long hall at right angles. Unfortunately, so few baths from Smooth Cilicia have been published that it is not yet possible to recognize a regional type of baths for this area.

The Larger Baths (Building 1)

This building lies at the westernmost reaches of Küçük Burnaz (map 4). Although the building appears to stand in isolation, it should be noted that new walls, previously covered in sand, have emerged since the creation of the plan. These walls stand east of Building 1 and fill in some of the gap between it and the rest of the site to the east. Although the north side of the building is almost completely exposed by bulldozing, the rest is filled with sand. Even half buried, however, Building 1 looks impressive, both for the area it covers and the height of its northern wall (fig. 45). The building comprises two parts (fig. 46). At its north side is a rectangular structure, identifiable as a reservoir, and to its south is a large multi-roomed structure. This arrangement finds parallels with the Smaller Baths just discussed, and the discovery of a hypocaust tile within Room A, would indicate that Building 1 was also a bath.

Figure 45. Building 1, general view

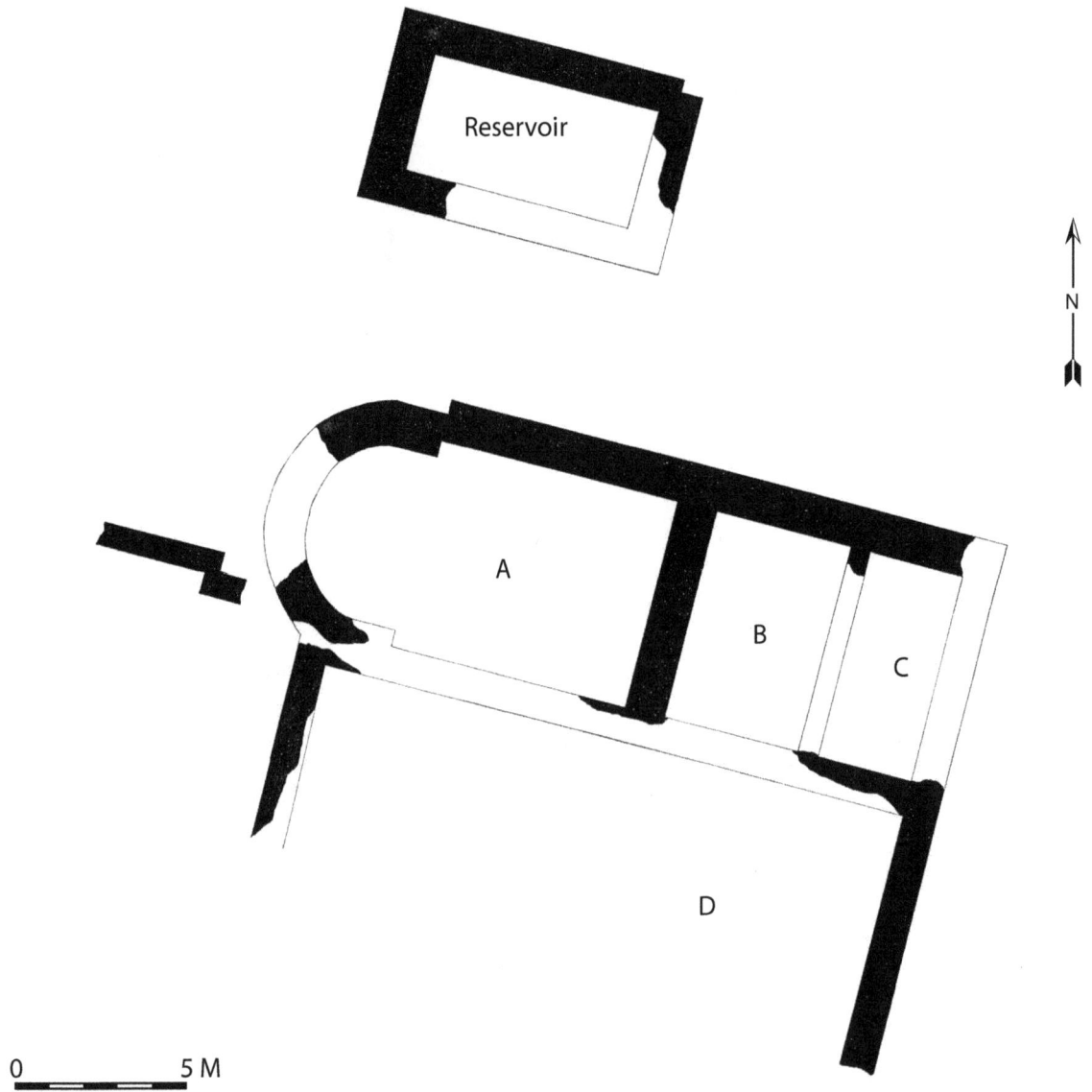

Figure 46. Restored plan of Building 1

Figure 47. Building 1, north wall of reservoir

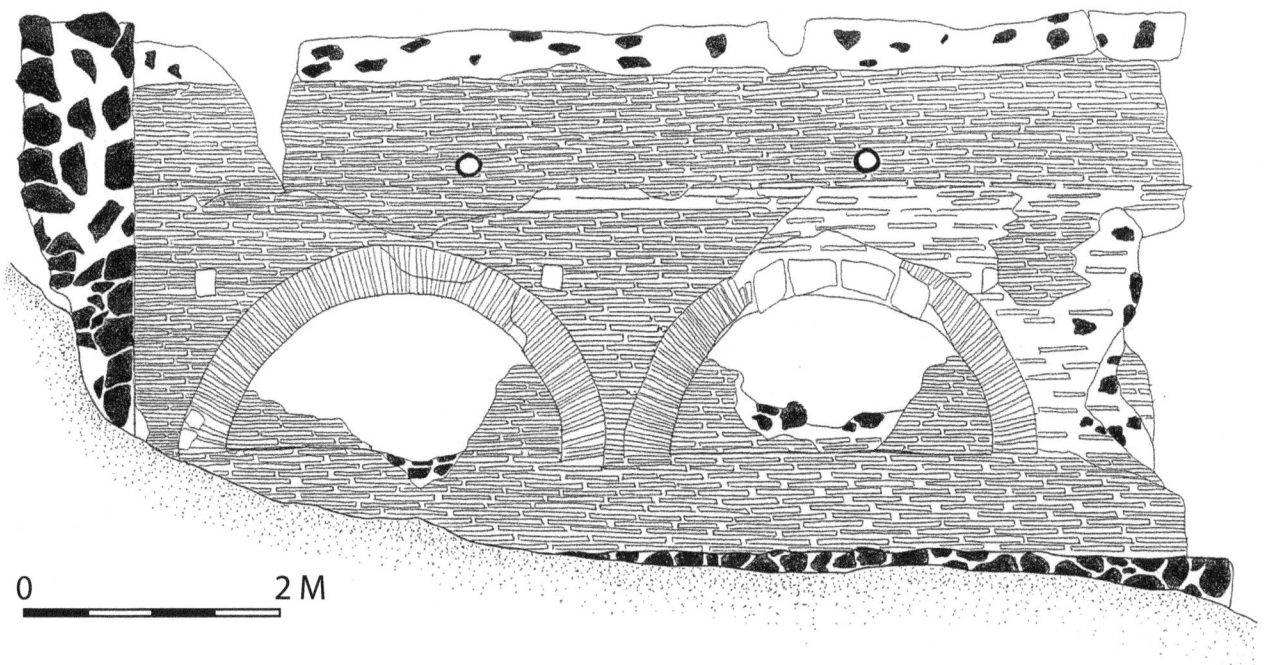

0   2 M

Figure 48. Building 1, drawing of the north wall of reservoir

The Reservoir

The rectangular reservoir measures 6.0 m N/S x 8.20 m E/W (figs. 47, 48). It is arranged on two levels, with a pair of vaulted chambers comprising the lower portion of the building and an open-air basin on top. The building is built in Type 5 masonry with the brick walling standing on a foundation of black basalt and white mortar. Traces of brick found on its top face indicate that the foundation originally possessed a brick coping. The height of the reservoir above its foundations is approximately 4 m but because of the sand level the exact height of the foundation cannot be ascertained.

Most of the western and eastern sides of the reservoir are visible, while the southern side is still buried in sand. The north face of the reservoir has been almost completely exposed, which is fortunate since this was the main side of the building. Approximately one meter above its foundations are two arches that open onto two barrel-vaulted water chambers. The arches are partially blocked by Type 5 walling, founded at the level of the springing of the arch, but inset 20 cm from the wall face. The blockage does not appear to have been a later addition, since the masonry matches that of the rest of the

Figure 49. Building 1, west wall of reservoir

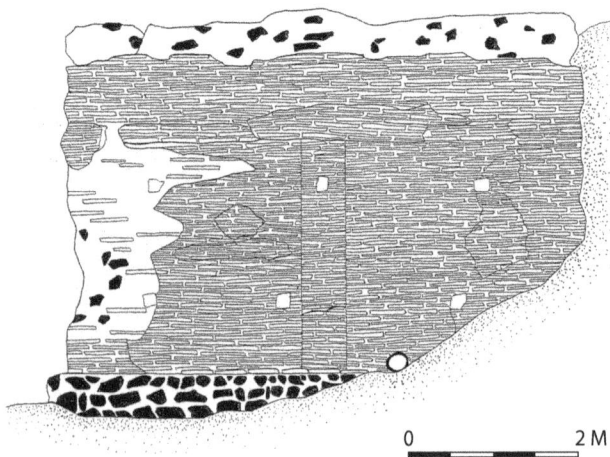

Figure 50. Building 1, drawing of the west wall of reservoir

Figure 51. Building 1, top of reservoir

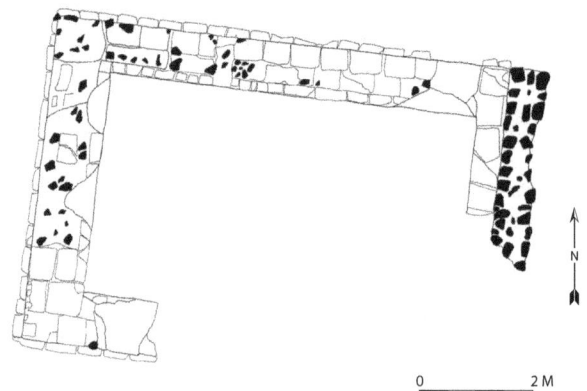

Figure 52. Building 1, drawing of top of reservoir

building. It is likely, however, that the arches were not completely closed off, since the blockages of both arches preserve at their western edges a flat surface that corresponds to the level of waterproof cement on the interior. It would seem that the arches were left with a small opening, which would allow access to the water within the building and afford entrance for maintenance.

Above the tops of the arches is a ledge composed of three outward-stepping bricks. The ledge may reflect the level of the bottom of the rooftop water basin. Above the ledge are two pipes, probably used to drain the rooftop basin when cleaning or during repairs. No doubt the pipes would have been plugged when the basin held water. Above the pipes the brick-faced wall continues for about half a meter to a point where the facing disappears leaving a mass of mortar and rubble. Although no facing is preserved on its outer sides, its inner face is lined with brick and forms the upper reaches of the rooftop water basin.

The west wall of the reservoir possesses both the brick ledge and the rubble and mortar core found at the top of the north wall (figs. 49, 50). Just above the stone foundation of the wall is a pipe that connects to the western inner chamber. In the center of the wall is a brick pilaster or buttress projecting 15

Figure 53. Building 1, interior of reservoir

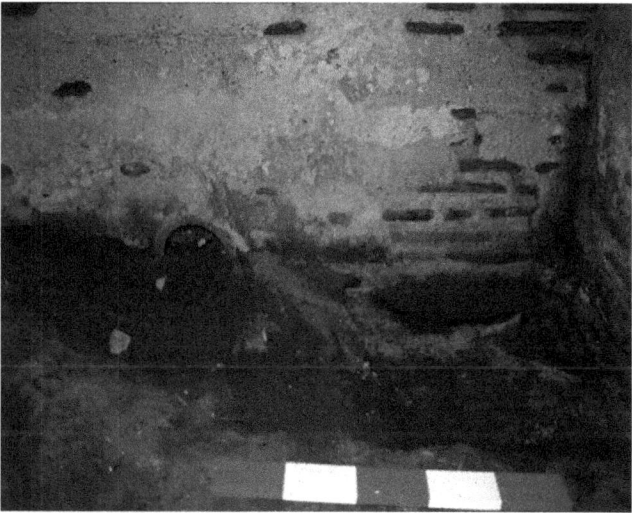

Figure 54. Building 1, interior of reservoir, detail with pipe

Figure 55. Building 1, interior of reservoir, detail of vaulting

cm from the wall face. It originally extended as high as the brick ledge, but its upper reaches have broken away. The purpose of the pilaster is unclear, although it is possible that a pipe was embedded in it that could siphon water into the basin from below.[18]

A wall of Type 3 masonry abuts the eastern wall of the reservoir (fig. 48). At first glance it would appear to be a later addition, but it may well have been part of the original design. If one combines the width of this wall with the length of the brick-faced north wall (not counting the foundation ledge) and then divides the building in half, one finds that the north face of the reservoir is neatly bisected at the midpoint between the two arches. This careful symmetry is probably not accidental, and thus it would appear that the reservoir was designed with the added width of the basalt wall in mind. The addition of a Type 3 masonry wall to the east face of the reservoir also occurs at the reservoir of the Smaller Baths. The purpose of the abutted walls is not clear, but they do not appear to have been later modifications.

On the top of the reservoir is a basin (figs. 51, 52). Today it is completely filled with sand and its depth cannot be measured, although its bottom probably coincided with the drains and ledge seen on the north face of the reservoir. The upper walls of the basin are formed on the north, south and west by the rubble and mortar mass mentioned above. In the east, the upper reaches of the Type 3 wall form the upper wall of the basin. It is significant that the width of the walls forming the east and west sides of the basin is identical, which strengthens the argument that the Type 3 wall was original to the reservoir. The inner walls of the basin are lined with brick and coated in waterproof cement. It is not clear how water entered the basin. Some rainwater could have helped to fill the pool, but it is more likely that water was piped in, perhaps through pipes secreted in the buttress to the west.

The lower level of the reservoir contained two chambers each roofed with a N/S-running barrel vault (fig. 48). The western chamber preserves more details than its neighbor (fig. 53). Although partially filled with sand, a section of its floor is visible, whose lowest layer was of black basalt set in mortar and stood at the same level as the foundation of the reservoir. Above that were a thick layer of white mortar and a layer of terracotta tile. At floor level one terracotta pipe leads eastward, into the adjacent chamber, and in the wall opposite another pipe leads outside (fig. 54). The walls are lined with

Figure 56. Building 1, north wall of bath building

waterproof cement, to a level 1.3 m above the floor, which coincides with the original height of the walls blocking the arches. This seems to reflect the intended maximum water level. It is not clear how water entered these chambers, except perhaps through the pipe in the west wall of the reservoir. There may have been other conduits that today are buried in the sand surrounding the building.

The walls and vaults of the chambers were constructed in Type 5 masonry. The bricks in the upper level of the vault are arranged so that they stand at right angles to the bricks of the lower sides of the vault (fig. 55). This pitched brick construction is typical of late Roman architecture in the east and will be discussed below.

The Bath Building

The plan of the main building of the Larger Baths is difficult to make out because sand fills all the rooms (fig. 46). Nevertheless it appears to consist of at least four rooms with the possibility of more. Running along the north side of the building is a 16 m-long wall (figs. 45, 56). Its height above the sand is 4 m but if its foundations lay at the same level as those of the reservoir, the wall would have stood at least 8 m

Figure 58. Building 1, Room A, detail of flue pipe in n. wall

tall. It is constructed in Type 2 masonry with several double bands of brick arranged approximately one meter apart. There are a number of holes in the wall, most of which were

Figure 57. Building 1, Room A, north wall

for scaffolding but others, larger and lined with brick, clearly have a different function, or could represent later modifications to the wall. On the exterior face of the wall are several layers of painted plaster, the lowest coat brickred in color.

Three rooms utilize this north wall. Room A, located at its western end, is nearly square, measuring 6.15 by 7.20 m. Both faces of the lower portions of the north wall are constructed in Type 2 masonry. The upper portions of the wall, however, have Type 2 masonry on the exterior and Type 5 masonry (brick-facing) on the interior, while sharing the same mortar and rubble core (fig. 57). This shift in materials may have been chosen to facilitate the vaulting of the roof (see below). In sections where the north wall has collapsed, pipes, whose interiors are blackened from soot, are visible running vertically through the wall (fig. 58). As was discussed in the context of the Smaller Baths (Building 2), the pipes may have served as flues to channel hot air and fumes out of the heating system under the floor of the room. From what can be seen of the eastern and southern walls of Room A, they appear to have been constructed of Type 5 masonry.

An apse, inset from the line of the north wall by 0.50 m, occupies the western side of Room A (figs. 46, 59, 60). The walls of the apse do not survive intact; only a large portion of wall standing along the northern side of the apse and small traces of walling to the south are visible. Nevertheless these fragments preserve some interesting architectural features. The outer wall of the apse, at its lower levels, was constructed of Type 2 masonry, a continuation of the long wall to the west, while its inner face of was of Type 5 masonry. At the upper reaches of the apsidal wall, however, the wall narrows to a construction of Type 6 masonry, mortared brick. Traces of vaulting indicate that the apse would have been covered with a half dome that has not survived. Traces of a small lateral arch in the north wall of the apse argue the presence of a window.

Pendentives occupy the northeastern, southeastern and northwestern corners of Room A (figs. 46, 57, 61). Judging from the low curve of the best preserved one (that in the northeastern corner, fig. 61), the pendentives supported a domical vault. Examples of domical vaults are known from Italy and

Figure 59. Building 1, Room A, apse

Roman Syria as early as the 2nd c. A.D. but become fairly commonplace throughout the Roman world by the 3rd c. and later.[19] As was the case in the vaulting in Room C in the Smaller Baths (Building 2), the domical vault and half-dome had a brick lining and was clad with an outer casing of mortar and rubble.

Room A was probably decorated in a fashion similar to Room A of the Smaller Baths. Fragments of marble revetment were found in this room, as well as stray bits of painted plaster. In the northeastern corner of the room the pendentive bears traces of yellow painted plaster and the join between it and the wall face is delineated in red.

Figure 60. Building 1, Room A, detail of apse

Figure 61. Building 1, Room A, pendentive in NE corner

The other rooms of the Larger Baths proved difficult to investigate because they were completely filled with sand. Room B, which lies east of Room A measures 5.95 by 4.20 m (fig. 46). Its walls are in Type 5 masonry. In the north the brick-faced wall abuts the long Type 2 masonry wall described above. There is no evidence for how this room was roofed. Even less can be said about Room C that lies west of Room B. Like Room B its walls are of Type 5 masonry and like Room B its northern wall abuts the outer Type 2 masonry wall (fig. 62).

South of Rooms B and C is Room D, which, like the others, is only partly free of sand. Its two visible walls, at the north and east, are constructed in Type 5 masonry. As was the case with Rooms B and C, an outer wall in Type 2 masonry abutted the eastern wall of Room D. This wall is built much like the long northern wall, with double bands of brick. A section near the northern end of the wall appears to have been repaired in brick. Like the north wall of the baths, this wall was covered in plaster (fig. 63).

Traces of walling south of Room A are on the same alignment as the rest of Building 1 and are constructed in Type 5 masonry. They may represent more of Building 1 or perhaps a related building.

Although the function of the individual rooms of Building 1 cannot be determined, it would seem that Building 1 was a bath, perhaps with an entrance in the east (Room C) and a heated room to the west (Room A). The identification is based on similar criteria used in the case of the Smaller Baths: a ready source of water, pipes in the walls, unusually shaped, highly decorated rooms, hypocaust tiles and window glass. While none of these alone would indicate securely

Figure 62. Building 1, Room C, north wall

Figure 63. Building 1 from the east

44

Figure 64. Building 5, from the south

that the building was used for bathing, combined they make the identification fairly likely.

Temple (?) (Building 5)

This building is located at the north end of the site, to the west of the Smaller Baths (Building 2), and was one of the buildings at Küçük Burnaz that suffered most from bulldozing (map 4). This is unfortunate since this building exhibits some features unique to the site. The damage to the building along with the build-up of sand is such that precise

Figure 65. Building 5, detail

dimensions for the building could not be obtained. The building is rectangular and faces roughly northeast at an orientation slightly more easterly than that of the other buildings of the site. The length of its northern face is approximately 5.70 m. From here the building runs at least 7 m towards the southwest. The building is in Type 1 masonry, with a limestone ashlar facing over a mortar and rubble core (fig. 64). The core was obviously deposited at the same time that the facing was installed; distinct tiers in the mortar correspond to the height of the ashlars. The sizes of the blocks vary; the average length is one meter with a width between 45 to 50 cm and a height of around 50 cm. The blocks were not clamped together, but were bonded with white mortar.

The foundations of the building have not been exposed, nor is the original top of the building preserved. Roughly in the center of the upper face of the core, however, is a pit (measuring 1.40 x 0.70 m) that is lined with limestone blocks (fig. 65). The purpose of this feature is not clear and it may be the result of looting.

Near the north side of Building 5 half of a marble pediment block was discovered. The marble is coarsely grained and white with grayish streaks, resembling marble from the Proconnesian quarries (color plate 3). It measures 1.75 m long and 0.57 m deep; the raking angle of the pediment block is 1.70 m long and preserves several clamp holes. The apex of the triangle has been cut away, forming a window within the block. It seems reasonable to associate the pediment block with Building 5, both because of its proximity to the building and also because Building 5 is the only building at

Figure 66. Building 6

Figure 67. Building 6, detail of masonry

Küçük Burnaz which used the kind of masonry, limestone blocks, which would have been harmonious with a marble pediment.

Figure 68. Building 6, detail of niche

Building 5 appears to have been highly decorated. During the 1994 survey, one limestone mosaic tessera was collected along with fragments of painted plaster and marble revetment. Members of the Hatay Museum who visited the site shortly after it was first bulldozed in 1987 report that they saw traces of a mosaic as well as limestone column drums in the vicinity of Building 5. During the 1994 season, however, there was no indication of the latter features. Building 5 aspired to some distinction, both in masonry and adornment. Obviously too little survives to indicate the function of this building, although it is tempting to identify the building as a temple.

The Eastern Arch (Building 6) and the Central Arch (Building 19)

The Eastern Arch (Building 6) stands at the eastern edge of the site, fronting the Küçük Burnaz stream (map 4, fig. 66). It is oriented N/S and measures 11.50 m in length, with each pier measuring 3.60 m N/S and 2.80 m E/W, with a space of 4.30 m separating the two piers. The arch is built in Type 1 masonry (fig. 67). Only the facing blocks from its lowest extremities are still in position; indentations in the core reflect the original position of blocks that have fallen away. The facing consists of ashlars of black basalt, with the average measurements of 65 x 40 x 33 cm. The quality of the stones in this instance is extremely high - the basalt is very dense with no holes or bubbles. The blocks are bonded together with a thin layer of white mortar.

The east faces of both piers are occupied with curved niches, measuring 1.10 m across and 55 cm deep (fig. 68). Their tops stand about 70 cm above the present ground level. The niches are faced with carefully carved wedge-shaped blocks. Such niches would perhaps have been used to hold life-size statues, so we must assume that the bottom of this building is around 2 m below the present ground level.

The Eastern Arch (Building 6) seems to have bounded the eastern side of the site. Visitors in antiquity may have entered the site through this arch, having moored their vessels at the river. The road this arch straddled can be postulated as running through the site towards the Central Arch. It is interesting to note that the Eastern Arch never seems to have formed part of a wall, and indeed, that the site never seems to have been fortified.

Figure 69. Building 19, from the west

Figure 70. Building 3, from the east

Figure 71. Building 3, from the north

Figure 72. Building 11

South of the Smaller Baths (Building 2) stand the remains of the Central Arch (Building 19, map 4, fig. 20). It has the same orientation as the Eastern Arch but is much more poorly preserved, with only its northern pier still standing (fig. 69). Although its facing has been stripped away, indentations for ashlar blocks can be seen in the rubble and mortar core. Also littered around the region of the arch are blocks of the same kind of fine quality basalt used for the ashlars facing the core of the Eastern Arch. On the western face of the north pier of the Central Arch one can see traces of a niche like those found on the eastern faces of the Eastern Arch.

A line drawn between the two arches gives us the best indication of the street system for the site. As mentioned above, the orientation of certain north-south running buildings (in particular Building 12) would indicate there were cross streets running perpendicular to this main thoroughfare.

Cisterns (Building 3 and 11)

Building 3 is located in the southeastern region of the site (map 4). It is a one-roomed building measuring 9.20 m N/S and 7.04 m E/W; much of its southern section is covered by a large sand dune (fig. 70). It is constructed from Type 3 masonry. Exceptional care was taken in the construction of the corners, which were built with large, nearly quadratic blocks. The most distinctive side is the northern face, which stands nearly 3.5 m above the present sand level (fig. 71). In the center of the north wall is a hole, either created by looters or perhaps the collapsed remains of an opening original to the building. Beneath this is a ledge, which runs along the north wall, widening the wall by 18 cm. The ledge is not found on the other sides of the building. The curvature of the top of the north wall indicates that it was covered with a barrel vault, perhaps of mortared rubble.

Although the interior of Building 3 is filled with sand it is clear that the inner walls were coated with waterproof cement. Its shape, rectangular with a barrel vault, is consistent with

Figure 73. Building 11, detail

that of Roman cisterns found in arid areas, such as North Africa.[20] Because most of the superstructure was above ground, aqueducts, rather than rainwater, usually fed such buildings, but here we may surmise that water was piped in perhaps via underground conduits.

The exterior of the cistern was plastered. The eastern wall preserves two layers, a lower coat of white plaster covered over by an upper coat of red. Abutting the southeastern corner of the building is a wall, which shares the same orientation and width as the eastern wall of the cistern but is situated some 10 cm to the east. Most of this wall is engulfed in sand, so there is no available data on its length. It is built in Type 2 masonry with a band of bricks near its preserved top. It is not clear whether this wall is a later addition to Building 3, or just a contemporary section of the building.

A series of wall remains in the southern area of the site comprise Building 11, which is probably another cistern (map 4). For the most part they consist of mortar and basalt rubble cores which have lost their facings. The best-preserved section lies to the west where the mortar and rubble core define a rectangular room measuring 5 m N/S and approximately 3.50-4.0 m E/W (fig. 72). The room was covered with a barrel vault, the spring of which can be seen just emerging from the sand. More rooms existed to the north, where more vaulting can be made out, and to the south, where the west wall of the room continues. The central room was lined in water-proof cement and embedded in its western wall was a vertical cut, probably for the insertion of a pipe, perhaps to conduct water from the roof into the chamber (fig. 73).[21] The room appears to have had some sort of hydraulic function and may have served as a cistern.

Figure 76. *Building 9, column drum*

North and east of the Smaller Baths (Building 2) is Building 4, measuring roughly 12 m from east to west (map 4). The poorly preserved walls appear to have been constructed in Type 2 masonry. This building is worthy of note, however, because of the high quality of its fittings. Fragments of marble revetment, plaster and window glass were recovered from around its walls, as well as a single mosaic tessera of olive green glass. Unfortunately, the remains of this building are too meager to comment on its plan or purpose, but it is possible that Building 4 somehow functioned in concert with the adjacent baths.

Building 4

Figure 74. *Building 9, base*

Building 9

A deep cut from a bulldozer exposed a variety of masonry fragments in a region midway between the two arches; the area has been designated as Building 9, although it is better described as an area of building activity (map 4). So violent was this disturbance that there was no indication of the original position of this material. Among the fragments was a rough limestone base measuring 50 x 28 cm and standing 25 cm tall (fig. 74). The upper face of the base had been hollowed out to support a rectangular object. Nearby was found the lower section of a round altar or base of limestone measuring 34 cm high with a top diameter of 41 cm (fig. 75). Its base preserves rough moldings.

Figure 75. *Building 9, limestone fragment*

Figure 77. *Building 13*

Figure 78. Building 7

The cut from the bulldozer also exposed two basalt column fragments (fig. 76), and an investigation of the reed bed in the vicinity recovered two more. The tallest stands at 78 cm with an upper diameter of 41 cm and a lower diameter of 44 cm (color plate 4). This drum was originally coated in plaster painted green with white stripes and brownish purple blotches, in imitation of marble (color plate 5). These drums must have been part of a fairly ornate building that stood along the road running between the two arches.

Building 13

Building 13 is a poorly preserved building standing near the northern edge of the site, south and west of the possible temple (Building 5). It consists of a section of E/W-running wall, with a preserved length of 5.80 m (map 4). At its eastern end is an apse, offset from the wall by 30 cm (fig. 77). It is constructed in Type 3 masonry, the stones ranging from 35-50 cm long and 20-30 cm high. Patches of white plaster adhere to the exterior of the building and more plaster can be found on the inner face of the apse. The numerous fragments of tiles surrounding the structure, indicate it had a tiled roof.[22]

Building 18

This building lies along the northern edge of the site and is represented by two very low stretches of wall, a long E/W-running wall and its south running cross wall at the west (map 4). The walls are constructed in Type 5 masonry and sit on a projecting basalt and mortar foundation. The arrangement is identical to that of the reservoir of the Larger Baths (Building 1). Unfortunately, too little of this building survives to guess its plan or function.

Figure 79. Building 10

Buildings 7, 8 and 12

Three other buildings, located in the southeastern quadrant of the site are preserved as low-lying walls built in Type 2 masonry (map 4, fig. 78). Their long and narrow dimensions could perhaps indicate that they functioned as storage buildings, or even as granaries, although too little survives to confirm this theory. Building 12 probably stood along a street (fig. 19), and it is likely that the positions of these buildings reflect the overall street plan of the site.

Buildings 10 and 14

Two final poorly preserved buildings, Buildings 10 and 14, consist of several small rooms. Both were constructed in Type 4 masonry - rough basalt facing with a mortar and basalt rubble core intermixed with the occasional brick fragment. Building 10 has a white limestone block built into one of its walls (fig. 79), perhaps reused from the possible temple (Building 5). One of the walls of Building 14 incorporates bits of reddish sandstone, a material not seen elsewhere on the site. Although the state of preservation in both these buildings is low, they seem to be of a later date than the rest of the buildings at Küçük Burnaz. They could have been domestic or had some industrial function since just west of Building 10 are sections of bedrock in which have been cut drains and a hole, perhaps for grinding.

LOOSE ARCHITECTURAL ELEMENTS

In addition to the buildings, stray architectural elements that relate to the buildings of Küçük Burnaz were collected. They are discussed generally here, with important features highlighted.

Pipes

Terracotta pipes were set into the walls of at least two buildings, the Smaller Baths (Building 2) and the Larger Baths (Building 1), and probably into one of the cisterns (Building 14), where a vertical groove in the wall face of one of the rooms appears to have accommodated a pipe. Thirty more fragments of pipe were collected at the site, mainly from the two bath buildings, but also from Building 4 and the other cistern (Building 3). None of these are preserved to their full length, although the pipes embedded in the north wall of Room A of the Larger Baths have an average length of 30 cm. This is somewhat shorter than the usual length of Roman pipes (45 to 70 cm), but these measurements apply to water pipes and do necessarily pertain to flues. The average inner and outer diameter of the pipes from Küçük Burnaz are 16 and 20 cm respectively, which is in keeping with the typical measurements of pipes of the Imperial Roman period. [23] As is typical of Roman pipes, these examples were designed to slot together with one end constricted to slide into the top of another pipe. In several cases mortar, used to bind the pipes together, still adheres to the joints.

Two basic fabrics were identified among the pipe fragments. One is a pale pink or buff clay with lime inclusions, occasionally preserving a white slip on the exterior. The other fabric is a dense red clay with lime inclusions, whose exterior bears heavy ridges. There are four examples of this type, one from Building 2, two from Building 4 and one a general find. From Antioch, pipes similar to these have been dated to the Byzantine period. [24]

Although not found in situ, it is obvious that some of the pipes conducted water, since they have calcium deposits in their interior, while others served as flues, since a black, sooty, material lines the inner faces of these pipes. The pipes embedded in the north wall of Room A of the Larger Baths were also discolored from contact with smoky air.

Rooftiles

Rooftiles were collected from virtually every quadrant of the site. Most were fragments of *tegulae* (pan tiles) and all appear to adhere to the same type: a flange with a square profile on one side, and on the adjacent side a second flange with a rounded profile inset 10 cm from the edge. Examples of cover tiles or *imbrices* were also found, mostly in the vicinity of Building 13. These take the form of the so-called Corinthian type, are roughly triangular, and measure 7.5 cm from apex to base. [25]

Although a few rooms, such as Room D in the Smaller Baths probably had a wooden roof, many more were vaulted. The amount of rooftiles collected at Küçük Burnaz may be explained by the vaults possibly having a wood frame roof, gabled or hipped, as is postulated for the Bath-Gymnasium Complex at Sardis. [26]

Hypocaust Tiles

Four round hypocaust tiles were collected at Küçük Burnaz, three from the region of the Smaller Baths (Building 2) and one near the Larger Baths (Building 1). These obviously served to support raised floors as part of the heating system for the two baths. [27] The three from the Smaller Baths are incomplete but have estimated diameters of 20 to 25 cm. [28] Their heights range from 4 to 4.5 cm and mortar used to bond one tile to another, still adheres to their top and bottom faces. Their fabric is very coarse with many large inclusions. The single example of a hypocaust tile from the Larger Baths has similar dimensions (diam. 21 cm, h. 3.5 cm) but has a dense dusky red fabric and large black basalt inclusions along with smaller red and white grits. The fabric is very close to that used in several clay basins found on the site, and that fact along with the appearance of black basalt grits may indicate that these are of local manufacture (below, page 76).

Window Glass

Window glass was found in association with three buildings at Küçük Burnaz: the Larger Baths (Building 1), the Smaller Baths (Building 2) and Building 4 (color plates 6, 7). No complete panes were found. The fragments average 2 to 3 cm long with a thickness ranging from 0.3 cm to less than 0.1 cm. The panes were created with the "muff" or cylinder-blown process, whereby glass was blown into the shape of a cylinder and, while still hot, was slit open and unrolled onto a flat surface.[29] This technique is recognized in most of the Küçük Burnaz fragments by the glossy finish on both sides of the fragments and the rows of parallel elongated bubbles which indicate that the glass was blown and stretched before cooling. One fragment has a rounded slightly thickened edge, which may have come from the top or bottom of the cylinder as it was blown. Several examples from the Smaller Baths (Building 2) belong to the matte/glossy type of Roman window glass and have striations on one side.[30] This may indicate they were created in a mold, but more likely the striations reflect the tray in which the panes were cooled after being unrolled.[31]

The colors and fabric found in the fragments of window glass are like those seen in the glass vessels discussed in the following chapter. They are blue-green, pale blue and olive green; naturally occurring colors in Roman glass. Also most pieces are bubbly and several have streaks of unmixed color in them, features characteristic of glass of the 4th and 7th c. A.D.

At each building where window glass was collected, the fragments could be divided into groups on the basis of color, fabric and thickness. These groups possibly represent fragments from individual window panes, although not enough is preserved to test this hypothesis. From the Larger Baths (Building 1) where 73 fragments were collected, there were three variations of window glass: a pale olive green glass with no bubbles, 0.1 cm thick; a pale blue-green bubbly glass, 0.5 cm thick; and a pale green bubbly glass, 0.1 cm thick. From the Smaller Baths (Building 2) 39 fragments were found which fall into a greater number of subdivisions: a pale purple bubbly glass, < 0.1 cm thick; a pale green bubbly glass, < 0.1 cm thick; a bright green bubbly glass, 0.3 cm thick; a pale green bubbly glass with striations on one side, 0.2 cm thick; a pale blue bubbly glass with striations on one side, 0.15 to 0.2 cm thick; an olive green bubbly glass with streaks of darker color and striations on one side, 0.15 cm thick; and a dark olive green glass with no bubbles and striations on one side, 0.25 cm thick. Four fragments were collected at Building 4: a fragment of green glass with large bubbles, 0.17 cm thick, a fragment of pale blue-green bubbly glass, 0.12 cm thick, and two fragments of olive green bubbly glass, 0.2 cm thick.

It is not surprising that the fragments of window glass were collected at or near the site of the two baths. There is much evidence for window glass being used in bath buildings of the Imperial period and later, particularly in the hot rooms where glazed windows both kept heat in and allowed additional solar heat to penetrate.[32] At Küçük Burnaz, the glass scatter was so wide that the original position of the panes could not be determined. However, in the Smaller Baths, windows were identified in Room C which was probably the caldarium, and in the Larger Baths there is a window in the apse of Room A, a room that also was probably heated. Unfortunately, no window frames were found.

It would be useful to be able to date the window glass with some precision, but this is not possible. The color and fabric are late Roman/early Byzantine in character, and could date from the 4th through the 7th c. A.D. The window glass fragments with striations from the Smaller Baths, may indicate that those panes date earlier than the unstriated examples found in the Larger Baths. Scholars, however, are not in agreement about the cause of the striations, nor when they appear, although they often seem earlier in date than non-striated examples.[33] It may be significant that there is no evidence for crown glass, circular plates of glass resembling dishes often set in stucco frames.[34] This type of window glass has been found at Gerasa and Samaria, although at the latter site flat pieces, such as those recorded at Küçük Burnaz, were also recovered.[35] According to Donald Harden, crown glass in windows supplanted flat glass in the East by A.D. 400.[36] Examples of flat glass from Anemurium, however, appear to date from the 5th through 7th c. so it would appear that flat glass was still being used after the invention of crown glass.[37] Further examples of window glass found in dated contexts are needed before it can be used as a dating criterion.[38]

DECORATIVE ELEMENTS

Painted Plaster

As described above, traces of painted plaster were found still attached to the interiors of both bath buildings. In Room A of the Smaller Baths, red plaster appears on the west wall between the corner and the door leading to Room B, and also on the lower portion of the groin vault in the SW corner of the room. In Room A of the Larger Baths, the pendentive in the NE corner was painted yellow with a red outline. Similarly, one of the basalt column drums associated with Building 9 had been plastered and painted to resemble variegated marble. Loose plaster fragments were recovered from the Larger Baths (22 pieces colored white, red, yellow and pale green), the Smaller Baths (ten pieces, colored white, green and red), Building 4 (six fragments, colored red), and the possible temple (Building 5) (seven red fragments). The fragments show that the color was applied to a thin plaster surface, which rested on a thick rendering of white mortar mixed with pebbles.[39] One of the pieces from the Building 5, which had lost its outer coating demonstrates that the rendering was gouged to help the topcoat bond to it. Some of the fragments show multiple layers of paint, indicating renovation of the decoration.

The exteriors of many of the buildings were painted as well. Rendering was found on the outer walls of one of the cisterns

(Building 3), the Larger Baths, the Smaller Baths, and Building 13. The first two preserve traces of red paint over the rendering. Other examples of painted plaster on the exterior of buildings are known from Rough Cilicia, where it is found on baths from Anemurium, Syedra and Antiochia ad Cragum. Their typical motif is horizontal and vertical lines painted over a pale background in imitation of ashlars.[40] In Lycia and Pamphylia there are further examples of buildings whose exteriors were painted to imitate isodomic masonry.[41] Not enough of the plastered exteriors of the buildings at Küçük Burnaz survive to ascertain whether they also imitated masonry.

Mosaics

Only two tesserae were found at Küçük Burnaz, one of white limestone (1.1 x 0.9 x 0.5 cm) from the possible temple (Building 5), and another of pale olive green glass with bubbles (0.8 x 0.6 x 0.4 cm) from Building 4. The bottom faces of both have a sandy mortar adhering to them. It may be concluded that mosaic floors were present at the site but since sand covers the lower surfaces of the buildings, they remain buried at this time.

Revetment

Nearly one hundred thin plates of marble, used as wall revetment or paving, were collected at Küçük Burnaz, and, with the exception of a few stray finds, all came from the two bath buildings and Building 4. Their thickness vary from slightly under 1 to more than 3 cm, with most averaging a thickness of 2 cm. Although none of the panels are preserved in their entirety, several fragments possess one or two original sides that are beveled. In addition to the pieces of marble plating, there are a few fragments with molded decoration that probably were originally located where the wall met the floor. Most of the fragments have at least one polished face, and some preserve saw marks on their undersurfaces to which mortar often adheres.

None of these fragments was found in situ, but it is likely that they encrusted the walls of the inner rooms of the baths. In Rooms A and B of the Smaller Baths (Building 2) nails were found still projecting from the walls, showing that nails, along with mortar, would have been used to secure the revetment.[42] A few of the thicker marble plates (those measuring 2.5 to 3.5 cm thick) may have been used for paving.[43]

None of the marble has undergone scientific analysis and thus it is difficult to identify the marble type with security, particularly in the case of white marble. Nevertheless several types of marble can be classified based on visual characteristics:[44]

Type 1: White marble with large granular crystals and distinctive thin gray bands (16 fragments). Proconnesian?[45]

Type 2: White marble with fine shiny crystals (9 fragments).

Type 3: Bright white marble with large shiny crystals (4 fragments). Thasian?[46]

Type 4: Whitish marble with large shiny crystals and small yellowish clouds (4 fragments). Phrygian "Beyaz"?[47]

Type 5: Dull grayish-white marble with large shiny crystals (6 fragments).

Type 6: Dull white marble with large crystals and brown veins (3 fragments). Phrygian "şeker"?[48]

Type 7: Uniformly gray marble with large shiny crystals (15 fragments). Phrygian "Kaplan postu"?[49]

Type 8: Green marble with distinct wavy veins ranging in color from whitish to dark green (20 fragments). Carystian.[50]

Type 9: Mottled-colored marble (white, yellow, purple and gray). The crystals in the white and yellow sections are very fine, coarser in the gray veins (13 fragments). Phrygian pavonazetto.[51]

Type 10: Wine-red colored stone with white dots (1 fragment). Purple porphyry.[52]

Since there is no known marble source close to Küçük Burnaz, all fragments seem to have been imported. It is likely that the marble would have arrived at Küçük Burnaz in blocks ready to be sawed into plates.[53] The marbles from Küçük Burnaz that could be tentatively identified on the basis of surface observation came from the Aegean or Anatolia (Carystian, Phrygian and Proconnesian) with the exception of the single piece of what appears to be purple porphyry from Egypt. These fragments, along with the marble pediment block from Building 5, connect Küçük Burnaz in a modest way to the vast network of marble trade that existed throughout the Roman Empire.

Much work, spearheaded by John Ward-Perkins, has been done on the distribution and use of marble in the Imperial period.[54] In the provinces a wide distribution of colored marbles from Imperial controlled quarries can be recognized by the 2nd c. A.D. Although the organization began to falter in the troubled the 3rd c., the listing of marbles in Diocletian's Price Edict demonstrates that the trade was still functioning in his day.[55] Certainly most quarries, including those represented at Küçük Burnaz, continued to function into the 6th c.[56] The purple porphyry quarries of Egypt may have stopped working by the mid-5th c.,[57] but the single fragment found at Küçük Burnaz could easily have been a reused piece.

CONCLUSIONS

Since no formal excavation took place at Küçük Burnaz there is subsequently no stratigraphic evidence for the date of the buildings studied on the site. A relative chronology for the buildings also seems problematic, since although the variety of building techniques used on the site appears at first glance to reflect separate phases of construction, the evidence from the individual buildings themselves indicates that this may not be the case. In both the Smaller and Larger Baths, there are many cases of external walls made of a basalt facing and inner walls faced with brick (Smaller Baths: Room C, B, and three walls of A; Larger Baths: Room A [upper reaches of the walls], B, C and D). Since most of these rooms are known to have been vaulted, the choice of brick over stone probably lay in the lighter weight and increased flexibility that that medium afforded.[58] The same reasoning holds for the use of bricks in apses. The relationship between Type 2 and Type 3 masonry is not so clear. In the Smaller Baths, Type 3 masonry is used for the walls of Room D, the north wall of Room A, and the outer wall of Room C. All walls appear to be integral parts of the original form of the Smaller Baths. Similarly, Type 3 masonry walls also abut the east sides of both the reservoirs, but in both cases the additions seem to be part of the original plan of the buildings. It may be that Type 3 masonry was a contemporaneous, more austere facing used in less important portions of a building.

Several cases of mixed masonry are known from the East. At Samosata one of the defensive towers was constructed with *opus reticulatum* on the exterior and *opus quasi reticulatum* on the interior, with both faces being contemporary,[59] and in the aqueduct at Aspendus can be found ashlar masonry, bricks and rubble facing, all stemming from a single construction phase.[60] Closer to home, the Baths in *Opus Mixtum* (the so-called Reticulate Baths) at Elaeussa in Rough Cilicia have exterior walls constructed with a stone facing but in certain rooms have interior walls of brick.[61]

It is, however, possible to suggest a tentative relative chronology for the buildings on the site. When the site was founded it was laid out on a grid. The arches (Buildings 6 and 19) were probably built at this time to emphasize the eastern entrance and the center of the community. Perhaps as part of the original layout of the site the Smaller Baths (Building 2) and its aqueduct were built, as well as most of the other buildings (Buildings, 3, 4, 5, 7, 8, 9, 11, and 12). The Larger Baths (Building 1) could also date to the initial phase of the site, but the greater dependence on brickwork may argue a slightly later date. It is possible that as the site became more heavily used, a second bath was needed to compliment the first. If the Larger Baths is a later addition to the site, then Building 18, which, although ruined appears to have been constructed exactly like the reservoir of those baths, might be its contemporary. Finally, Buildings 10 and 14 may have been constructed later since their masonry includes reused material.

An examination of the building techniques found at Küçük Burnaz may reveal some further chronological indicators for the architecture. Mortar and rubble cored buildings faced with ashlars or small stones, were common in parts of Asia Minor by the Augustan period.[62] However, the use of this building technique, in imitation of the *opus caementicium* of the west, was not uniformly adopted, but seems to have been spread in part as a result of direct Roman influence.[63] It is not clear when the technique was adopted in Cilicia, but it was certainly in use by the second half of the 1st c. A.D.[64] The use of fired brick appears in the architecture of Asia Minor during the early 2nd c. A.D. and expands in the 3rd. Brickwork is found at Ephesus (in the Library of Celsus and the Harbor Baths), at Pergamum (in the Kızıl Avlı), and at Aspendus (in the basilica and aqueduct), just to name a few sites.[65] While these examples superficially resemble traditional Roman *opus testacaeum*, where the bricks face a core of concrete, they are in fact solid mortared brick. This appears to have been a typical technique of Asia Minor and the forerunner of Byzantine solid brick architecture. However, it has long been noted that in Cilicia (specifically at Augusta), bricks were used as a facing over a mortar and rubble core, conforming more closely with western Roman brickwork.[66] In Antioch *opus testaceum* was also the norm from the 2nd through 4th c. A.D.[67] As has been demonstrated, the brickwork found at Küçük Burnaz falls into this pattern.

There are several aspects of the brickwork found at Küçük Burnaz which may help date the buildings: the size of the bricks, their ratio to the mortar which binds them together, the use of bands of bricks with stone masonry, and the manner in which they are used in vaulting.

In the west, particularly Italy, there were a variety of standard sizes for bricks. The more common were the *bessales* (each side measuring 19 cm), the *pedales* (34 cm), the *sesquipedales* (44 cm), and the *bipedales* (59 cm). The last two were often subdivided into triangles whose pointed ends achieved an especially secure bond with their concrete facing.[68] In Asia Minor the bricks were usually square, measuring 30-35 cm, the equivalent of the Italian *pedales*.[69] Occasionally oblong bricks were used, but triangular bricks were rare. This of course was due to the fact that these bricks were not designed to face a concrete core. There are a few instances in the East where triangular bricks do occur, specifically at Elaeussa and at Antioch, where the bricks were used as facings. In the former, the triangular bricks appear in the baths dating to the late 1st c. A.D, while at Antioch they are found in several buildings of the 2nd and 3rd c., but are not used during the 4th c. and later, when oblong bricks are preferred.[70] This may suggest that the use of triangular bricks in Cilicia and Northern Syria was a feature of the High Empire, one that disappeared by the Late Roman period. At Küçük Burnaz, the square bricks have an average length of 30-35 cm and an average thickness of 3.5 cm. Rectangular bricks occur in the lining of the reservoir of the Larger Baths. Although some bricks have deeply impressed lines dividing them into triangles, no triangular brick was found at the site. This may imply that the brickwork dates after the end of the 3rd c., at the time when triangular bricks were abandoned in Antioch.[71]

Much attention has been devoted to the relationship of the height of the brick to the height of the mortar, and this has resulted in a fairly secure chronological indicator of buildings, particularly in Italy.[72] A rule of thumb is that the mortar joints between the bricks tend to become greater over time. In the west during 1st c. A.D., for example, the thickness of the mortar was half that of the brick, but by the late 3rd c. the relative thickness of the mortar and brick was equal. Less work has been conducted on brick architecture in the East, though much valuable information has recently become available thanks to the endeavors of Dodge, Ginouves and Deichmann.[73] For brickwork in Asia Minor, Dodge has developed a table comparing the thickness of bricks to the thickness of their mortar over time.[74] Unfortunately, there is a higher degree of irregularity than seen in similar tables on brickwork from Italy or Greece, probably due to a lack of well-dated and adequately recorded brick monuments from Asia Minor. Dodge suggests that the most significant chronological indicator is probably the height of the mortar, but she cautions that this should be used only as a general indicator of date.[75] At Küçük Burnaz, the average brick height is around 3.5 cm and the mortar is virtually the same. No examples from Dodge's table match these measurements, but if one follows her suggestion of using the height of the mortar as a chronological guide, then the brickwork at the site should date to the 4th or 5th c.[76] In comparison, at Antioch, Bath C makes use of square bricks measuring 3.0-3.5 cm per side with a height of 3.7 cm. The mortar height is slightly more than that of the brick. These baths are dated A.D. 350-400.[77]

Another use of brick found in Asia Minor that may be significant for our understanding of the date of the buildings at Küçük Burnaz is the insertion of bands of brick between broader bands of stone facing. At Küçük Burnaz this is found in many examples of Type 2 masonry. In Italy this technique is known as *opus mixtum*, where the bands of brick, like the stone facing they accompany, do not penetrate deep into the core.[78] In Asia Minor is found a similar technique, but here the bands of brick run all the way through the mortar and rubble core of the wall. Examples occur during the late 2nd c. A.D. at Sardis and Ancyra, and during the 3rd c. A.D. at Nicaea. The building technique is also well known from the 5th c. Theodosian walls in Constantinople.[79] There are isolated examples of true *opus mixtum* in the East, however, in Cappadocia, Paphlagonia/Pontus and in Syria. All appear to date between the Flavian to Trajanic periods.[80] In Cilicia *opus mixtum* occurs in the so-called Reticulate Baths at Elaeussa, which also date to the late 1st c., and in buildings from Küçük Burnaz's neighbor, Epiphaneia, usually considered to be late Roman in date.[81] At Küçük Burnaz there are bands of brick used in Type 2 masonry, and can best be seen in the reservoir and aqueduct of the Smaller Baths (Building 2), and the outer walls of the Larger Baths (Building 1). The latter bear a strong resemblance to the late 3rd c. curtain walls from Nicaea, although these are not constructed in true *opus mixtum*.[82] The buildings with the brick bands at Küçük Burnaz could possibly date to the Flavian or Trajanic period, but may in fact be Late Roman, based on the nearby examples from Epiphaneia and the similarity with Nicaea.

A final noteworthy aspect of the brickwork is how it is used in barrel vaults. Typically the bricks in barrel vaults were arranged radially in vousoirs. In the three completely preserved vaults found in the lower sections of the reservoirs of the Smaller and Larger Baths, however, the upper portion of the vaults have pitched brick vaulting, where the bricks have been laid end to end across the vault. Thus when one looks up at the vault, one sees that the bricks of its sidewalls are at right angles with the bricks of the vault itself. Although pitched brick construction was rarely used in the West it was fairly common in the East and seems to have developed from mudbrick vaulting techniques found in early Egypt and Mesopotamia.[83] The earliest know example in Asia Minor is found in the subbuilding of the basilica at Smyrna, which dates to the later 2nd c. A.D. The 3rd c. basilica at Aspendus also has pitched brick vaulting and in the 5th and 6th c. it

becomes a common technique in Constantinople. Although pitched brick vaulting from Küçük Burnaz examples could date as early as the 2nd c, A.D., the greater frequency of the architectural in Late Roman times may suggest it belongs to that era.

The manner in which bricks were used in the architecture at Küçük Burnaz does not provide a precise date for their construction, although when taken together they present an argument for the buildings being dated to the 4th or 5th c., during Late Roman times. The use of the pendentive for the domical vault in Room A of the Larger Baths (Building 1) also points to its construction in that era. The evidence for the window glass, which admittedly does not have to be original with the period of construction of the two baths, conforms to a Late Roman date.

An observation remains concerning Roman architecture in Cilicia. John Ward-Perkins was the first to note that Cilicia was unique in Asia Minor because the use of building materials in this region resembled Italo-Roman work, both in building and technique. He based this observation on a fairly small number of sites: Elaeussa, Corycus and Epiphaneia.[84] The "Roman" traits he observed at these settlements were: the use of a material very close to concrete (seen at the harbor mole at Elaeussa and the baths at Corycus), the use of *opus reticulatum* (seen at the so-called Reticulate Baths at Elaeussa) and the use of bands of bricks as bonding courses (seen at the so-called Reticulate Baths at Elaeussa and at various buildings at Epiphaneia). He suggested the reason behind this adoption of Roman forms was due to a weak Hellenistic building tradition in the region, which left Cilicia all the more easily influenced by new architectural techniques. The phenomenon can also be seen in Pisidia and Pamphylia.[85]

Recently Marc Waelkens has re-addressed the question of Italian elements in the architecture of Cilicia.[86] While citing the Rough Cilician examples given by Ward-Perkins (Corycus and Elaeussa), he also brought into the discussion architecture from the Smooth Cilician cities of Augusta and Anazarbus. The Italian element he noted there was the use of concrete with a brick facing, *opus testaceum*. While supporting the explanations given by Ward-Perkins for why Cilicia took on Roman building techniques so readily, Waelkens also suggests that the presence of the Roman army, particularly in Smooth Cilicia in the late Roman period, may have helped transmit these traditional Italian forms.

Both Ward-Perkins and Waelkens based their assertions on a handful of sites in Rough and Smooth Cilicia. Although knowledge of Rough Cilicia is improving, primarily thanks to excavations at Anemurium and recent work at Elaeussa, the existing information concerning the architecture of Smooth Cilicia is still somewhat impressionistic. This makes the present study of the buildings at Küçük Burnaz all the more significant, particularly since it is clear that the architecture fits the pattern suggested by Ward-Perkins and Waelkens. Italo-Roman elements found at Küçük Burnaz include the use of high quality mortar and rubble (resembling true Roman concrete), the insertion of bands of brick in stone facing as bonding courses which do not run through the core (like *opus mixtum*) and brick facing over a concrete-like core (like *opus testaceum*). The possibility that these Italic elements may have been brought to the settlement at Küçük Burnaz by the military will be addressed in the Conclusion of this work.

---

[1] Ward-Perkins 1958, 83.

[2] For a discussion of these, see below, pages 51-53.

[3] See Chapter 6, pages 78-81. A handful of medieval sgraffiato ware sherds were collected at Building 2 indicating the building was briefly reoccupied.

[4] Hellenkemper and Hild 1986, 127-28.

[5] Adam 1994, 255-56; Hodge 1992, 279-91.

[6] Also seen farther east. At Dura Europos there is a rectangular reservoir raised on three vaulted subbuildings built into the southern side of Bath E3. See Brown (1936, 94).

[7] See Rosenbaum, Huber and Onurkan (1967, 31-32) who do not identify the building as a reservoir. In a visit to Selinus, however, the author could clearly see that the top of the building was a basin lined with waterproof cement. Although the aqueduct skirts the reservoir, there must have been some sort of connection between the two.

[8] See Gough (1956, 172-75, figs. 2-3) for the "West Building" (interpreted as a large meeting hall) and the "Building with Pendentives" (baths), and Akok (1957, 18, figs. IX and XVI) for Building A (Gough's "West Building") and Building B (Gough's "Building with Pendentives").

[9] Several nails, mostly iron but one copper, were found still imbedded in the north wall face. These pins served to hold heavier fragments of marble in position. See below, pages 52-53.

[10] Such an arrangement is documented in the Bath-Gymnasium Complex at Sardis. Yegül 1986, 143-44.

[11] For a discussion of flues see Yegül (1992, 357) and Rook (1978, 270 and 1979a, 303-308).

[12] Sardis: Yegül 1986, 128; Augusta: Akok 1957, fig. XXIII.32.

[13] Walls were heated using such devices as lugged tiles (*tegulae mammatae*), which were attached to walls by pins, or by hollow bricks (*tubuli*) built into the walls. Both these systems allowed hot air to flow up from the furnace along the walls and out through the roof. A third system, which used spacer pins set into the wall to support tiles, was particularly common in Lycia. See Yegül (1992, 363-65), Adam (1994, 268-70) and Farrington (1995, 101-104). Pins were found in the walls of both Rooms A and B. In the case of Room A only three were found, too few to postulate their function, although the presence of numerous fragments of marble revetment argues that the pins were used to attach the plates to the wall. More pins were found in the east wall of Room B, but since they are clustered above the doorway they could not have been part of the heating system.

[14] Although apses are more commonly found in the caldaria of baths of southern Turkey, frigidaria with apses have been identified in Baths B at Tlos and the North Baths at Patara. Farrington 1995, 4.

[15] It was suggested above that there may have been a doorway in the north wall of Room C. Although this is not a typical feature of caldaria, several caldaria in Lycian baths were equipped with doorways leading to the outside. Farrington 1995, 12-13.

[16] As is found in some Lycian baths. Farrington 1995, 14-16.

[17] Yegül 2003, 64-65; Yegül 1992, 291-304; Farrington 1995, 31-34; Onurkan 1967, 69-85.

[18] See Adam (1994, 255) and Hodge (1992, 300-02). In the reservoir built into the south wall of Bath M7 at Dura Europos a buttress was built into the interior of its lower chamber which may have supported a pipe used to send water to its upper chamber. Brown 1937, 88.

[19] Ward-Perkins 1947, 179. The domical vault was one of the earliest devices used to place a dome over a square space. It is referred to by a bewildering assortment of technical names (pendentive dome, sail dome, handkerchief vault, *volta a vela*, *Hängekuppel*) but can be recognized by its low curvature and by the unified curve formed by the vault and the pendentives. This distinguishes it from the true dome, which rests on independent spherical triangular pendentives (Krautheimer 1967, 362 for a diagram). The true dome, featured in Byzantine churches such as Hagia Sophia, developed later than the domical vault, although the two existed side by side in early Byzantine times. Domical vaults from the 2nd c. A.D. are known from Italy (Sedia del Diavolo, a tomb outside of Rome on the via Nomentana, Rivoira 1925, 152-55) and Syria (West Baths at Gerasa, Fisher 1938, 23). For debates on the origins and development of the pendentive see Creswell (1932, 304-23), Ward-Perkins (1947), and Davies (1953, 63-67).

[20] Hodge 1992, 58-62.

[21] For an illustration of this type of arrangement see Adam (1994, fig. 608).

[22] Because the ceramic evidence indicates that the site was active into the late 6th c. A.D., it is logical to assume that there may have been a church on the premises. The orientation and apse of Building 13 make it a possible candidate for a church, but so little is preserved that this can only be speculation.

[23] Adam (1994, 254) presents the average diameter of Roman pipes as between 13 and 20 cm. See also Hodge (1992, 106-15) for a discussion of pipes.

[24] Fisher 1934, 2, fig. 3.

[25] Little work appears to have been done on Roman rooftiles in the eastern Mediterranean. For discussions concentrating on Britain and Northern Europe, see Bodribb (1987, 5-33) and Rook (1979a, 295-301).

[26] Yegül 1986, 128.

[27] Yegül 1992, 357-61; Rook 1978.

[28] Adam (1994, 266-68) gives the average length of a square hypocaust tile as 20 cm.

[29] For a discussion of the process see Harden (1961, 41-49), and Boon (1966, 41-45).

[30] A pane of window glass in the Afyon Museum also exhibits striations on one side. See Lightfoot (1989, 29).

[31] Matte/glossy or mold-made window glass was created by pouring molten glass into a tray. Evidence for this technique can be seen in the two finishes of the two faces of the glass, the upper surface is shiny and lower one is dull because it was set into a shallow mold. Also this type of glass tends to be somewhat thicker than that made with the cylinder-blown technique. However, Harden (1961, 44-45) argued that this

was not a technique employed by the Romans, and explained the matte surface of the glass as being created when one face of the opened cylinder was laid on the iron surface to cool. Other scholars, however, do not appear to have abandoned the idea of mold-made windows; see Lightfoot (1989, 28) and Stern (1985, 48-50). Whatever the mode of manufacture, glossy/matte windows are generally thought to date to the 1st and 2nd c. A.D., although examples are found at Anemurium dating to Late Roman times (see below note 37). For dates of matte/glossy glass see Harden (1974, 280).

[32] See Yegül (1992, 383, n. 85) for a list of baths with glazed windows from heated rooms. Stern (1999, 458-64) in discussing the inclusion of window glass in the Price Edict of Diocletian, cites texts from Oxyrhynchus which deal with large amounts of window glass for baths.

[33] Supra n. 31.

[34] Harden 1961, 40.

[35] For Gerasa see Bauer (1938, 514, 546 and pl. XXXVb). For Samaria see Crowfoot (1957, 421).

[36] Harden 1961, 43.

[37] Stern (1985, 48-50) identifies some panes as being made with the "muff" process and others as mold-made.

[38] Few examples of window glass have been published from Turkey. Examples exist in the Afyon Museum, published by Lightfoot (1989, 28-29), and fragments from 5th -7th c. contexts have been published by Stern (1985, 48-50). Von Saldern (1980, 91-92) also presented window glass from Sardis, mostly from the shops and Bath-Gymnasium Complex, made with the "muff" process. No examples of crown glass were reported from Sardis. Window glass produced in the muff technique was also recovered in a recent survey at Olba (Rough Cilicia), and has been tentatively dated from Roman to late Roman/early Byzantine times. See Erten (2003, 149-52).

[39] For a basic discussion of rendering see Adam (1994, 216-20).

[40] Onurkan 1967, 81.

[41] Farrington 1995, 112.

[42] For a discussion of the technique see Farrington (1995, 111-12), Adam (1994, 227-28) and very recently Ball (2002).

[43] Dodge 1988a, 218.

[44] See Dodge (1992, 153-59) for a gazetteer of important Roman quarries, and Röder (1971) for a thorough discussion of Phrygian quarries.

[45] Dodge 1992, 154.

[46] Ibid. 154.

[47] Röder 1971, 255.

[48] Ibid. 255.

[49] Ibid. 255.

[50] Dodge 1992, 156.

[51] Dodge 1992, 156; Röder 1971, 255.

[52] Dodge 1992, 158.

[53] Fant 1993, 154.

[54] For example see Dodge (1988a), (1988b) and Fant (1993). Recently Hazel Dodge and Bryan Ward-Perkins have collected John Ward-Perkins' essays and lectures on the marble trade, see Dodge and Ward-Perkins (1992).

[55] Fant 1993, 153; Erim and Reynolds 1970, 133.

[56] Dodge 1992, 153-159; Mango 1985, 14.

[57] Mango 1985, 14; Dodge 1992, 158.

[58] Ward-Perkins (1958, 85-86) recognized pre-Byzantine (late Roman) brickwork as a common secondary material used for specific constructional details such as apses, vaults and in baths. He admitted that it was difficult to distinguish original brickwork from later repairs.

[59] Tırpan 1989, 523.

[60] Ward-Perkins 1955, 120-21.

[61] Spanu 1999, 106-07.

[62] Waelkens 1987, 94-100.

[63] Ibid. 101-102.

POTTERY

The pottery catalogued in this volume was collected during two campaigns, the initial survey by Özgen/Gates in 1991 and the intensive survey by the author in 1994. Most fragments are small, many quite worn, and in no case do we possess the whole profile of a vessel. However, by studying the ware types, the fabrics and, where possible, the vessel forms and decoration, the broadest chronological range of occupation of the site can be ascertained.[1]

The study of pottery from Küçük Burnaz must rely heavily on the published results of neighboring excavations. Unfortunately, no Roman period site in the Plain of Issus has been excavated. For the period in question, the two closest well-published sites are Tarsus and Antioch.[2] Useful information also comes from sites slightly further afield, from Anemurium in Rough Cilicia and Porsuk at the northern entrance to the Cilician Gates.[3] Sites in the Levant, such as Samaria and Tel Anafa, are also useful for comparanda, as are the excavations on Cyprus.[4]

The catalogue is divided into the categories of fine ware, plain ware and amphorae of the Roman and Late Roman period, followed by a discussion of medieval glazed ware. The entries are organized in the following manner:

Catalog number, followed by the field number (preceded by SID ["Site in Dunes"]) and findspot. Those sherds found during the 1991 survey often do not have a precise findspot. Those from the 1994 survey are recorded either in terms of the building at which they were found or the pass in which they were collected.[5]

Dimensions in centimeters. The following abbreviations are used: p. h. = preserved height, p. l. = preserved length, th. = thickness, w. = width, est. r. diam. = estimated rim diameter (taken from the inside of the rim), est. f. diam. = estimated diameter of the foot (taken from the inside of the foot), p. dim. = preserved dimensions.

Description
Comparanda
Tentative date

Because of the fragmentary nature of the pottery, it has not been possible to organize the catalog by vessel shape. Rather, it has been arranged by diagnostic type, beginning with bases, since they are, at least in the case of the fine wares, the most securely identified. The bases are followed by rims, handles and decorated body sherds. Where possible, the fragments have been discussed in order of the dates at present assigned to their production.

FINE WARES

Eastern Sigillata A (ESA)

As has now been well established, Eastern Sigillata A is a ware that developed around 150 B.C. It is the most common sigillata found in the Eastern Mediterranean, and is especially common in the region of Syro-Palestine. The center of production for ESA has not yet been established, although it would appear to have been located in the region of Syro-Palestine, either on the coast or possibly inland, most likely coming from a series of workshops located in the same general geological region.[6] By the 3rd c A.D., ESA was superseded by African Red Slip.

All the fragments of sigillata-type pottery found at Küçük Burnaz presented the typical characteristics of ESA, that is to say a pale pinkish or yellowish fabric with a red or orange-red slip. No examples of other contemporary eastern sigillatas, such as Eastern Sigillata B, Çandarlı Ware, or Cypriot Sigillata, were identified from the site, nor could any western sigillatas be recognized. Certainly the lack of other wares in this assemblage could be an accident of recovery or preservation. This pattern, however, is typical for the Eastern Mediterranean, where ESA was the dominant sigillata type.[7]

The 191 fragments of ESA pottery collected at Küçük Burnaz fall into three different fabric groups.

Type 1: This is the most common type with 126 examples. The fabric is pinkish orange in color and ranges from Munsell 7.5 YR 7/6 to 5 YR 7/4.[8] The fabric is fairly hard and fine, although occasionally there can be small lime inclusions present. The slip ranges from orange (2.5 YR 6/8) to dark red (10 R 5/8-4/8) and is rarely well preserved.

Type 2: This type, with 42 examples, has a very fine pale yellow fabric (2.5 YR 8/3), with occasional tiny red inclusions. The slip tends to be very worn on most fragments but where preserved is a dark reddish orange (10 R 5/8-4/8).

Type 3: There are 21 examples of this fabric type, which is recognized by the presence of golden micaceous inclusions,[9] sometimes accompanied by small black and white inclusions. The fabric is pinkish orange (7.5 YR 8/4) with a rather fugitive orange slip. It is interesting to note that nearly all examples of heavy low ring feet are in this fabric (see catalogue entries **P2-P9**).

It is possible that these divisions reflect different sources for the three ESA fabrics seen at Küçük Burnaz. Kathleen Kenyon identified two different fabric types of ESA at Samaria, where she was able to recognize both through visual observation and spectrographical analysis.[10] However, recently a spectographical analysis of examples of ESA fabrics from Tel Anafa exhibiting differences in color, hardness and texture demonstrated that despite their variations they were all the same clay. The variances were due to the firing temperature of the kiln.[11] Thus the possibility must be considered that the three fabric types could possibly come from the same clay source. Of the micaceous examples whose shape could be identified (Type 3), however, all seem to date to the Augustan period, perhaps indicating a source for ESA specific to that time.

Because of the size of the fragments in this assemblage and the fact that no whole profiles exist, it is difficult to identify with complete security what precise form they follow. The two most extensive typologies of ESA, by Hayes[12] and Waagé[13] have proven useful in the identification of this material, in addition to comparanda from other sites. In general these typologies are based on the form of the entire vessel, often depending on the relationship between rim and base. Since few sherds from Küçük Burnaz preserve both these features, these typologies are being used with caution.

Bases

Thirty-four bases were collected, but only those whose stance could be ascertained have been catalogued.

P1 (SID 94.178, Building 2), fig. 80
P. h. 2.3, wall th. 0.4, est. f. diam. 2.8
Foot of a round-sided bowl or cup, portions of the foot, floor and wall preserved. Deep half-round molding on the exterior of foot below where the wall meets the foot. The clay is pale and fine, and the slip is glossy red all over (10 R 5/8), although more brown on the underside.
ESA Type 2
Similar to Antioch 164
Mid-1st c. B.C.

P2 (SID 94.387, Pass 9), fig. 80
P. h. 1.5, wall th. 0.5, est. f. diam. 8.7, floor th. 0.2
Base of a small plate or saucer, joined from two fragments. Portion of foot, floor and wall preserved. The exterior of the wall has a slight angle and the foot has a beveled exterior profile. The clay is orange and micaceous, with brown, white and black inclusions. Interior is badly abraded, but some red slip is preserved; more adheres to the exterior (2.5 YR 6/8).
ESA Type 3
Antioch 125 or 117
1st c. B.C.

P3 (SID 94.173a, Pass 10), fig. 80
P. h. 1.6, wall th. 0.9, est. f. diam. 1.5, floor th. .0.4
Base of a plate, portion of the foot, floor and wall preserved. Slight beveling on the exterior of the ring foot, just above the resting surface. Groove encircles the floor of the plate. Clay is pinkish-orange and very fine. Red slip preserved on interior and exterior (2.5 YR 6/8).
ESA Type 1
Hayes (1987) ESA Form 3; Antioch 405a-f, 116n, or 126x
Late 1st c. B.C. - first half of the 1st c. A.D.

P4 (SID 91.155, from the 1991 survey), fig. 80
P. h. 3.9, wall th. 0.9, est. f. diam. 10, floor th. 0.6
Base of a plate, portion of foot, floor and wall preserved. Interior of the vessel forms an even curve from wall to floor. Clay is pinkish-orange and micaceous with small black inclusions. Red slip preserved on interior and exterior (10 R 5/8).
ESA Type 3
Antioch 405a-f, 116n, or 126x
Late 1st c. B.C. - first half of the 1st c. A.D.

P5 (SID 91.125 + SID 94.501, from the 1991 survey and Building 4), fig. 80
P. h. 4.2, est. f. diam. 10.0, wall th. 0.6

Base of a plate, joined from two fragments, portions of the foot, floor and wall preserved. Clay is pinkish orange and micaceous with small black inclusions. Traces of red slip on exterior (2.5 YR 6/6).
ESA Type 3
Antioch 405a-f, 116n, or 126x
Late 1st c. B.C. - first half of the 1st c. A.D.

P6 (SID 94.62, between Buildings 2 and 3), fig. 80
P. h. 1.2, wall th. 0.7
Very worn, only a part of the ring foot preserved. Clay is yellow and very fine. Slip is only faintly preserved on the interior of the vessel; slip on the exterior is red (10 R 5/8).
ESA Type 2
Augustan ?

P7 (SID 94.40, between Buildings 2 and 3), fig. 80
P. h. 1.5, wall th. 0.7
Very worn, only a part of the ring base preserved. Clay is micaceous with traces of small black inclusions. No slip preserved on the interior, faint traces of red slip on the exterior.
ESA Type 3
Augustan ?

P8 (SID 94.312, general find), fig. 80
P. h. 1.6, wall th. 0.9
Small fragment of a plate or shallow bowl, some wall preserved but almost none of the floor. Incised lines found on exterior wall just above the foot and midway up the interior face of the foot. Clay is pale pinkish-yellow and micaceous with small black and white inclusions. Only scant traces of red slip found on foot.
ESA Type 3
Augustan ?

P9 (SID 94.419, Building 3), fig. 80
P. h. 1.5, floor th. 0.5
Base with ring foot, portion of floor preserved. Clay is very fine and micaceous with black and white inclusions. Traces of slip preserved on the interior.
ESA Type 3
Similar to Antioch 116
Augustan ?

P10 (SID 91.154, from the 1991 survey), fig. 80
P. h. 5.5, wall th. 0.4, est. f. diam. 7.5, floor th. 0.2
Base of a bowl, portion of the foot, floor and vessel wall preserved. Interior of vessel forms an even curve from wall to floor, indicating this may have originally had a hemispherical profile. Foot is distinguished from the exterior wall by a shallow groove. Clay is micaceous with white (lime?) inclusions. Reddish-orange slip preserved on interior and exterior (10 R 6/8).
ESA Type 3
In general, close to Tarsus 401, Samaria 24 and Antioch 465p-468
Second half of the 1st c. A.D.

P11 (SID 94.413, Building 3), fig. 80
P. h. 1.4, wall th. 0.7, est. f. diam. 7.5, floor th. 0.3
Base of a plate, portion of foot, floor and wall preserved. There is a shallow groove on the exterior where the foot meets the wall of the vessel. The clay is orange and very fine, micaceous with a few inclusions. Traces of slip preserved on the interior.
ESA Type 3
Similar to Hayes ESA Forms 30 and 33 and Antioch 407 or 412
First half of the 1st c. A.D.

P12 (SID 94.522, Building 4), fig. 81
P. h. 1.0, wall th. 0.6, est. f. diam. 6.2, floor th. 0.3

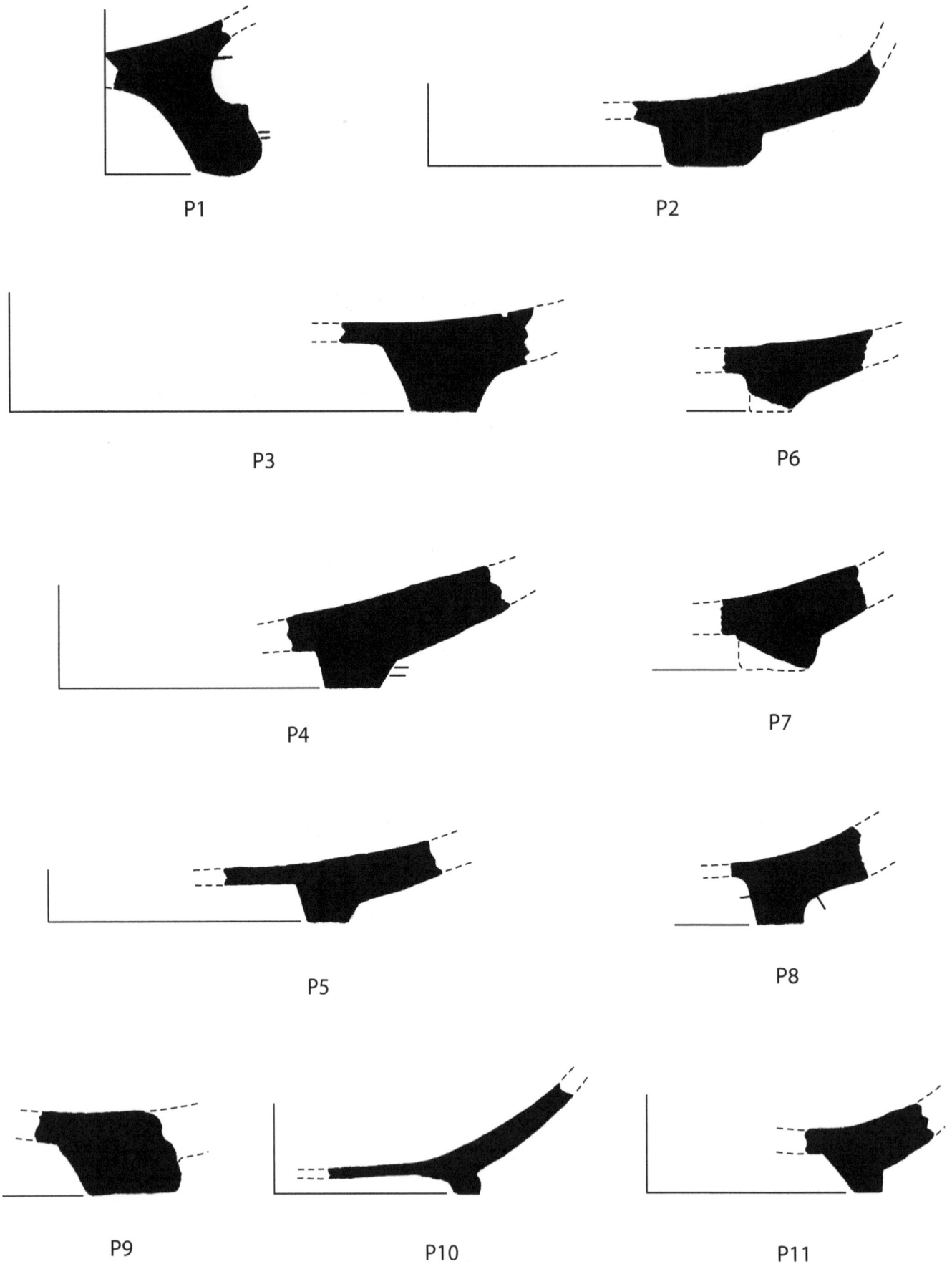

Figure 80. Profiles of ESA bases, **P1-P11**, Scale 1:1

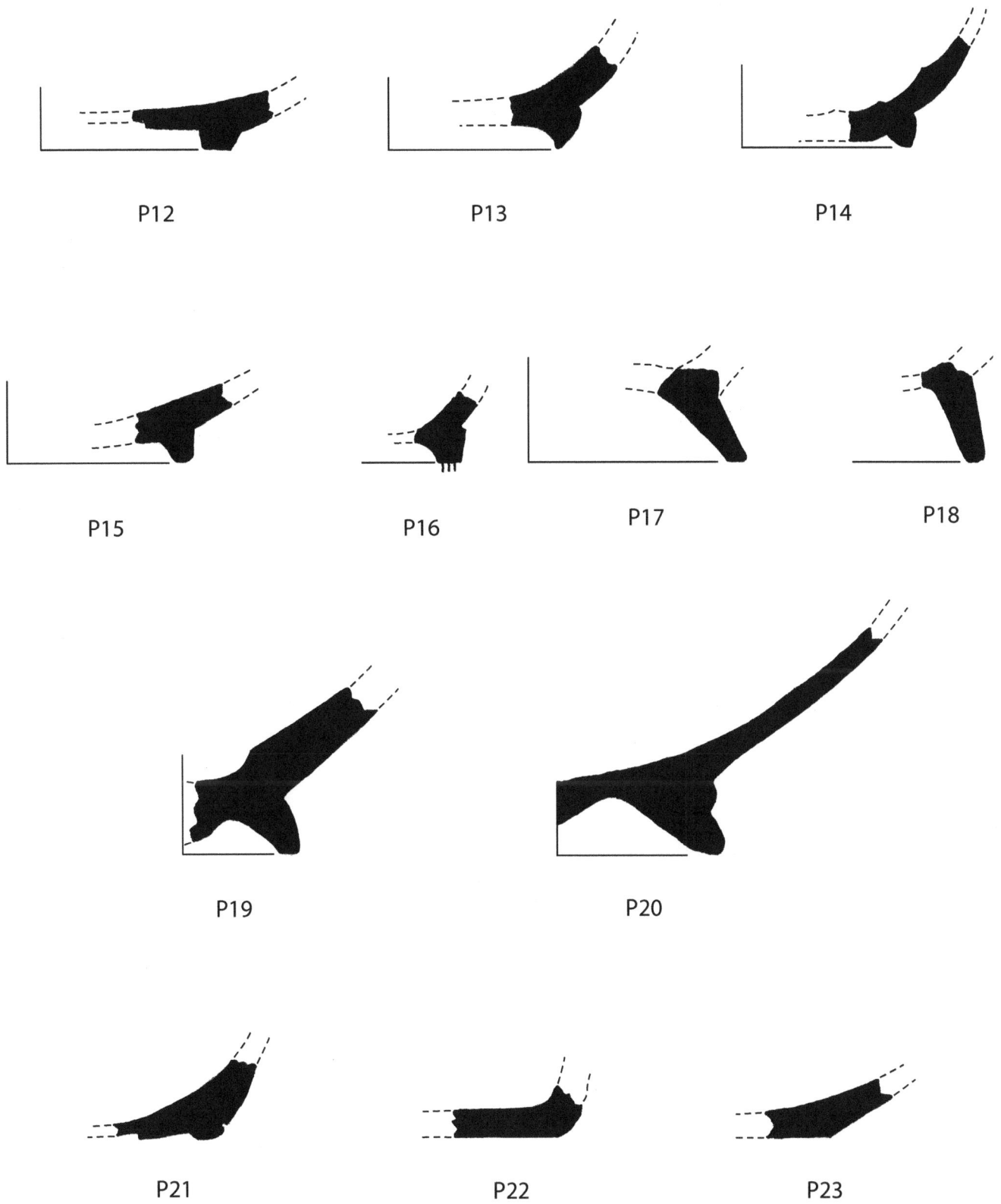

*Figure 81. Profiles of ESA bases, **P12-P23**, Scale 1:1*

Ring base fragment, portions of foot, floor and wall preserved. Interior of foot rises in a step. Clay is orange and fine. Dark orange slip is present on both the interior and exterior.
ESA Type 1
Similar to Hayes ESA Form 30 and Antioch 412f
A.D. 25-50

P13 (SID 94.176a, Building 2), fig. 81
P. H. 1.8, wall th. 0.6, est. f. diam. 6.2, floor th. 0.6
Base with pointed ring foot, section of foot, floor and wall preserved. Clay is buff and fairly fine. Burnt-orange colored slip preserved on interior and exterior (10 R 4/6).
ESA Type 2
Similar to Hayes ESA Form 45 and Antioch 453
First half of the 1st c. A.D.

P14 (SID 94.179, Building 2), fig. 81
P. h. 2.2, wall th. 0.3, est. f. diam. 6.2
Base of a pitcher with ring foot, portions of foot, floor and wall preserved. Ring foot is triangular in section. Interior has distinct carinated ridges. Clay is fine. Red slip exists on exterior and interior (10 R 5/8).
ESA Type 1

P15 (SID 94.58, between Buildings 2 and 3), fig. 81
P. h. 1.3, wall th. 0.4, est. f. diam. 6.2
Base with ring foot, portions of the foot and wall preserved, only a small trace of floor present. The exterior of the foot is slightly rounded and has a small groove where it meets the wall. An incised groove circles the interior of the vessel. The clay is pale orange, and fine. Reddish-orange slip on the interior and exterior (10 YR 5/6-6/6).
ESA Type 1

P16 (SID 94.362, Pass 9), fig. 81
P. h. 1.6, wall th. 0.4
Base with low ring foot. Part of wall and floor preserved. Clay is pale yellow and fine. Slip is dark orange (2.5 YR 7/6).
ESA Type 1

P17 (SID 94.97, between Buildings 2 and 3), fig. 81
P. h. 1.8, wall th. 0.3, est. f. diam. 7.5
Fragment from a cup (?) with outward splaying foot; part of the foot, the floor and beginnings of the wall of the vessel preserved. Clay is pale yellow and very fine. Red slip preserved on exterior and interior of vessel (2.5 YR 6/8).
ESA Type 1
Similar to Hayes ESA Form 50 and Antioch 465
A.D. 60/70-100

P18 (SID 94.198, Building 3), fig. 81
P. h. 1.3, est. f. diam. 6.2
Small section of a high foot, similar to **P17**. A trace of floor is preserved but no wall. Clay is pale and fine. Red slip on all original surfaces (10 R 5/8).
ESA Type 1
Second half of the 1st c. A.D. (?)

P19 (SID 94.291, between Buildings 3 and 9), fig. 81
P. h. 3.0, wall th. 0.6, est. f. diam. 2.4
Base with high foot, portions of the floor and wall preserved. The foot is triangular in section and protrudes outward on its interior face. A concavity in the floor of the vessel matches the protrusion. Striations exist on exterior of foot. Clay is pinkish and fine with a few inclusions; scanty traces of red slip.
ESA Type 1

P20 (SID 94.231, Building 2), fig. 81
P. h. 4.8, wall th. 0.4, est. f. diam. 4.8
Base with high foot, portions of the floor and wall preserved. Foot is triangular in section. Exterior face stands vertical and has a rounded bulge. Interior of foot projects. Interior of base forms a smooth unbroken curve. Clay is pale and very fine; cloudy and fugitive red slip (10 R 5/8) adheres to the interior and exterior, and appears to have been applied through dipping. Possibly a lid.
ESA Type 1

P21 (SID 94.359, Building 2), fig. 81
P. h. 1.5, wall th. 0.6
Base with low foot, portions of the wall and floor preserved. Foot is low and rounded and separated from the wall on the exterior by a groove. The interior of the foot rises in two steps. The clay is orange and fine with a few small white inclusions. Orange slip adheres to the interior and exterior (10R 6/8).
ESA Type 1
Similar to Hayes ESA Form 57 and Antioch 627 or 640a
First half of the 2nd c. A.D.

P22 (SID 94.298, Building 2), fig. 81
P. l. 2.5, wall th. 0.5
Flat base with no foot, part of the vessel wall preserved. A slight ridge on the interior marks the shift from floor to wall. Clay is fine and yellowish, red slip on interior and exterior (10 R 5/8).
ESA Type 2
Similar to Antioch 630-635 and Hayes ESA Late Form E. Hayes classifies such footless vessels as local to the regions of Tarsus and Antioch.
Antonine

P23 (SID 94.515, Building 4), fig. 81
P. h. 1.0, wall th. 0.4
Flat base with no foot, part of the vessel wall preserved. Clay is orange and fine. Interior slip is deep red (10 R 6/8), while the exterior slip is more orange (2.5 YR 7/8).
ESA Type 1
Similar to Antioch 634 and 635 and Hayes ESA Late Form E
Antonine

Rims

With very few exceptions the ESA rim sherds collected at Küçük Burnaz are so fragmentary that it is almost impossible to determine to which precise form they might have belonged. Some are so small that one cannot accurately obtain the stance or diameter. Of the 29 rim sherds collected at Küçük Burnaz, only those examples whose stances have been securely obtained are listed here. They are classified by general shape, and have been tentatively assigned a form and date.

Incurving Rim

This rim shape could apply to many of the plates classified as Hayes ESA Forms 3 and 4, (dating to the end of the 2nd c. B.C. to the last decade of the 1st c. B.C.) and Antioch 124-126, which extend into the early 1st c. A.D. One example of an incurving rim (**P28**) with a nearly semi-circular profile could possibly be from an Antonine form.

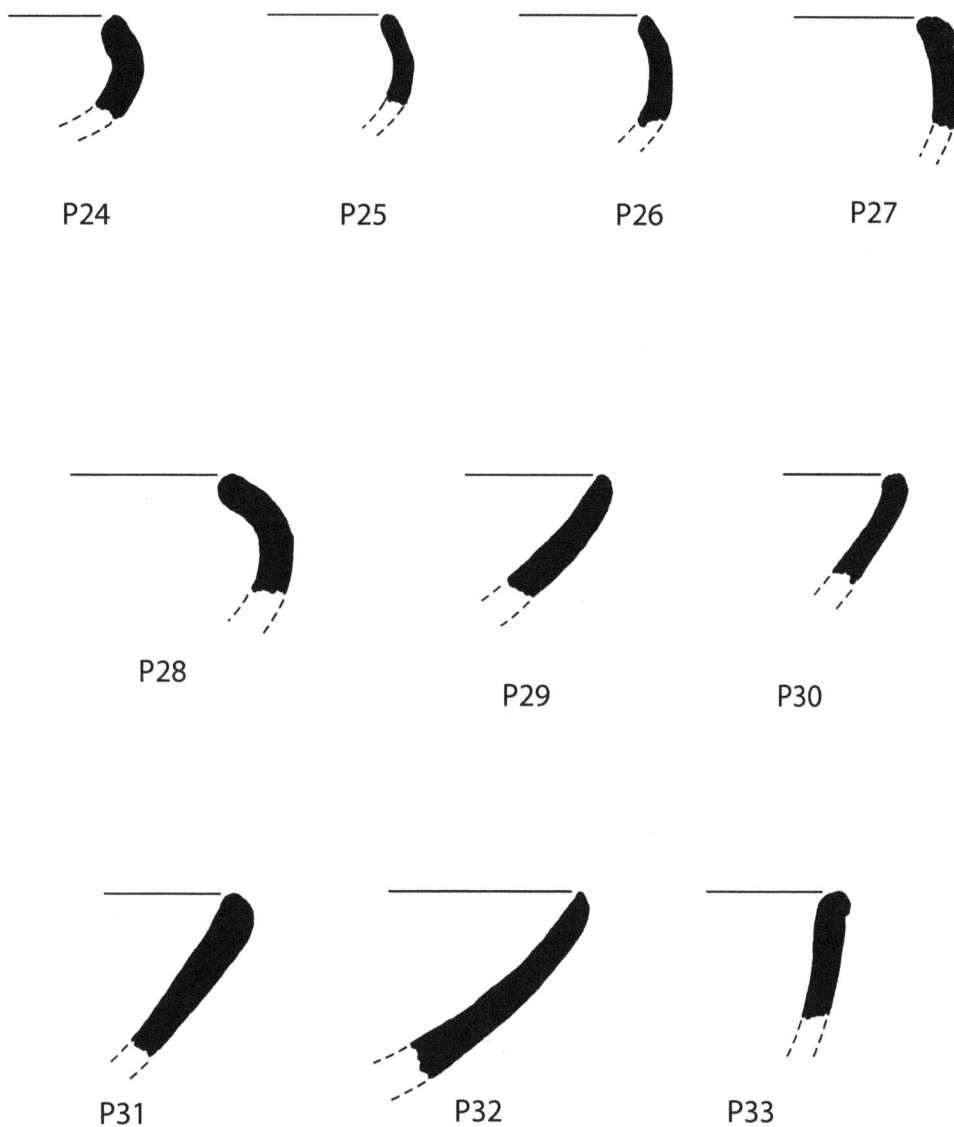

P24   P25   P26   P27

P28

P29   P30

P31   P32   P33

*Figure 82. Profiles of ESA rims, **P24-P33**, Scale 1:1*

P24 (SID 94.300, Building 2), fig. 82
P. h. 1.5, wall th. 0.4
Rim fragment, too small to obtain diameter. Clay is pale and very fine, red slip on interior and exterior (10 R 5/6). Some striations on the interior.
ESA Type 1

P25 (SID 94.462, Building 3), fig. 82
P. h. 1.7, wall th. 0.3
Rim fragment, too small to obtain diameter. Clay is pinkish and fine, red slip on interior and exterior (10 R 5/6). Striations on both surfaces.
ESA Type 1

P26 (SID 94.489, between Buildings 3 and 9), fig. 82
P. h. 1.9, wall th. 0.4
Rim fragment, too small to obtain diameter. Clay is orange with tiny white inclusions. Minute traces of slip on interior and exterior. Striations on both faces.
ESA Type 1

P27 (SID 94.372, Pass 9), fig. 82
P. h. 1.7, wall th. 0.3 m, est. r. diam. 20.0
Rim fragment with a rounded band on the exterior below the lip. Clay is pale orange with small white inclusions. Traces of reddish slip on interior and exterior (2.5 YR 6/8). Striations on the exterior.
ESA Type 1

P28 (SID 94.83, between Buildings 2 and 3), fig. 82
P. h. 1.1, wall th. 0.3
Rim fragment, too small to obtain diameter. Rim curves inward, creating a semicircle. Clay is pale yellow and very fine. Red slip is preserved on interior and exterior (10 YR 5/8) with rough striations on both surfaces.
ESA Type 1
Possibly Hayes ESA Late Form G and Antioch 653
Late 2nd c. A.D?

Curved or Inclined Rim

These rims are compatible with those of deep plates of Augustan date identified by Hayes as ESA Form 5 and seen at Antioch as Form 151.

P29 (SID 94.206, Building 3), fig. 82
P. h. 2.2, wall th. 0.4
Inclined rim with a rounded lip, too small to determine diameter. Clay is pale; red slip adheres to interior and exterior (10 R 5/6).
ESA Type 1

P30 (SID 94.375, Pass 9), fig. 82
P. h. 1.4, wall th. 0.4
Inclined rim with a rounded lip, too small to determine diameter. Clay is pale and fine with a few small red inclusions. Fugitive red slip adheres to the exterior, which also bears faint striations.
ESA Type 2

P31 (SID 94.317, Building 2), fig. 82
P. h. 2.4, wall th. 0.7, est. r. diam. 15
Inclined rim with a rounded lip. Clay is pale orange and fairly fine with tiny traces of "mica." Slip is brownish-orange, slightly mottled and flaking off in places (10 YR 5/8). Striations on both the interior and exterior of vessel wall.
ESA Type 3

P32 (SID 94.173B, between Buildings 2 and 3), fig. 82
P. h. 3, wall th. 0.5 m, est. r. diam. 15
Inclined rim fragment. Lip is slightly curved. Clay is pale and fine. Orange-red slip preserved on interior and exterior (10 R 6/6).
ESA Type 1

P33 (SID 94.364, Pass 9), fig. 82
P. h. 1.7, wall th. 0.4
Inclined rim fragment with squared lip. Clay is very fine with tiny white inclusions. Red slip is present on all original surfaces (2.5 YR 6/8).
ESA Type 1

P34 (SID 94.45, between Buildings 2 and 3), not illustrated
P. H. 1.8, wall th. 0.5
Inclined rim fragment, too small to determine diameter. Partially encrusted with cement-like sand. Where visible a brownish-red slip covers the interior and exterior of sherd (10 R 5/3-5/4). Ridges are visible on exterior and interior.
ESA Type 1 (?)

Handle

Only one handle in ESA fabric was collected.

P35 (SID 94.229, Building 3), not illustrated
P. l. 2., w. .018, th. 0.7
Vertical handle fragment, rectangular in profile. Two grooves decorate its exterior. Clay is pale and fine; dark red slip adheres to all original surfaces (10 R 5/8).
ESA Type 1

Decorated Body Sherds

One hundred and thirty one body sherds in ESA fabric were collected at Küçük Burnaz, all but four coming from open vessels. The following three sherds have rough rouletting on their exteriors and may belong to the same vessel, since they were all found in the vicinity of the Smaller Baths (Building 2).[14]

P36 (SID 91.144, from the 1991 survey, east of Building 2), not illustrated
P. dim. 3 x .2.4, wall th. 0.4
Convex body sherd. Clay is pale and very fine. Interior and exterior are coated in a thin red slip (10 R 6/8). Exterior decorated with an incised horizontal line, rouletting below.
ESA Type 1

P37 (SID 94.181, Building 2), not illustrated
P. h. 1.2, p. l. 1.4, wall th. 0.3
Convex body sherd. Clay is pink and fine. Red slip is glossy and thick on the interior (2.5 YR 5/8), but is very worn on the exterior. Exterior preserves rouletting.
ESA Type 1

P38 (SID 94.184, Building 2), not illustrated
P. h. 1.4, p. l. 2, wall th. 0.3
Body sherd, profile is slightly curved. Clay is pink and fine. Red slip on the interior and exterior (10 R 5/8). Exterior preserves rouletting.
ESA Type 1

General Remarks

Although the earliest ESA fragment, **P1**, dates to the mid-1st c. B.C., most of the examples (**P2-13, P24-27, P29-35**) are slightly later, dating to the late 1st c. B.C. through the mid-1st c. A.D. Thus the initial period of occupation of Küçük Burnaz would appear to be sometime in the mid to late 1st c. B.C., with much activity for the next fifty years. There are a few examples (**P17, P18, P22, P23**) that appear to date from the second half of the 1st c. - 2nd c. A.D., but these are less securely identified. Based upon this evidence, it would seem that the site at Küçük Burnaz flourished during the first fifty years of this era, at which point activity at the site diminished.

Late Roman Red Wares

Ninety-four fragments of Late Roman Red Ware were collected, adhering to two basic wares: African Red Slip and Phocaean Red Slip Ware (Late Roman C Ware).

African Red Slip (ARS)

African Red Slip Ware - a name popularized by John Hayes, who has made the critical study of the ware - was produced in various workshops in North Africa from the 2nd through the 7th c. A.D.[15] It was exported widely, including to Syro-Palestine where it was the dominant ware in Tarsus and Antioch from the mid-3rd through the early 5th c. A.D. During the 5th c. A.D. African Red Slip was supplanted by Phocaean Red Slip Ware, but re-emerged later in the 6th c.[16]

Thirty-two fragments of African Red Slip were collected at Küçük Burnaz. The fabric of these is consistent - fairly coarse with white (lime) inclusions, small brown or black inclusions and often traces of "mica." The thin slip is usually the same color as the fabric (and thus often indistinguishable from it) or a shade or two darker. The fabrics collectively fall within the Munsell 10 R range, specifically between the following: 7/8, 6/8, 5/8, 6/6, 5/6.

As is the case with the ESA examples, the following pieces have been catalogued by diagnostic type and, when possible, arranged chronologically within each type.

Bases

Of the eight base fragments identified, four are so worn that it was impossible to identify with any certainly their original form, and they have not been catalogued. Two of these, however, are probably examples of Hayes ARS Form 50, dating to *c.* A.D. 250-300. Three of the better-preserved examples are flat bases with minute ring feet, similar to Hayes ARS 58 B.8, dated to A.D. 290/300-75.

P39 (SID 94.46, between Buildings 2 and 3), fig. 83
P. dim. 3.2 x 4.0, floor th. 0.3 thickening to 0.5

Fragment from the floor of a plate with double groove decoration. Sherd is flat but thickens towards the region of the grooves. Clay and slip are red and barely distinguishable from each other. The slip is on the interior only.
Bases such as this one, with a flat floor and grooves describing a tondo can be found on a variety of forms.
Similar to Hayes ARS 27.1, 31.4, 42, 48, 58-60.
2nd - 5th c. A.D.

P40 (SID 91.3, from the 1991 survey), fig. 83
P. dim. 2.5 x 2.3, floor th. 0.4
Stamped floor fragment from a bowl. Clay is pale red and micaceous. No trace of slip. Sherd preserves a stamp of a palm branch and a cloverleaf whose stem projects towards the palm.
Similar to Hayes ARS 67[17]
Mid-4th to early 5th c. A.D.

P41 (SID 95.232, Building 4), fig. 83
P. h. 1.0, wall th. 0.8, floor th. 0.6
Small fragment of a plate with a low rounded foot. Trace of foot, floor and wall preserved. Clay is red and rather granular with small red and brown inclusions. Slip is the same color as the clay and exists on the interior only. Base is stamped with a motif of four concentric circles with whirling fringe around the outermost circle. Next to the circle motif is a trace of what may be a palm frond or perhaps a chevron.
Similar to Hayes ARS Form 67; decoration compatible with Hayes ARS Style A (iii), Type 37v.[18] Very similar to Anemurium 255.[19]
Mid-5th c. A.D.

P42 (SID 94.197, Building 3), fig. 83
P. h. 1.8, wall th. 0.3, floor th. 0.2
Small fragment of a base with low ring foot. Trace of foot, floor and wall preserved. Foot is triangular in section and is demarcated from the vessel wall by a small groove. Clay is hard and is the same color as the red slip.
Similar to Hayes ARS Form 105, #6 or #13
580-660 A.D.

Rims

Nearly all of the eleven rims in ARS fabric are quite small, many too small to determine their diameter. The five rim fragments whose stances could not be determined have been omitted from the catalogue.

P43 (SID 91.116, from the 1991 survey, Building 2), fig. 83
P. h. 1.8, wall th. 0.5
Rim of a straight walled dish, two grooves on exterior below the rim. Clay is red with some black inclusions. Slip is red on the exterior and a deeper shade on the interior.
Similar to Hayes ARS Form 9, #16
Second half of the 2nd c. A.D.

P44 (SID 91.6, from the 1991 survey), fig. 83
P. h. 3.5, wall th. 0.5
Rim of a steep straight walled dish. Clay is red and micaceous with some black inclusions. Slip is red, and nearly the same color as the fabric. Fine striations appear on the interior, just below the rim.
Similar to Hayes ARS Form 31, #2 or #6
Early to mid-3rd c. A.D.

P39

P40

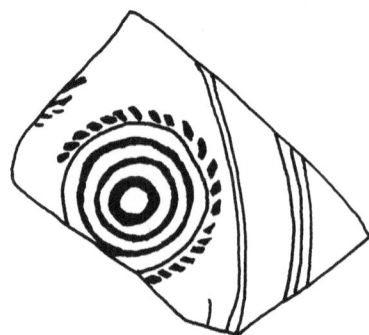

P42

P41

P43

P44

P45

P46

P47

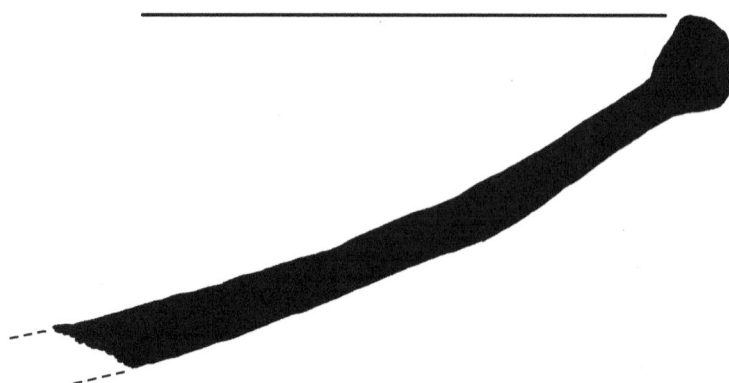

P48

*Figure 83. Profiles of ARS sherds, **P39-P48**, Scale 1:1*

P45 (SID 94.247, Building 1), fig. 83
P. h. 3.5, wall th. 0.4
Rim of a steep straight walled dish. Clay is red and micaceous, with some white inclusions. Slip is red, and nearly the same color as the fabric. Fine striations appear on the exterior.
Similar to Hayes ARS Form 31, #4
Mid-3rd c. A.D.

P46 (SID 94.336, Building 5), fig. 83
P. h. 1.9, wall th. 0.4
Rim from a high straight walled dish. Clay is hard and red; slip is a shade darker.
Possibly like Hayes ARS Form 50, #46
Mid-3rd through late 4th c. A.D.

P47 (SID 94.487, between Buildings 3 and 9), fig. 83
P. l. 3.6, wall th. 0.5
Fragment of a flaring rim in two parts, too small to obtain diameter. Clay is fine and red, slip is the same color.
Close to Hayes ARS Form 67
Late 4th c. A.D.

P48 (SID 94.246, Building 18). Fig. 83
P. h. 11.4, wall th. 0.9
Knobbed rim of a shallow bowl; in two fragments. Striations on the exterior below the lip. Clay is orange and soft, micaceous, with white inclusions. No slip survives.
Hayes ARS 104C
A.D. 525-600

General Remarks

A few of the ARS examples (**P43-45**) may date to the 2nd and 3rd c. A.D., and reflect sporadic activity at Küçük Burnaz. The more securely dated fragments (**P40-41**, **P46-47**) however, date to the 4th and 5th c. A.D. Two examples of ARS (**P42** and **P48**) are later in date. While the identification of **P42** is rather tentative, that of **P48** is more secure. This rim, dating to A.D. 525-600, is the latest Red Ware fragment found on the site, and probably gives a date for the end of activity at Küçük Burnaz.

Phocaean Red Slip Ware (Late Roman C Ware)

This ware, originally described by Hayes under the name Late Roman C Ware (LRC),[20] was later renamed Phocaean Red Slip Ware (PRS), when it was determined that a source of production of the ware was in Phocaea in Asia Minor.[21] Phocaean Red Slip was the main competitor to African Red Slip in the east, especially from the early 5th c. A.D. onward. In Tarsus and Antioch it was particularly common throughout the 5th and 6th c., disappearing sometime in the 7th.[22]

John Hayes has laid out the characteristics of fabric and manufacture. The fabric is a fine-grained red clay with small lime inclusions, brownish red in color with a thin red slip. The interior surfaces are smoothed with a spatula and the exterior often has fine corrugations.[23]

At Küçük Burnaz 58 examples of Phocaean Red Slip were collected, and these can be divided into two basic fabrics. The first, of which there are 35 examples, is identical to Hayes' description, having a Munsell of 10 R 7/6 or 6/8 and a slightly darker slip. The second, however, is much more orange in color (2.5 YR7/8 - 6/8) and contains small white (lime) inclusions. The texture is extremely soft, almost talc-like in some examples. About one-third of the examples are micaceous. Twenty-three examples in this type fabric were collected, all following Phocaean Red Slip forms, especially Form 3. It is likely that this soft fabric represents low-fired examples of Phocaean Red Slip. [24]

Bases

P49 (SID 91.9, from the 1991 survey), fig. 84
P. h. 6.0, wall th. 0.4, est. f. diam. 8.0
Base of a bowl with a low foot, in two fragments. Portions of foot, floor and wall preserved. Clay is reddish and fine with a few inclusions. Slip is red. Interior of the vessel has been smoothed by a spatula; exterior has fine corrugations.
Similar to Hayes LRC Form 3[25]
Mid-5th through mid-6th c. A.D.

P50 (SID 91.36, from the 1991 survey, area of Building 1), fig. 84
P. h. 3.3, wall th. 0.3, est. f. diam. 18.7
Base of a bowl with a low foot. Portions of foot, floor and wall preserved. Small ridge on interior of ring foot. Clay is red and fine with a few small white inclusions. Slip is red. Interior of the vessel is smooth, while the exterior has fine corrugations.
Similar to Hayes LRC Form 3
Mid-5th through mid-6th c. A.D.

P51 (SID 94.240, Building 18), fig. 84
P. h. 1.3, est. f. diam. 16.2, floor th. 0.3
Small fragment of a base with a low foot. Traces of foot, floor and a small portion of vessel wall preserved. Exterior of foot has several rounded bands. Clay is reddish with white inclusions. Slip is red.
Similar to Hayes LRC Form 3
Mid-5th through mid-6th c. A.D.

P52 (SID 91.156, from the 1991 survey), fig. 84
P. h. 1.7, wall th. 0.4, est. f. diam. 17.5, floor th. 0.2
Base of a bowl with a low foot. Portions of foot, floor and wall preserved. Clay is orange and soft with a few small white inclusions. Slip is red. Interior of the vessel is smooth, while the exterior has fine corrugations.
Similar to Hayes LRC Form 3
Mid-5th through mid-6th c. A.D.

P53 (SID 91.38, from the 1991 survey, area of Building 1), fig. 84
P. dim. 5.9 x 5.5, floor th. 0.2
Sherd with a stamped human figure; probably from the floor of a bowl. Sherd is slightly convex and preserves a swirl from the potter's wheel on its underside. Clay is red and fine with a few small white inclusions. Slip is slightly redder than the fabric. Stamp portrays a naked male figure, arms, legs and face in profile, torso in a three-quarter view. Both arms are bent at the elbow and drapery flows behind the figure's shoulders. An exact parallel (made from the same stamp) was found at Capernaum on the Sea of Galilee.[26] The Levantine example is more complete and reveals that the figure is Bacchus, holding a bunch of grapes in his left hand.[27] Stamped human figures in this ware have been dated to the 5th and early 6th c. A.D. and tend to appear on LRC Form 3 bowls.
Mid-5th through mid-6th c. A.D.

P49

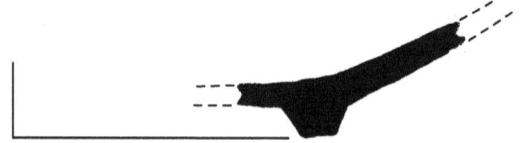

P50

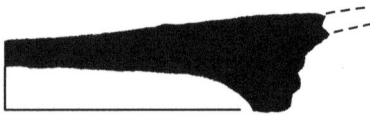

P51

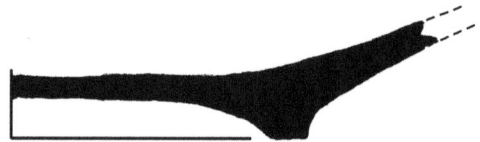

P52

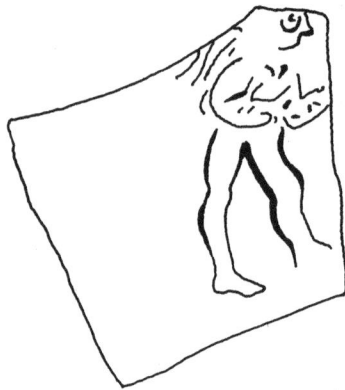

P53

P54

P55

P56

Figure 84. Profiles of LRC (Phocaean Ware) bases, **P49-P56***, Scale 1:1*

P57

P58

P59

P60

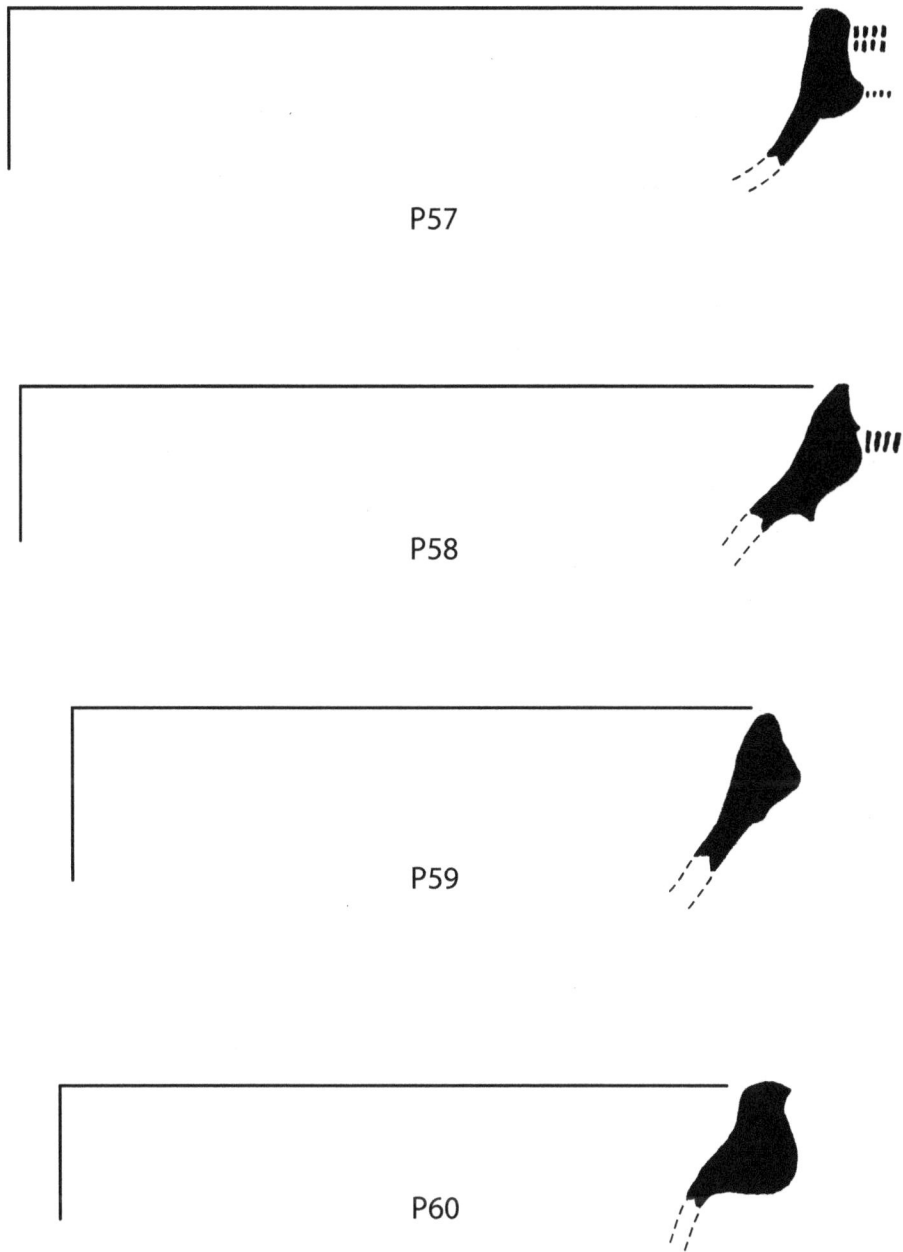

*Figure 85. Profiles of LRC (Phocaean Ware) rims, **P57-P60**, Scale 1:1*

P54 (SID 94.430, Building 3), fig. 84
P. dim. 2.1 x 1.8, floor th. 0.3
Floor of a plate (?) from two pieces; stamped with a flower (?) motif. Clay is reddish orange and traces of red slip are present on both faces.

P55 (SID 94.168A, Pass 11), fig. 84
P. h. 1.5, wall th. 0.4, est. f. diam. 10.0, floor th. 0.2
Base of a bowl with a low foot. Portions of foot, floor and wall preserved. Clay is orange and soft, micaceous with some white inclusions. Red slip adheres to the interior and exterior of base.
Hayes LRC Form 3
Mid-5th through mid-6th c. A.D.

P56 (SID 94.190, Building 3), fig. 84
P. h. 2.0, wall th. 0.4, floor th. 0.3
Small fragment of a base with a low foot. Portions of foot, floor and wall preserved. Clay is orange and micaceous with some small dark inclusions. Red slip adheres to the interior and exterior of base.
Hayes LRC Form 3
Mid-5th through mid-6th c. A.D.

Rims

P57 (SID 91.4, from the 1991 survey), fig. 85
P. h. 3.0, wall th. 0.2, est. r. diam. 22.5
Flanged rim of a bowl; rouletting on rim. Clay is reddish yellow with some fine white inclusions. Traces of red slip adhere to the rouletting and to the region below the rim as well as to the interior. Striations on the interior and exterior of the vessel.
Hayes LRC Form 3
Mid-5th through mid-6th c. A.D.

P58 (SID 94.417, Building 3), fig. 85
P. h. 1.5, wall th. 0.3, est. r. diam. 23.7
Flanged rim of a bowl. Top of rim has a rouletted band. Clay is soft and reddish orange, micaceous with a few white inclusions. Traces of slip on interior and exterior.
Hayes LRC Form 3
Mid-5th through mid-6th c. A.D.

P59 (SID 94.241, Building 18), fig. 85
P. h. 2.2, wall th. 0.4, est. r. diam. 18.7
Flanged rim of a bowl. Clay is soft and orange. Traces of red slip on the interior of the vessel.
Hayes LRC Form 3
Mid-5th through mid-6th c. A.D.

P60 (SID 94.305, Building 18), fig. 85
P. h. 2.1, wall th. 0.4, est. r. diam. 18.7
Flanged rim of a bowl. Clay is soft and reddish yellow, fairly fine with small white inclusions. No slip survives.
Hayes LRC Form 3
Mid-5th through mid-6th c. A.D.

General Remarks

The recovered fragments of Phocaean Red Ware can be firmly dated between the mid-5th and the mid-6th c. A.D. This may have been a period of intense activity at Küçük Burnaz, considering the amount of fragments collected. It is also possible that this is an accidental statistic of recovery.

Thin-walled Ware

This ware is a class of lightweight pottery characterized by having very thin walls (1-2 mm thick). Several typologies of thin-walled wares exist, all concentrating on its production and distribution in the Western Mediterranean.[28] The ware developed in Northern Italy, the earliest examples are from the 2nd c. B.C. and at least in the west production appears to have ceased by the end of the 2nd c. A.D. In the Eastern Aegean after about 80 A.D., two provincial centers of production began to dominate, the first at or near Phocaea and the second in the region neighboring the Dardanelles. These products were exported widely throughout the 2nd and early 3rd c A.D.[29]
Typical shapes in thin-walled ware are delicate drinking vessels, beakers, mugs and bowls, styled in imitation of vessels in other mediums such as metal or glass. They were designed to compliment plates and bowls in the heavier sigillata wares.[30] Although some vessels were wheel-made, most were mold-made in order to achieve the thin walls. Common decoration includes rouletting and barbotine. Also, the surfaces of these vessels are often very rough or sandy to the touch, achieved by the potter brushing grit onto the exterior and/or interior of the pot, or sometimes dipping the vessel into a gritty compound. Sometimes a thin black resinous coating covers the exterior of the vessel.

Waagé mentions in passing the presence of thin-walled ware at Antioch.[31] At Tarsus it is referred to as "Sanded Ware" and is described as fine, hard and compact with a small amount of mica.[32] In the Tarsian examples the color varies from red to buff to greenish buff and the vessels are often covered with a thin reddish-brown or brownish-black glaze to achieve a metallic sheen. The ware appears at Tarsus in 1st c. A.D. contexts and the publisher speculated that it was imported from the west.

At Küçük Burnaz the fabric is virtually indistinguishable from one used for cooking pots (described below). Two fragments, however, have been placed in the Thin-walled Ware category on the basis of shape. Both have reddish fabric (2.5 YR 5/8) fabric with white inclusions.

P61 (SID 94.314, Building 2), fig. 86
P. h. 2.3, wall th. 0.2, est. rim diam. 8.7
Fragment of a collarino-type mug with slightly outward flaring rim, trace of thin-walled body preserved. Shallow band below rim. Clay is red with white inclusions.[33]
1st - 3rd c. A.D.

P62 (SID 94.326, Building 2), fig. 86
P. h. 1.8, wall th. 0.2
Fragment with a vertical rim, probably from a drinking vessel or mug. Vessel wall is thickened below the rim before sloping outwards. Clay is reddish with few inclusions.

General Conclusions

The fine ware pottery from Küçük Burnaz reflects continuous occupation of the site from the middle of the 1st c. B.C.

through the end of the 6th c. A.D. These parameters accord well with what is known about the history of the region, which was stabilized and brought under Roman control in the mid-1st c. B.C., and was lost to the Persians in the late 6th c. A.D. We can speculate that certain periods may have enjoyed more intense activity at Küçük Burnaz, namely from the late 1st c. B.C. through the mid-1st c. A.D., and during the mid-5th through mid-6th c. A.D. This hypothesis is based on the greater number of diagnostic sherds identified from those two periods.

PLAIN WARES

This category contains both coarse and cooking wares. Although more than 1500 plain ware sherds were collected, few could be recognized in the assemblages published elsewhere. While this may be explained by the fact that the ceramics from Küçük Burnaz exist only in fragments, it should also be noted that few publications from the region include a study of the plain wares.[34] Since it would be impossible (and not useful) to present examples of all plain wares collected at Küçük Burnaz, four fabrics, particularly prevalent at Küçük Burnaz and distinctive enough to perhaps be recognized elsewhere, will be described. The catalogue for each fabric is comprised of all diagnostics identified.

Fabric 1

This is a thin-walled fabric, related to that used in the thin-walled vessels described above. Some 200 examples were collected, all extremely thin, with a wall thickness of 1-3 mm (color plate 8). The fabric is hard-fired and ranges from dark red (2.5 YR 6/6), to light reddish brown (5 YR 6/4), to a greenish color (10 YR 7/4). Most fragments have lime inclusions as well as tiny black and red grits, and some fragments are micaceous. The exteriors can have a surface decoration of wheelridging or rouletting, and some pieces have a dark, mottled slip. The form seems to be a stew pot, with a narrowing of the neck, two vertical handles, and a rounded bottom. It appears to be similar to Evrin's Type 3a1 cookpot from Tarsus, which she assigns to the Late Roman period.[35]

Bases

P63 (SID 94.558, general find), not illustrated
Wall th. 0.2
Base with low, false ring foot. Portion of vessel wall preserved. Clay is reddish yellow with white and red inclusions.

P64 (SID 94.559, Building 2), fig. 86, color plate 8, lower right
Est. base diam. 8.0, wall th. 0.2
Base with low, false ring foot. Portion of vessel wall preserved. Clay is pink with many white and inclusions and fewer red ones.

P65 (SID 94.557, general find), fig. 86

Est. base diam. 7.5, wall th. 0.2
Base with low, false ring foot. Portion of vessel wall preserved. Clay is reddish yellow with white and red inclusions. Same shape and fabric as **P63**.

Rims

P66 (SID 94.313, Building 2), fig. 86
P. h. 1.0, wall th. 0.2, est. rim diam. 10.0
Overhanging rim, trace of globular vessel preserved. Top of rim has a shallow ridge near its outer edge. Clay is red with white inclusions.

P67 (SID 94.320 + SID 94.541, Building 2), fig. 86, color plate 8, top
P. h. 1.6, wall th. 0.3, est. rim diam. 11.2
Two joining fragments of a vessel; portions of the rim and globular body preserved. Rim has a sharp carination on its outer face. Clay is pale red with many voids and small white inclusions. Whitish incrustations on interior and exterior.

P68 (SID 94.530 + SID 94.531, Building 2), fig. 86
P. h. 2.9, est. rim diam. 11.2
Two joining fragments of a vessel; portions of the rim and globular body preserved. Rim has a sharp carination on its outer face. Profile of rim similar to that of P67. Clay is pale brown and micaceous with small brown inclusions.

P69 (SID 94.323, Building 2), fig. 86
P. h. 1.2, wall th. 0.3, est. rim diam. 15.0
Fragment of a globular (?) vessel with an everted rim. Clay is pinkish with white inclusions. Surface is pitted.

P70 (SID 94.529, Building 2), fig. 86
P. h. 1.8, est. rim diam. 15.0
Small fragment of an everted rim, preserving a small portion of the vessel wall. A fine ridge exists below the rim. Clay is pinkish orange with pale brown inclusions.

P71 (SID 94.357, Building 2), fig. 86
P. h. 1.8
Small fragment of a vertical rim, thick and square in section. Clay is pinkish-red with small white inclusions.

Handles

P72 (SID 91.10, from the 1991 survey), not illustrated
P. l. 4.1, w. 1.4, th. 0.8
Upper portion of a vertical handle that attached near the rim of the vessel. Handle is ovoid in section. Fabric is reddish-yellow and micaceous, with white, red, and black inclusions.

P73 (SID 91.141, from the 1991 survey), not illustrated
P. l. 3.0, w. 1.5, th. 0.8
Worn fragment of a curved handle, ovoid in section, top face faceted. Clay is reddish with large white inclusions and small dark ones.

P74 (SID 94.279, Building 2), color plate 8, second row from top, center
P. l. 2.5, w. 1.7, th. 0.7, wall th. 0.3
Lower half of a vertical handle, portion of wall preserved. Handle is oval in section with shallow grooves on the sides and along the exterior surface. Three raking grooves are on the vessel wall, just below the handle. Clay is pinkish-red with darker red inclusions.

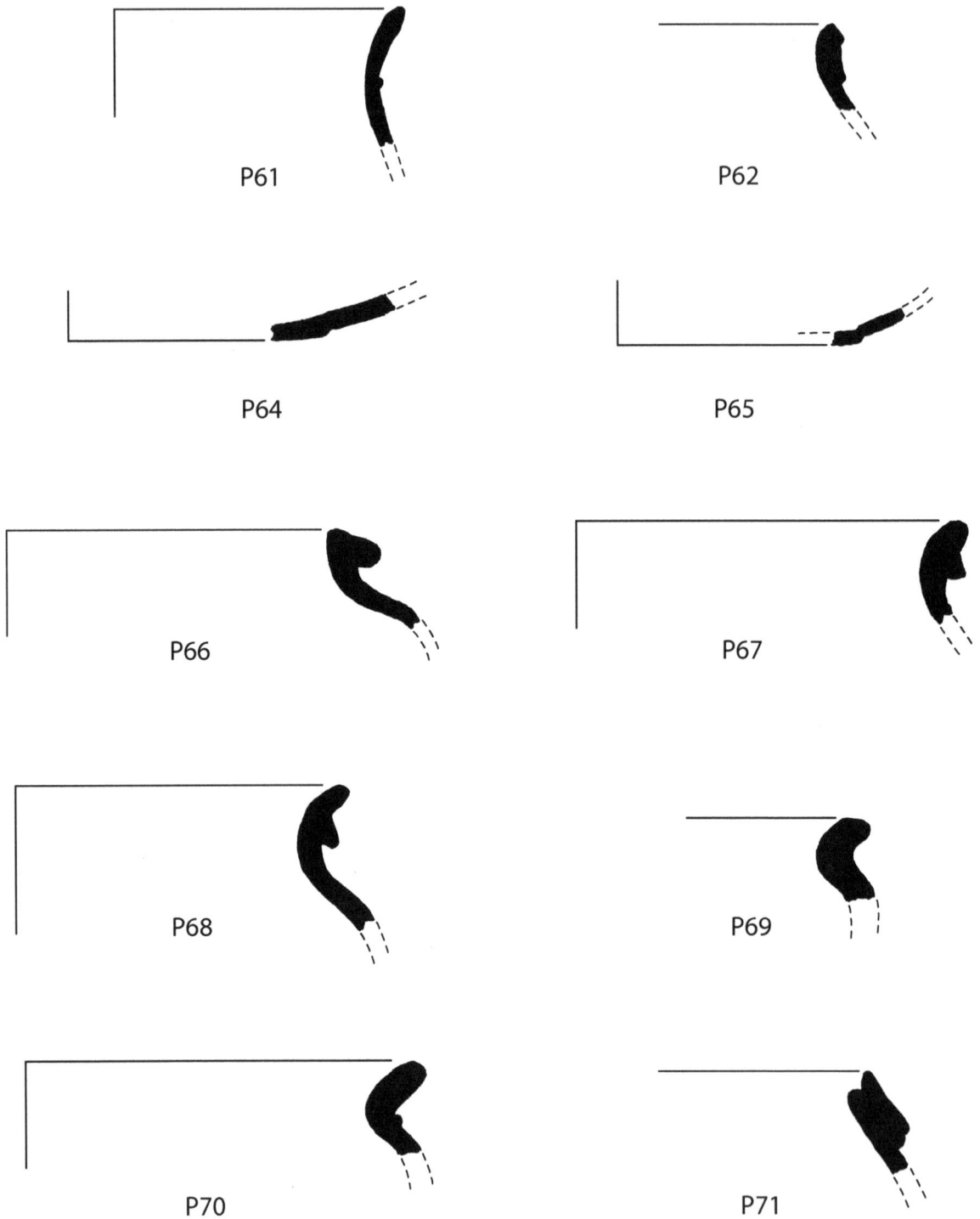

Figure 86. Profiles of Plain Ware Type 1, **P61-P71**, *Scale 1:1*

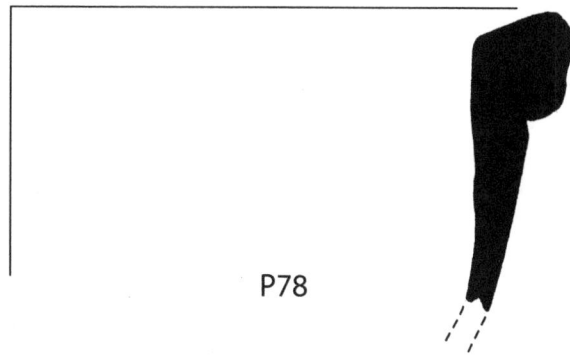

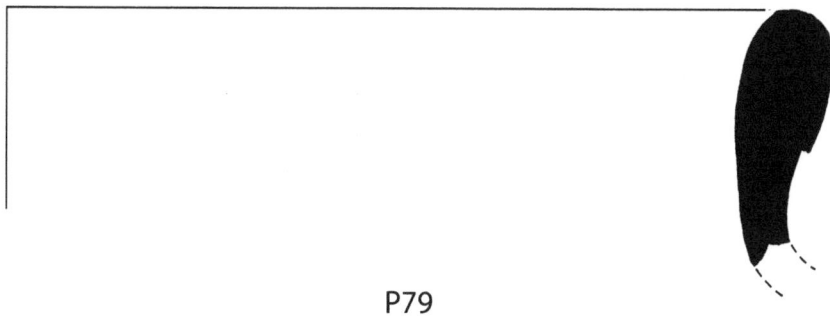

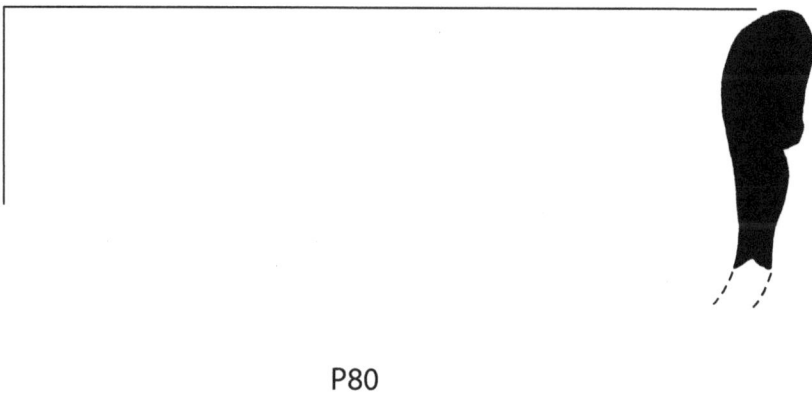

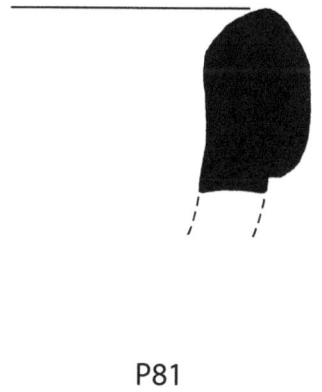

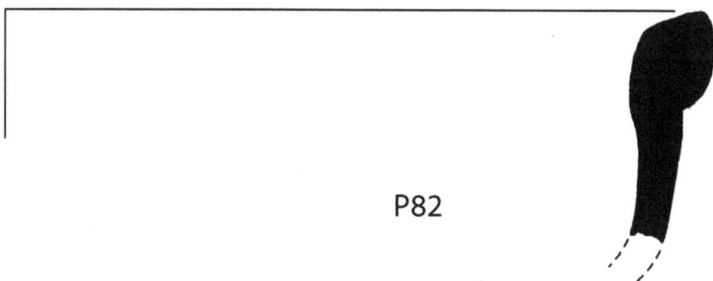

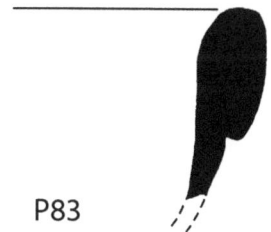

*Figure 87. Profiles of Plain Ware Type 2, **P78-P83**, Scale 1:1*

P84

P85

P 86

P87

P88

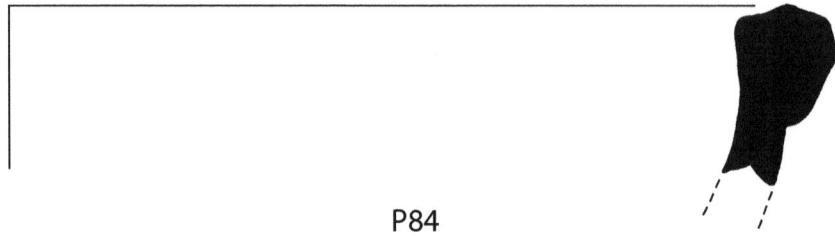

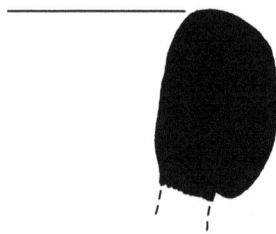

*Figure 88. Profiles of Plain Ware Type 2, **P84-P88**, Scale 1:1*

P75 (SID 94.316, Building 2), not illustrated
P. l. 4.4, w. 1.8, th. 0.7
Lower half of a vertical strap handle. Handle is a flattened oval in section.
Clay is pale brown, micaceous with dark brown inclusions.

Decorated body sherds

P76 (SID 94.331, Building 2), not illustrated
P. h. 3.1, wall th. 0.2
Body fragment preserving the base of a vertical handle. Below the handle is an incised band of curved roulettes below an incised line.
Clay is reddish-yellow with tiny white and brown inclusions.

P77 (SID 94.428, Building 3), color plate 8, second row from top, left
P. h. 2.4, wall th. 0.2
Body fragment preserving an incised decoration of zig-zags between two lines. Clay is fine and reddish, micaceous with tiny white and blue inclusions.

Fabric 2

This fabric is very soft to the touch, almost talc-like. It is reddish-orange in color (ranging between 5 YR 6/8 and 2.5 YR 5/4) and contains small lime inclusions, black grits and is occasionally micaceous (color plate 9). Its texture is similar to that found in the underfired examples of Phocaean Red Slip Ware described above. Over fifty fragments in this fabric were collected, all rim and body sherds. All the rims are upright and thickened; some of the body sherds are wheel-ridged. The closest identifiable parallels are coarse ware basins with a similar rim, found in an early Byzantine cistern from Samos. These basins were in association with Phocaean Red Slip/Late Roman C vessels, Form 3, and thus can be dated mid-5th - mid-6th c. A.D.[36]

Rims

P78 (SID 91.22, from the 1991 survey), fig. 87, color plate 9, top row, center
P. h. 4.6, wall th., 0.5, est. rim diam. 16.2
Thickened rim, some wall of the vessel preserved. A reddish brown slip adheres to the interior and exterior.

P79 (SID 94.69, between Buildings 2 and 3), fig. 87
P. h. 03.6, wall th., 0.5, est. rim diam. 23.7
Thickened rim, some wall of the vessel preserved.

P80 (SID 94.73, between Buildings 2 and 3), fig. 87, color plate 9, middle register, left
P. h. 3.6, wall th., 0.7, est. rim diam. 22.5
Thickened rim, slightly pointed at its outer edge.

P81 (SID 94.92, between Buildings 2 and 3), fig. 87, color plate 9, bottom register, right
P. h. 3.0, wall th. 1.0
Thickened rim in two fragments, slightly pointed at its outer edge.

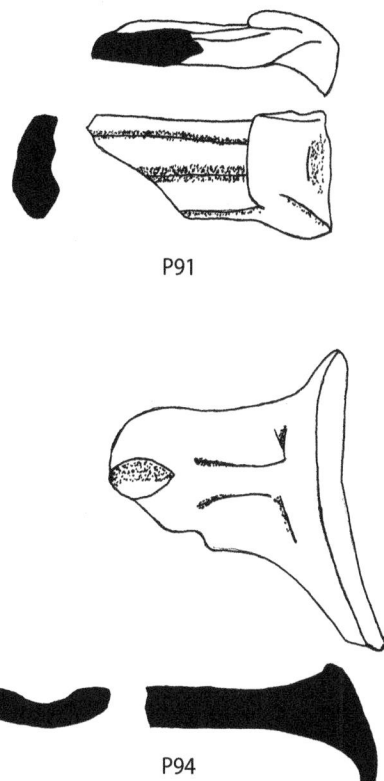

Figure 89. Profiles of Plain Ware Type 3, P91, P94, Scale 1:2

P82 (SID 94.80, between Buildings 2 and 3), fig. 87
P. h. 3.6, wall th., 0.6, est. rim diam. 23.7
Thickened rim, slightly pointed at its outer edge.

P83 (SID 91.123, from the 1991 survey), fig. 87, color plate 9, bottom register, left
P. h. 2.0, wall th. 4.0
Thickened rim, slightly pointed at its outer edge.

P84 (SID 91.127, from the 1991 survey), fig. 88
P. h. 2.0, wall th. 9.0, est. rim diam. 22.5
Thickened rim, top surface is slightly beveled.

P85 (SID 91.128, from the 1991 survey), fig. 88
P. h. 2.9, wall th. 0.5
Thickened rim.

P86 (SID 94.221, Building 3), fig. 88
P. h. 2.6, wall th. 0.5
Extremely worn fragment with a thickened rim, slightly pointed on upper exterior face.

P87 (SID 94.416, Building 3), fig. 88, color plate 9, middle register, right
P. h. 2.8, wall th. 0.9
Fragment with a thickened rim, broken at juncture with body of vessel.

P88 (SID 94.434, Pass 9), fig. 88
P. h. 3.4, wall th. 0.4
Fragment with a thickened rim, portion of body preserved.

Fabric 3

This fabric is a distinctive gray color (ranging from 7.5 YR 6/1 and 10 YR 7/1). The clay is very dense and has fine lime inclusions and is occasionally micaceous (color plate 10). Twenty-three fragments in this fabric were recovered; all the diagnostics were handles for either pitchers or cooking pots.

P89 (SID 94.39, between Buildings 2 and 3), color plate 10, bottom register, right
P. l. 3.8, w. 3.2, th. 1.5
Fragment of a handle, oval in section with a groove running down the center of its exterior face.
P90 (SID 94.50, between Buildings 2 and 3), color plate 10, top register, left
P. l. 4.5, w. 2.3, th. 1.1
Fragment of a strap handle, oval in section, although one of the short sides is squared. Two parallel grooves decorate the top of the handle.

P91 (SID 94.94, between Buildings 2 and 3), color plate 10, middle register, left, fig. 89
P. l. 6.2, w. 2.5, th. 1.0
Fragment of a handle and its connection with rim of vessel. Top of handle has two parallel grooves.

P92 (SID 94.288, between Buildings 3 and 9), color plate 10, bottom register, left
P. l. 2.8, w. 2.8, th. 0.7
Fragment of a curved handle with gently curved grooves on exterior.

P93 (SID 94.393, Building 3), color plate 10, top register, right
P. l. 2.8, w. 1.4, th. 1.0
Fragment of a handle with two parallel grooves on exterior.

P94 (SID 94.475, between Buildings 3 and 9), color plate 10, middle register, right, fig. 89
P. l. 5.5, w. 3.2, th. 0.8
Fragment of a handle of a cooking pan, trace of rim preserved. Groove runs along the top of the handle, ending in a thumb-shaped depression.

P95 (SID 94.535, Building 2), color plate 10, top register, middle
P. l. 4.2, w. 2.6, th. 1.0
Fragment of a handle with a parallel groove on exterior.

Fabric 4

This fabric is a dark, nearly purple color (Munsell 2.5 YR 4/3 to 6/7) and is extremely dense. Characteristic are the many black inclusions and the fewer white (lime inclusions). The vessels in this fabric all appear to have been broad bowls or basins. The fabric is similar to that used in a hypocaust tile from the Larger Baths (above, p. 551), and may be of local manufacture.

P96 (SID 94.55, Building 2), fig. 90
P. l. 22.0, p. h. 4.8
Rim fragment of a broad basin, diameter too wide to be measured.

P97 (SID 94.65, between Buildings 2 and 3), fig. 90
P. h. 2.6, wall th. 0.6, rim diam. 22.5
Fragment of an inward curving rim.

P98 (SID 94.474, between Buildings 3 and 9), fig. 90
P. h. 2.9, wall th. 0.8
Fragment of an inward curving rim, too small to obtain diameter. Similar in shape to **P97**.

P99 (SID 94. 354, Building 2), fig. 90
Rim fragment from a broad basin.

P100 (SID 94.86, between buildings 2 and 3), fig. 90
P. h. 1.4
Rim fragment from a basin?
P101 (SID 94.202, Building 3), fig. 90
P. h. 1.3, rim diam. 23.75
Rim fragment from a basin?
P102 (SID 94.448, Building 3), fig. 90
P. h. 2.3, wall th. 0.3, rim diam. 18.7
Rim fragment from a basin?

AMPHORAE

As would be expected from its seaside location, many fragments of amphorae were recovered in the survey of Küçük Burnaz. Of the 85 amphora diagnostics collected, most were small fragments of handles and difficult to identify.[37] Two amphora forms can be recognized with some security: the Pinched-handle amphora and the Late Roman 1 amphora. Fragments belonging to these two forms have been catalogued below, as well as a few other amphora fragments of interest.

Pinched-handle amphorae

This amphora, also known as Zemer type 41, is characterized as having a tall phalliform toe (often with a mushroom cap), a large cylindrical body (usually ridged), a nearly horizontal shoulder and a short cylindrical neck. The handles are distinctive, attached at right angles to the neck and to the shoulder. A thick groove exists on both the horizontal section of the handle and on the vertical. A pinched corner is formed where the two sections meet. Nicholas Rauh, in the course of his survey of western Rough Cilicia, has identified the form in at least five fabrics and considers it the standard local amphora of the region.[38] Caroline Williams also identified the type at Anemurium in Rough Cilicia. There the fabric is orange in color (2.5 YR 5/8 or 4/8) and gritty with small white lime particles as well as red and black colored grits and mica or silica flakes. Sometimes the color of the fabric can be darker (10 R 3/6). Often the exterior of the amphora is covered with a yellowish-white slip or a thin reddish-purple wash. At Anemurium the pinched handle amphora is practically the only amphora type represented in the Roman levels, appearing in the 1st or early 2nd c. and continuing through the 4th c. A.D. It appears to have been locally made, since a kiln site

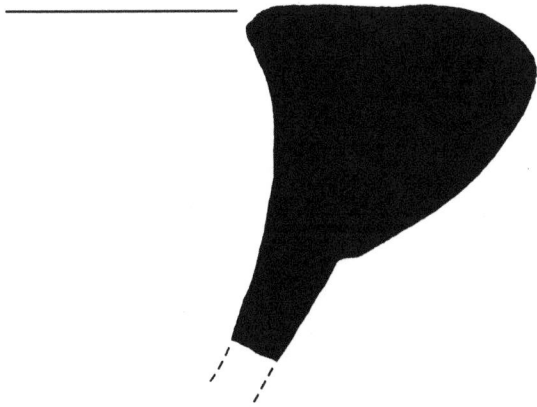

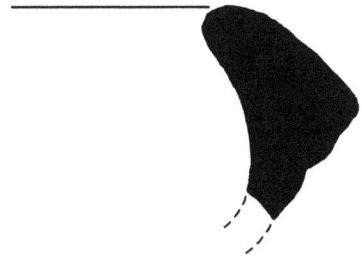

P97

P96

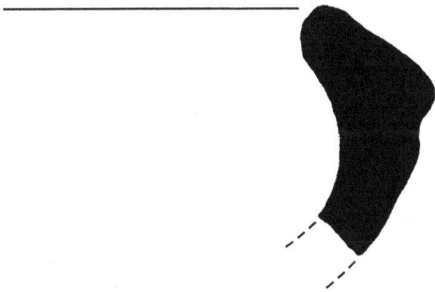

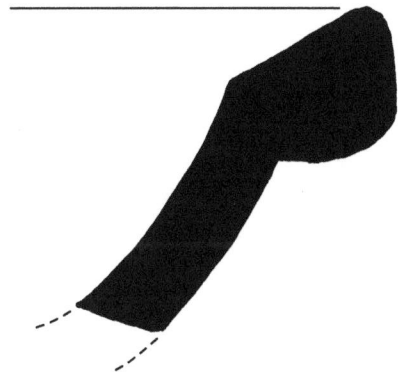

P98

P99

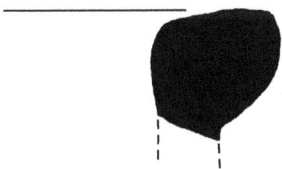

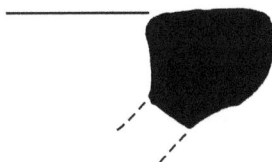

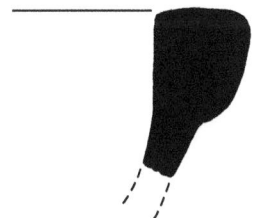

P100

P101

P102

Figure 90. Profiles of Plain Ware Type 4, **P96-P102***, Scale 1:1*

was discovered in the region of Anemurium. Examples of this amphora have been found elsewhere, both in the red colored fabric like that of Anemurium, and in other fabrics.[39]

At Küçük Burnaz three handles were found whose fabric is consistent with that of Anemurium (2.5 YR 6/8). A very worn amphora toe may also belong to this form.

P103 (SID 91.158, from the 1991 survey), fig. 91
P. h. 6.5
Fragment of a handle, nearly complete. Clay is red and fairly soft with lime inclusions, micaceous with black inclusions.

P104 (SID 94.269, Pass 10), not illustrated
P. dim. 4.2
Fragment of a handle, only the pinched corner preserved. Clay is red and fairly soft and micaceous with large lime and small black inclusions.
P105 (SID 94.423, Building 3), not illustrated
P. h. 6.5
Fragment of a handle, nearly complete. Clay is red and dense, micaceous with lime inclusions.

P106 (SID 94.495, between Buildings 3 and 9), not illustrated
P. h. 8.5
Fragment of a cylindrical toe. Clay is red and soft, micaceous, with large lime and small red inclusions.

Late Roman 1 amphora (Bii amphora)

This amphora has a wide distribution, ranging from the Sudan to Britain, and is one of the most common amphorae found on Late Roman sites, dating from the 5th through the mid-7th c.[40] It is characterized by a rounded base with a nipple toe, thin, ridged walls, and a cylindrical neck with a plain thickened rim. The handles are twisted so that the two or three deep grooves on their exterior curve around.[41] The fabric is hard and sandy with lime inclusions dark grits and mica and ranges from a pink color (7.5 YR 8/2-4) to a reddish-yellow (5 YR 7/6).[42] Occasionally there is an exterior wash and *tituli picti*. By analyzing thin-sections of examples of this ware from Carthage, Peacock concluded that the Gulf of Issus was a possible source of production.[43] This suggestion appears to be confirmed by the subsequent discovery of several ateliers of LR1 amphorae found around the gulf: two in the region of Seleucia Pieria, two near of Rhodopolis (Rhosus), and two in the vicinity of Yumurtalık (ancient Aegeae).[44]

It is not surprising, then, that several examples of this amphora were found at Küçük Burnaz. Only handles have been identified; three of these (**P107-109**) have the pinkish-buff fabric (7.5 YR 8/3) while the fourth (**P110**) is pinkish-yellow in color (5 YR 7/6). The latter matches the fabric of LR1 amphorae from Anemurium and Berenice, while the former is similar to the fabric of LR1 amphorae from Carthage.[45]

P107 (SID 91.35, from the 1991 survey, area of Building 1), not illustrated
P. l. 11.0, w. 2.1
Handle fragment, upper section broken, point of attachment to

amphora body preserved. Clay is pink and fairly fine with small reddish inclusions and large lime inclusions that erupt out of the surface. Surface is slightly paler pink in color, perhaps the results of a wash.

P108 (SID 91.99, from the 1991 survey), not illustrated
P. l. 9.4, w. 3.0
Handle fragment, lower section broken, point of attachment to amphora neck preserved. Clay is pink and fairly fine, micaceous with small black and white gritty inclusions.

P109 (SID 94.456, Building 3), not illustrated
P. l. 10.4, w. 2.5
Handle fragment. Clay is pink with white and brown inclusions.

P110 (SID 94.353, Building 2), fig. 91
P. l. 8.1, w. 3.5
Handle fragment, lower section broken, point of attachment to amphora neck preserved. Clay is pinkish yellow and micaceous, with lime inclusions and brown grits.

Miscellaneous Amphora Fragments

P111 (SID 91.153, from the 1991 survey), not illustrated
P. h. 8.5, w. 2.7
Handle fragment, lower section broken, point of attachment to amphora neck preserved. Handle is oval in section. Clay is pink and hard with many black inclusions (5 YR 8/3).[46]

P112 (SID 94.2, Building 1), fig. 91
P. h. 8.5, wall th. 8.0
Neck and shoulder of an amphora. Clay is reddish and hard with fine black inclusions (5 YR 7/6). A yellowish wash coats the exterior on which is a painted inscription in red letters.

P113 (SID 91.31, from the 1991 survey), fig. 91
P.h. 4.0, est. rim diam. 5.0
Portion of rim and handle. Fabric is pink and coarse with many lime inclusions as well as small red, black and brown inclusions (7.5 YR 7/4).

P114 (SID 94.208, Building 3), fig. 91
P.h. 3.7, est. rim diam. 6.2
Portion of rim and handle. Fabric is pale brown and fairly coarse, with large lime inclusions, a few large black inclusions and tiny brown ones (10 YR 8/3).

General Conclusion

The dates of these fragments range from as early as the 1st to as late as the 7th c. Although it could easily be an accident of preservation or collection, it is interesting to note that certain amphorae typically found throughout the Eastern Mediterranean in the Late Roman period, the Gaza Amphora (Peacock-Williams Class 49) and the Palestinian Bag-shaped Amphora (Carthage Late Roman 6) appear to be lacking at Küçük Burnaz. Similarly, these types are also absent or very rare at Anemurium.[47] In a recent survey of amphora ateliers in the Gulf of Issus, not only were many LR 1 type workshops identified (see above) but also workshops creating a Pseudo-Coan type amphora with a bell-shaped neck.[48] Unfortunately no fragments of that amphora type were identified at Küçük Burnaz.

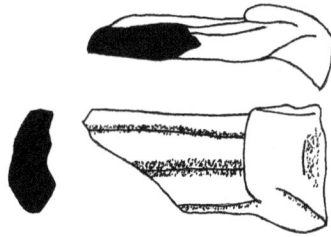

P91

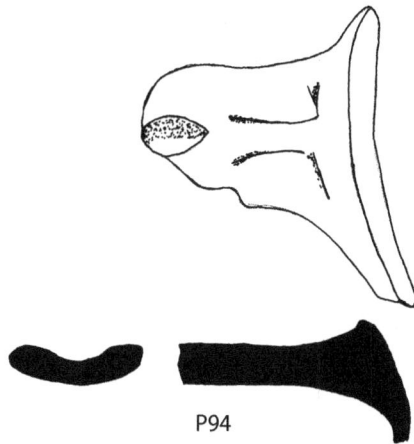

P94

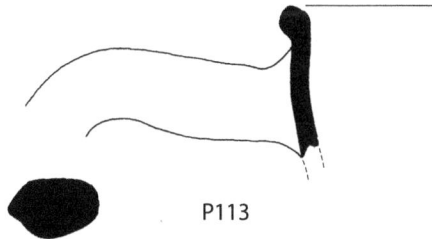

P113

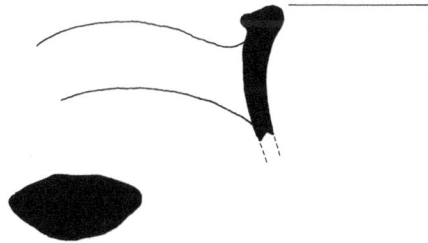

P114

*Figure 91. Profiles of amphorae, **P103**, **P110**, **P112-P114**, Scale 1:2*

MEDIEVAL POTTERY

Thirty fragments of medieval pottery were collected at Küçük Burnaz, all from the vicinity of the Smaller Baths (Building 2). Scott Redford, who is at present publishing the medieval pottery from nearby Kinet Hüyük (Issus), examined the fragments briefly in 1996 and concluded that they all date to the 13th c. Thus at least one building on the site was reoccupied during the time that the region was part of the Kingdom of Armenian Cilicia.[49]

Three types of glazed ware were identified: polychrome glazed sgraffiato ware, monochrome glazed sgraffiato ware and plain glazed ware. Glazed sgraffiato ware was the most prevalent type of decorated pottery in Asia Minor, Anatolia, North Syria and Cyprus during the 12th and 13th c.[50] In Cilicia examples have been published from Anemurium, Corycus, Tarsus, and Mopsuestia (Misis).[51] In the region south of Küçük Burnaz, sgraffiato ware has been published from Antioch and the neighboring coastal site of Al Mina.[52] The recent excavations at Kinet Hüyük are also reporting a quantity of this ware.[53]

In the publication of the excavations at Aşvan Kale in Eastern Anatolia, Stephen Mitchell presented a kiln site dating from the 12th-13th c., which produced sgraffiato ware. The evidence from the wasters found there gives a clear account of the process used to create sgraffiato ware. After the vessel was thrown it was dried to a leather hardness and covered in a white slip. Decorative incisions were scratched through the slip and the vessel was fired. Glaze was then applied, dark colored glaze in the incisions and other colors elsewhere, and the vessel was fired for a second time.[54]

Four examples of polychrome glazed sgraffiato ware were found at Küçük Burnaz (**P116-P119**). All have a hard pink fabric (7.5 YR 7/3) with some lime inclusions. The glazes range between various shades of green and yellow, with dark green or brown glaze pooled in the incisions. All the fragments come from open vessels, judging from the placement of the glaze. One piece (**P117**) may come from a goblet,[55] and the rest appear to have come from plates or bowls, the latter being the most common shape for glazed sgraffiato ware of the 13th c.[56] The largest sherd of the catalogue, **P116**, is a fragment of a bowl with a carinated lip whose shape and decoration has parallels at Al Mina.[57]

A simpler type of sgraffiato is made using the same technique described above but utilizing a single color of glaze. Four fragments of monochrome glazed sgraffiato ware were recovered from Küçük Burnaz (**P120-123**). Three are green-glazed with dark green or black glaze in the incisions. Their fabric matches that of the polychrome glazed sgraffiato ware. The fourth fragment (**P123**) has a bright yellow glaze and a friable red fabric (10 R 5/8) and may have come from a separate source. **P122** may be from a closed vessel, while the rest come from plates or bowls. The remaining sherds appear to be from plain glazed vessels, although it is possible that some come from sgraffiato ware vessels whose incisions are not preserved on the particular sherd. All but one fragment is green-glazed. With a few exceptions, the fabric is slightly more pink (5 YR 7/4) than that of the sgraffiato ware, sometimes micaceous and often having lime inclusions. As was the case with the sgraffiato ware fragments, many of the plain glazed sherds appear to have come from bowls or plates. Fragments from more utilitarian vessels can be identified: pieces of a cookpot with brown glaze and a friable fabric (**P133**) and a rim from a green-glazed oil lamp (**P134**). The shapes recovered from the Smaller Baths (Building 2) at Küçük Burnaz, open shapes (bowls or plates) a closed shape (a jug or pitcher) as well as a cooking pot and lamp would appear to be a household assemblage.

It is likely that the most of the pottery is local.[58] As mentioned above, glazed sgraffiato ware has turned up at most cities and towns occupied in the medieval period in Anatolia and Northern Syria. Rather than coming from a single source, it has been suggested that most regions produced their own sgraffiato ware during this period.[59] Certainly the evidence from Aşvan Kale confirms this theory. Although wasters and half-finished pieces have been found at Misis,[60] and unglazed incised sherds, wasters and a kiln trivet have been found at Kinet Hüyük,[61] it is likely that the fragments from Küçük Burnaz came from a closer source, Epiphaneia. Here, walking over freshly plowed fields in 1997 and 1998, the author identified not only countless polychrome sgraffiato ware sherds, but also numerous kiln tripods (fig. 11). These three-legged kiln separators came into vogue in the 13th c., replacing the older ox-yoke kiln furniture.[62]

The small assemblage of medieval pottery found at Building 2 possibly represents a family or a few families squatting in the remains of the Smaller Baths. This indicates that in the 13th c. the building was in good enough repair to be occupied. It is even possible that the aqueduct may still have been functioning. The occupants may have come from nearby Epiphaneia, perhaps drawn to the seashore for fishing.

P116 (SID 91.5, from the 1991 survey), color plate 11, top register
P. h. 4.2, wall th. 0.4
Polychrome glazed sgraffiato ware. Fragment of a bowl with broad carinated rim. Inner edge of rim preserved, outer edge broken, portion of body preserved. Interior of the bowl has traces of light and dark green glaze; incised bands encircle the upper portion of the bowl, a more elaborate incised decoration on interior. Top face of rim has an incised leaf ribbon pattern with light green, dark green and mustard yellow glaze. The underside of the rim has a yellowish-green glaze and a dull brownish glaze extends partially down the exterior of the bowl.

P117 (SID 91.108, from the 1991 survey; Building 2), color plate 11, lower register, right
P. h. 1.1, wall th. 0.5
Polychrome glazed sgraffiato ware. Vertical rim from a goblet (?). One side has a yellowish-green glaze with two incised bands, the other side has a dark green glaze.

L2

L3

L4

L5

L6

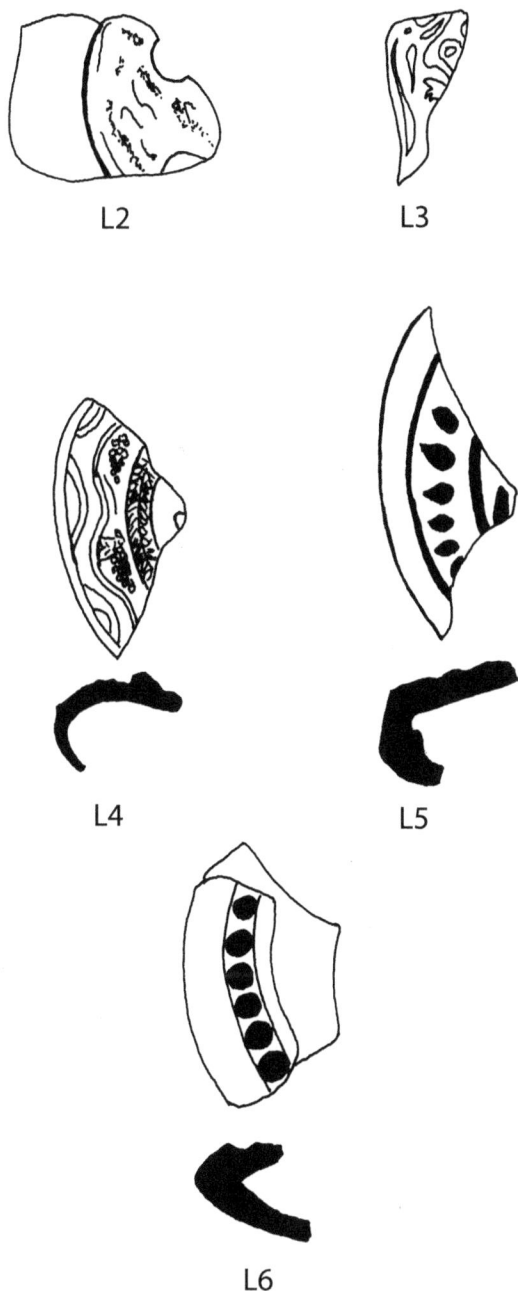

*Figure 92. Profiles of lamps, **L2-L6**, Scale 1:1*

P118 (SID 91.105, from the 1991 survey; Building 2), color plate 11, bottom register, center
P. dim. 2.9 x 1.8, wall th. 0.4
Polychrome glazed sgraffiato ware. Curved body sherd from an open vessel; glaze on concave side only. Glaze is yellow with some mottled mustard and green coloring. One incised line.

P119 (SID 91.107, from the 1991 survey; Building 2), color plate 11, bottom register, left
P. dim. 2.2 x 1.4, wall th. 1.2
Polychrome glazed sgraffiato ware. Curved body sherd from an open vessel; glaze on concave side only. Glaze is greenish-yellow with some mustard-yellow mottling. Two incised lines preserved.

P120 (SID 91.111, from the 1991 survey; Building 2), not illustrated

P. dim. 2.8 x 4.3, wall th. 0.9
Monochrome sgraffiato ware. Curved body sherd from an open vessel; glaze on concave side only. Glaze is light green with a metallic sheen; one incised line preserved.

P121 (SID 94.260, Building 2), not illustrated
P. dim. 3.0 x 2.2, wall th. 0.6
Monochrome sgraffiato ware. Curved body sherd from an open vessel; glaze on concave side only. Glaze is light green; one incised line preserved.

P122 (SID 91.109, from the 1991 survey; Building 2), not illustrated
P. dim. 2.5 x 1.6, wall th. 0.5
Monochrome sgraffiato ware. Curved body sherd from a closed vessel; glaze on convex side only. Dark green metallic glaze, two faintly incised lines preserved.

P123 (SID 91.110, from the 1991 survey; Building 2), not illustrated
P. dim. 2.2 x 1.7, wall th. 0.3
Monochrome sgraffiato ware. Curved body sherd; glaze on concave side only. Glaze is mustard-yellow, one incised line preserved.

P124 (SID 94.174a, Building 2), not illustrated
P. h. 3.2, est. rim diam. 21.2, wall th. 0.7
Plain glazed ware. Fragment of rim and body preserved. Square rim with a ridge running around its top face. Bright green matte glaze on top of rim and interior of vessel.

P125 (SID 91.106, from the 1991 survey; Building 2), not illustrated
P. h. 2.1, est. rim diam. 21.2, wall th. 0.5
Plain glazed ware. Fragment of rim and body preserved. Thick, outward projecting rim, bulge below the rim on the exterior of the vessel. Thick dark green glaze extends from the interior of the vessel over the rim to the exterior where it halts just above the bulge.

P126 (SID 91.112, from the 1991 survey; Building 2), not illustrated
P. dim. 2.9 x 3.5, wall th. 0.4
Plain glazed ware. Curved body sherd from an open vessel; shiny bright green glaze on concave side only.

P127 (SID 94.175a, Building 2), not illustrated
P. dim. 2.0 x 2.7, wall th. 0.6
Plain glazed ware. Curved body sherd from an open vessel; bright green glaze on concave side only.

P128 (SID 94.182, Building 2), not illustrated
P. dim. 4.5 x 3.6, wall th. 0.5
Plain glazed ware. Curved body sherd from an open vessel; bright green glaze on concave side only.

P129 (SID 94.315, Building 2), not illustrated
P. dim. 0.9 x 0.5, wall th. 0.5
Plain glazed ware. Curved body sherd from an open vessel; bright green glaze on concave side only.

P130 (SID 94.183, Building 2), not illustrated
P. dim. 4.5 x 3.0, wall th. 0.6
Plain glazed ware. Curved body sherd from an open vessel. Concave side covered with a dull olive- green glaze; a splash of the same glaze appears on the other side of the sherd.

P131 (SID 91.118, from the 1991 survey; Building 2), not illustrated
P. dim. 3.0 x 2.6, wall th. 0.8
Plain glazed ware. Curved body sherd from an open vessel. Concave side covered with a moss- green glaze, the other side is partially covered with a yellowish-green glaze.

P132 (SID 91.115, from the 1991 survey; Building 2), not illustrated
P. dim. 3.9 x 3.1, wall th. 0.5
Plain glazed ware. Curved body sherd from an open vessel; one side bears a trace of a relief band. Green glaze covers both faces of the sherd.

P133 (SID 94.258, Building 2), not illustrated
P. dim. 1.5 x 0.7, wall th. 0.4
Plain glazed ware. Body sherds from a cooking pot; dark brown glaze, shiny and crackled, covers one side.

P134 (SID 94.327, Building 2), not illustrated
P. h. 2.1, wall th. 0.3
Plain glazed ware. Rim fragment from an oil lamp. Pale green glaze on exterior face.

LAMPS

Six small fragments of lamps were collected at Küçük Burnaz, although none is complete enough to reconstruct its original form. Three of the lamps were mold-made (**L2-L4**). Fragment **L2** bore a relief figural decoration on its discus, and the other two fragments have a molded vegetal decoration on their shoulders. On the better preserved fragment **L4** the pattern is clearly a vine with grapes, a typical feature of Broneer Type XXVIII lamps. This lamp type dates to the 3rd and 4th c. A.D. and typical shoulder decorations include wavy lines, a herring bone pattern, or a vine pattern. The discus is often plain, or may be decorated by a ray pattern, a rosette, or occasionally by a figured relief.[63] Example **L4** has the vine pattern as well as a herring bone pattern along the rim of the discus.

Waagé published a few locally made lamps from the Antioch region similar to **L4**. These he classified as his Type 50e, and compared them with Broneer Type XXVIII. Although the published photographs are somewhat blurred, the examples 147-149 appear to have a vegetal/vine motif on their rims and their relief discs are each surrounded by a band with herring bone decoration. [64] Waagé dates the type to the 4th c. A.D. More recently, additional examples of this type of lamp have come to light in Tarsus.[65]

The final two lamp fragments, **L5** and **L6**, have a stamped decoration of ovules on their rims. The fabric of both is quite coarse and soft and in general these two appear less well made than the mold-made fragments.

The catalogue presented below the follows the same organization as seen in the pottery catalogue.

L1 (SID 94.189, from Building 3), not illustrated
P. l. 3.8
Shoulder fragment. Fabric is fine and pale pink (2.5 YR 7/6), fugitive red slip on exterior (10 R 6/8).

L2 (SID 94.212, from Building 3), fig. 92
P. dim. 2.8 x 2.0
Fragment of a mold-made lamp, portion of discus preserved. Fabric is pink and micaceous (7.5 YR 8/4). Discus preserves half of a fill hole and relief decoration too worn to identify. Rim is undecorated.

L3 (SID 94.12, from between Buildings 2 and 3), fig. 92
P. dim. 2.3 x 1.0
Fragment of shoulder from a mold-made lamp; perhaps from the region where the nozzle begins. Fabric is fine and pale brown (10 YR 8/4), micaceous with a few black inclusions. Vine pattern (?) in relief.

L4 (SID 94.329, from Building 2), fig. 92
P. dim. 3.8 x 1.4
Fragment of a mold-made lamp in three joining pieces, portion of shoulder and lower body preserved and a bit of the discus. Fabric is fine and pink (7.5 YR 8/3). Traces of burning along outer edge. Shoulder is decorated with curving vines and bunches of grapes in relief. Discus is framed by a herring bone patterned band. A trace of relief decoration is visible on the discus.

L5 (SID 94.253, from Pass 6), fig. 92
P. dim. 4.5 x 2.9
Fragment of a lamp from three joining pieces, portions of shoulder and tondo preserved. Fabric is pale brown (10 YR 8/3), coarse and soft, with many small brown inclusions. Shoulder is decorated with stamped ovules between two raised bands. A trace of relief decoration on discus.

L6 (SID 94.555, from Building 2), fig. 92
P. dim. 3.0 x 2.2
Fragment of a lamp, portion of shoulder and lower body preserved. Fabric is pale brown (10 YR 7/3), gritty with brown and white inclusions. Shoulder is decorated with stamped ovules.

GLASS

Approximately 225 fragments of glass were collected at Küçük Burnaz. The pieces came from the most heavily bulldozed areas of the site, particularly around the Smaller and Larger Baths (Buildings 2 and 1). About half of the fragments collected were identified as window glass and have been discussed already.[66] The remainder came from a variety of vessels, all made in the blown glass technique.[67]

Since the pieces are extremely fragmentary and few shapes can be identified, it is useful to examine the fabric and color of the glass to make some tentative conclusions as to their date.[68] The natural color of glass is blue/green, the color resulting from the levels of iron in the raw materials from which the glass was made. Variations in shade are a consequence the amount of iron present and the firing conditions.[69] During the 1st and 2nd c. A.D. blue/green glass predominated although strongly colored glass, created by adding a colorant, also was produced. Truly colorless glass, achieved by adding a decolorant, became popular in the 2nd and 3rd c., with high quality examples disappearing by the 4th c. A.D. During the 5th c. in the Eastern Mediterranean the naturally colored blue/green glass prevailed, but the quality declined, with many bubbles and dark impurities appearing.[70] During this time a common color, in Anatolia at least, was olive green.[71]

The glass collected at Küçük Burnaz embraces a very limited range of colors. Of the 95 vessel fragments, 60 are pale blue or green, 32 are olive green and three are colorless. Although a few fragments of blue/green glass appear fairly well made with few bubbles, most of the glass is quite bubbly and may be guessed to date to the 4th c. or later.

Very little glass has been published from the excavations at Antioch and Tarsus. Fortunately, Marianne Stern has taken an interest in the glass of Cilicia, having studied the glass from Anemurium in Rough Cilicia and the glass vessels in the Adana Museum.[72] According to Stern there were two periods of heightened glass production in Cilicia, the first occurring in the 2nd and 3rd c. A.D. and the second in the 5th-7th c. A.D. Stern suggests that there may have been a glass industry in Cilicia during the first period of production. Certain specific forms - especially thin-walled cups - are found repeatedly in the region and are likely to be local. Further evidence for glass working exists from the Late Roman/Byzantine period. Epitaphs from Rough Cilicia (Corycus and Seleucia) refer to glass workers, and two glass kilns were excavated at Anemurium. Farther east at Mopsuestia lumps of unworked blue glass have been reported.

The following catalogue presents the most distinctive diagnostics collected. Since in most cases the precise form of the vessel cannot be ascertained, the catalog is arranged by diagnostic form and within that form by degree of color, from blue to blue/green to green to olive green. The entries are follow the arrangement set for the pottery catalogue.

Bases

The twelve best preserved of the nineteen bases collected at Küçük Burnaz have been catalogued. They can roughly be divided into two types: those with tubular base rings (**G1-5**), and those with applied coil bases (**G6-7**).[73] Both types can be associated with a wide variety of forms. Two of the bases (**G1** and **G6**) of pale blue/green glass with no bubbles, may possibly date to the 2nd or 3rd c. A.D. The latter may belong to a beaker, judging from its narrow diameter and vertical sides. One small rounded base in blue/green glass is the bottom of an unguentarium (**G8**), although its precise form cannot be identified. Another distinctive base (**G9**) is flat with a series of pinched projections running around the edge.[74]

One base (**G12**) probably belonged to a stemmed goblet, or a "wine-glass," common in the Eastern Mediterranean from the 5th through the 7th c.[75] In Rough Cilicia, the form is known from Anemurium,[76] Alahan,[77] and most recently, Olba.[78] In Smooth Cilicia examples have been reported from Mopsuestia and Kadirli.[79] Despite the appellation, "wine-glasses," such vessels may also have been used as lamps.[80] At the Necropolis Church at Anemurium several were found with the remains of bronze wick holders still inside of the vessels.[81] Since the Küçük Burnaz "wine-glass" fragment was found at Building 2, it may have been used to help light the baths.

G1 (SID 94.G56, Building 2), fig. 93
P. h. 2.5, wall th. 0.1, est. base diam. 4.0
Pale green glass. Concave base with pushed-in hollow tubular base ring. No pontil scar.

G2 (SID 94.G33, Building 5), fig. 93

P. h. 1.1, wall th. 0.1, est. base diam. 3.0
Pale blue/green glass, bubbles. Concave base with tubular base ring.

G3 (SID 98.G96, general find), fig. 93
P. h. 8.0, wall th. 0.2, est. base diam. 5.0
Olive green glass, bubbles. Concave base with tubular base ring.

G4 (SID 91.G20, from the 1991 survey), fig. 93, color plate 12, lower register, right
P. h. 2.2, wall th. 0.2
Olive green glass, bubbles. Base with outward splaying tubular base ring.

G5 (SID 94.G24, from Building 3), fig. 93
P. h. 1.8, wall th. 0.1, est. base diam. 9.0
Olive green glass, bubbles. Base with upright tubular base ring.

G6 (SID 94.G53, from Building 2), fig. 93
P. h. 2.0, wall th. 0.2, est. base diam. 5.0
Very pale green/colorless glass. Base with shallow flattened bottom with an off-centered tool mark, applied coil base of varying thickness.

G7 (SID 94.G54, from Building 2), figs. 93, 95, top register, center
P. h. 1.5, wall th. 0.1, est. base diam. 5.0
Pale green glass, many bubbles. Base with applied coil base ring.

G8 (SID 94.G32, general find), fig. 93
P. h. 3.0
Pale green glass, bubbles. Lower portion and base of an unguentarium. Flat base; pontil scar. Vessel is a flattened oval in section.

G9 (SID 94.G48, between Buildings 2 and 3), figs. 93, 95, bottom register, right
P. h. 1.1, est. base diam. 6.0
Pale green glass, bubbles. Flat base with pinched projections. No pontil scar preserved.

G10 (SID 94.G43, between Buildings 2 and 3), fig. 93
P. h. 1.2, wall th. 0.2, est. base diam. 7.0
Pale blue glass, bubbles. Base with folded foot.

G11 (SID 95.G93, Building 2), fig. 93
P. h. 1.4, est. base diam. 6.0
Olive green glass, bubbles. Base with tubular base ring.

G12 (SID 94.G40, between Buildings 2 and 3), figs. 93, 95, bottom register, center
P. h. 2.5, est. base diam. 6.0
Olive green glass, bubbles. Base, stem and trace of body from a "wine-glass." Tubular ring base; hollow stem projects into the vessel floor in the form of a knob.

Rims

Twelve rim fragments were collected, but only the seven whose diameter could be ascertained have been included in the catalogue. All were created by means of fire rounding, where the sheared-off edge of the vessel was heated to produce a smooth, rounded rim.[82] Nearly every example has tool marks (faint linear abrasions) on the exterior just below the rim. The rims share a fairly narrow diameter (6.0-8.0 cm) and may have come from beakers or goblets. The presence of bubbles and other impurities indicate a Late

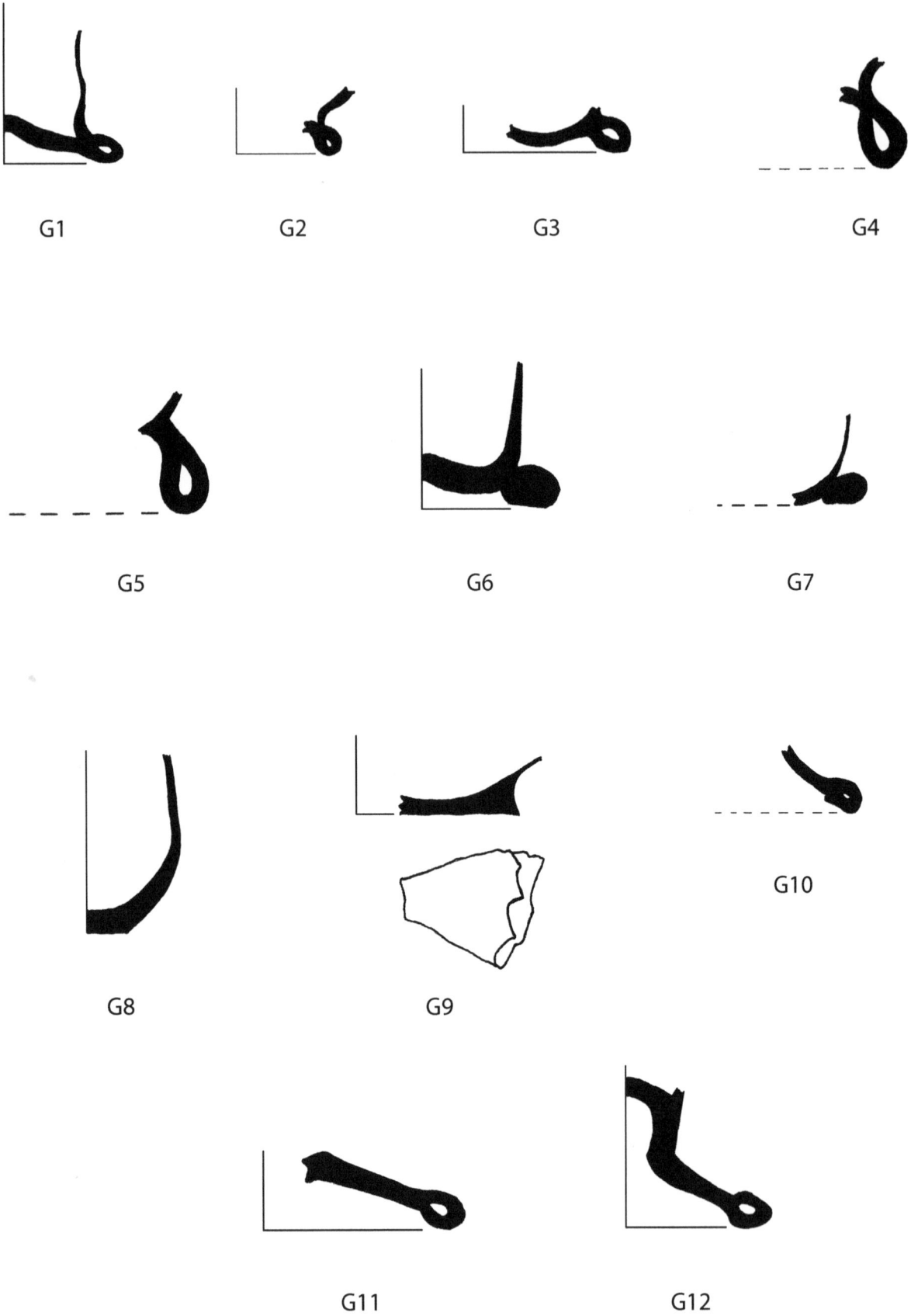

*Figure 93. Profiles of glass vessel bases, **G1-G12**, Scale 1:1*

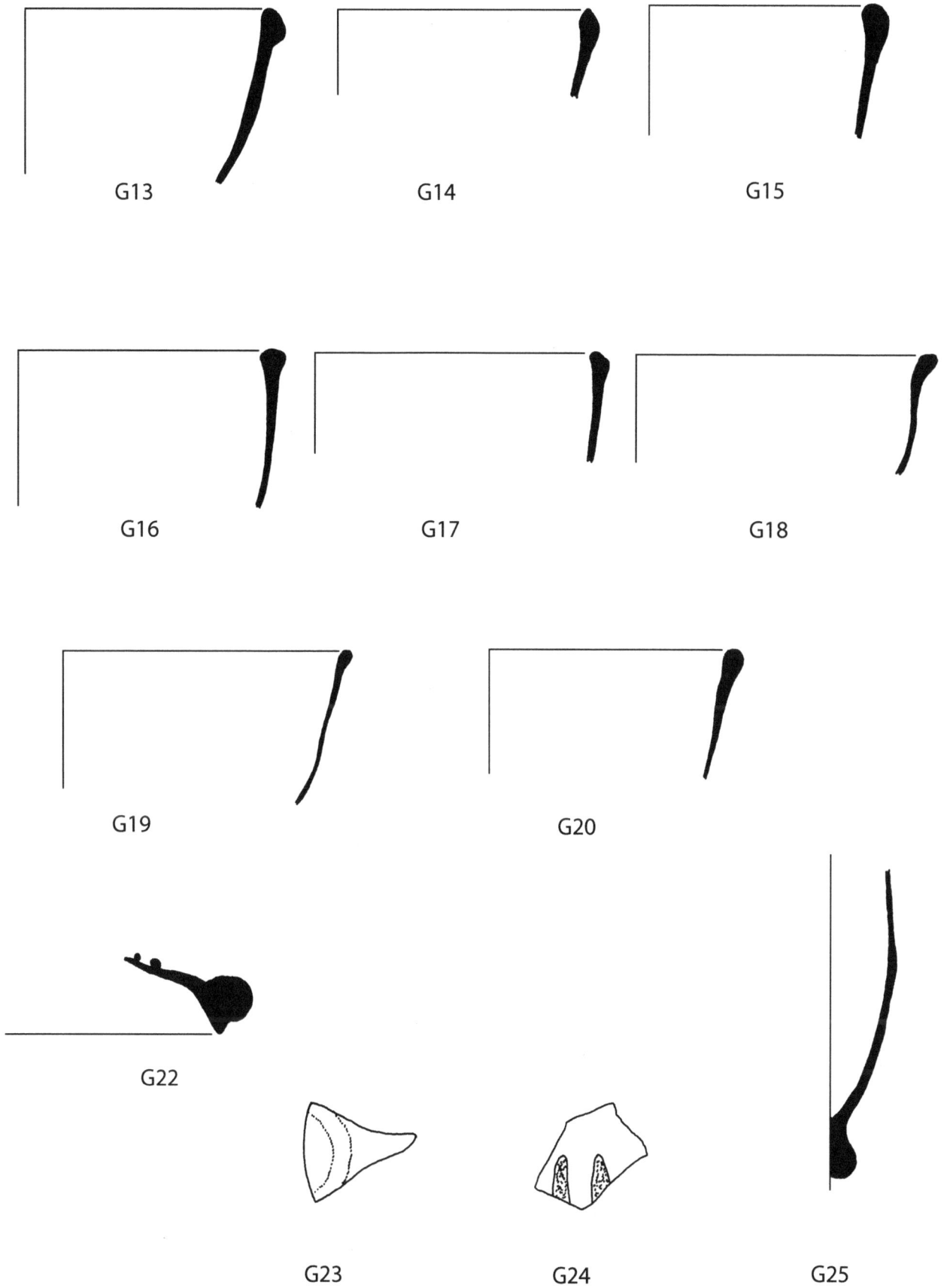

*Figure 94. Profiles of glass vessel rims and miscellaneous shapes, **G13-G20**, **G22-G25**, Scale 1:1*

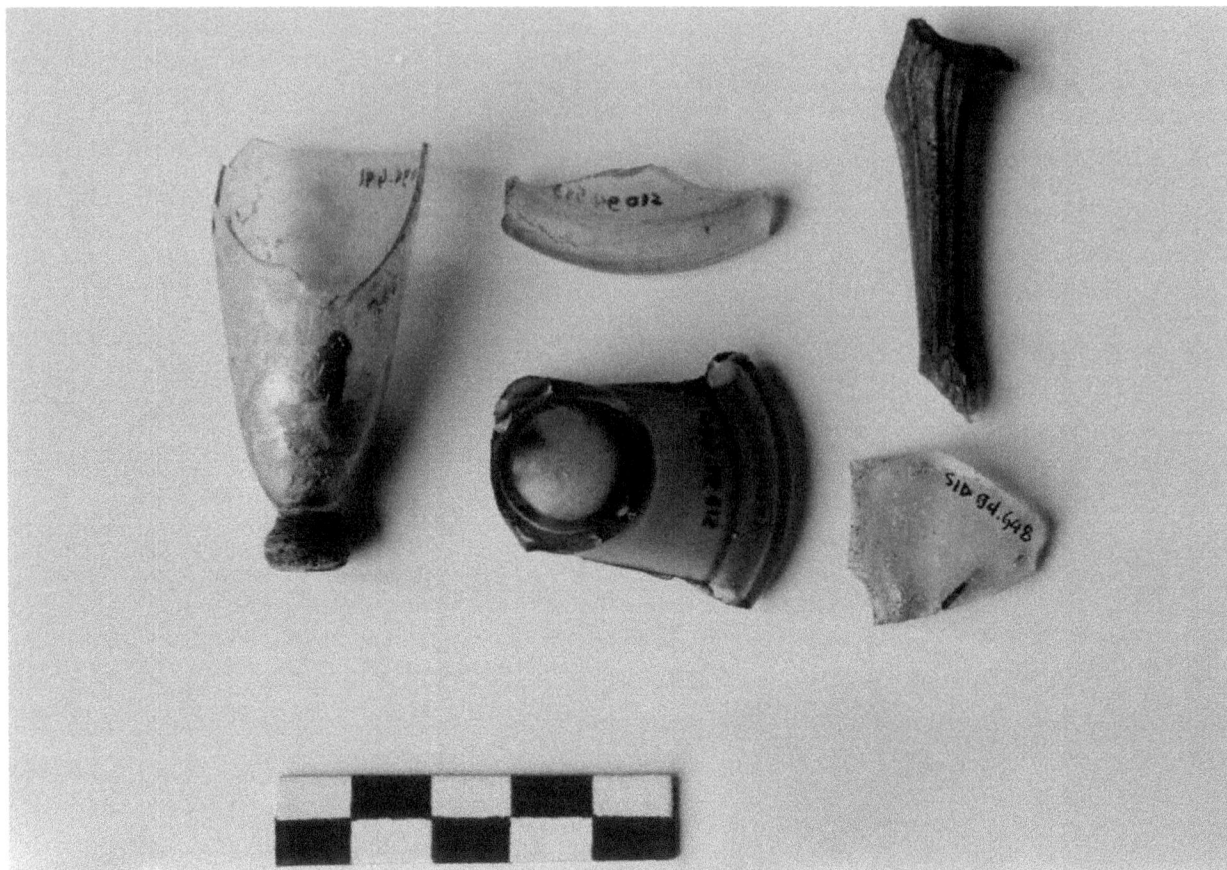

Figure 95. Examples of glass vessels

Roman/Byzantine date. **G13** however, may be slightly earlier, since it has few bubbles and is pale blue in color.

G13 (SID 91.G19, from the 1991 survey), fig. 94, color plate 12, top register
P. h. 3.1, wall th. 0.1, est. rim diam. 8.4
Pale blue glass, few bubbles. Rim rounded and thickened in flame. Tool marks along the exterior.

G14 (SID 94.G23, from Building 3), fig. 94
P. h. 1.6, wall th. 0.1, est. rim diam. 8.7
Pale blue/green glass, bubbles. Rim rounded and thickened in flame. Tool marks along the exterior.

G15 (SID 95.G94, from Building 2), fig. 94
P. h. 2.4, wall th. 0.1, est. rim diam. 7.5
Pale blue glass, large bubbles. Rim rounded and thickened in flame. Tool marks along the exterior.

G16 (SID 94.G29, general find), fig. 94
P. h. 2.7, wall th. 0.1, est. rim diam. 8.7
Pale olive green glass, bubbles. Rim rounded and thickened in flame. Tool marks along the exterior.

G17 (SID 94.G30, general find), fig. 94
P. h. 2.0, wall th. 0.1, est. rim diam. 10.0
Pale green glass, bubbles. Rim rounded and thickened in flame. Tool marks along the exterior.

G18 (SID 94.G50, from Building 2), fig. 94
P. h. 2.0, wall th. 0.2, est. rim diam. 10.0
Pale green glass, bubbles. Rim rounded and thickened in flame. Tool marks along the exterior.

G19 (SID 94.G51, from Building 2), fig. 94
P. h. 2.7, est. rim diam. 10.0
Pale green glass with olive green streaks, bubbles. Rim rounded and thickened in flame. Tool marks along the exterior.

G20 (SID 94.G49, from Building 2), fig. 94
P. h. 2.3, wall th. 0.2, est. rim diam. 8.7
Olive green glass with dark green specks, bubbles. Rim rounded and thickened in flame. Tool marks along the exterior.

Other diagnostics

Only one handle was found at Küçük Burnaz (**G21**), as well as what appears to be a fragment of a lid decorated with trailing (**G22**).[83] Two body sherds possess other forms of decoration. One (**G23**) has a portion of a circle in relief and was probably made with the expanded mold-blown technique.[84] The other (**G24**) is a fragment of colorless glass with abraded lozenge-shaped facets. Wheel-abraded decoration is commonly found in vessels of the 4th c. A.D.[85]

One final fragment worthy of note is the lower portion of a suspension lamp (**G25**); a bell-shaped beaker with a knob base.[86] The lamp would have been suspended or placed in a metal holder. It falls into the typology developed for Sardis by von Saldern, his Type 4, which he places in the 5th to 7th c. A.D.[87]

G21 (SID 94.G42, between Building 2 and 3), fig. 95, top register, right
P. l. 5.1, w. 0.6, th. 0.4

Olive green glass with striations, bubbles. Narrow ribbed handle.

G22 (SID 91.G21, from the 1991 survey), fig. 94, color plate 12, bottom register, left
P. h. 1.5, wall th. 0.1, est. rim diam. 17.5
Bright "apple green" colored glass, bubbles. Fragment of a lid (?). Top decorated with two glass trails running parallel to the rim.

G23 (SID 94.G34, Pass 9), fig. 94
P. dim. 2.2 x 1.7, wall th. 0.2
Pale green glass, bubbles. Body sherd from a globular expanded mold-blown vessel (?). Preserves a portion of a circle in relief.

G24 (SID 94.G55, between Buildings 2 and 3), fig. 94
P. dim. 1.5 x 1.0, wall th. 0.2
Colorless glass, bubbles. Body sherd with shallowly abraded vertical grooves or lozenges.

G25 (SID 94.G41, from between Buildings 2 and 3), figs. 94, 95, left
P. h. 5,5, wall th. 0.2, est. base diam. 1.5
Pale green glass, large bubbles. Fragment of a suspension lamp, portion of body and applied wound base knob.

Conclusions

Although some of the examples possibly date to the 2nd or 3rd c. A.D., the majority seems to date to the 4th c. or later. Certain forms, such as the "wine-glass" and suspension lamp, definitely date to the 5th c. and later. The assemblage at Küçük Burnaz appears to illustrate Stern's assertion of a florescence of glass forming in Cilicia in the Late Roman/Byzantine period.

COINS

Only two coins were collected at Küçük Burnaz. One (**C1**) was brought to the author by a local fisherman, who found it in a ditch north of the northern limits of Passes 1 and 2. Originally there were many more coins (the fisherman admitted he had sold them to some tourists sometime previous) and thus the coin may have been part of a hoard. The small bronze coin, although very worn, had a draped turreted female head on the obverse, and on the reverse a two-lined legend beginning with ΕΠ. During the 2nd and 1st c. B.C. many cities in Cilicia began to mint bronze coinage in their own name. Often the obverse of these coins bore the image of a woman wearing a turreted crown, Tyche, as a symbol of the city.[88] It is very likely that **C1** is a coin from nearby Epiphaneia. Examples of coins minted by that city during the 1st c. B.C. have a draped turreted bust of Tyche on the obverse, and on the reverse a seated Zeus holding a spear and a Nike. The accompanying legend reads: ΕΠΙΦΑΝΕΩΝ ΤΗΣ ΙΕΡΑΣ ΚΑΙ ΑΣΥΛΟΝ.[89]

The second coin, **C2**, was collected at Building 4 and is a bronze coin of Constantine I. The obverse bears a draped, diademed bust of Constantine facing to the right, accompanied by the legend CONSTAN[TINUS AUG]. The reverse has two soldiers facing one another with an object in between

and the partial inscription [GLOR]IA EXERCI[TUS]. The coin resembles the "Gloria Exercitus" coins issued around A.D. 330 in Constantinople, whose reverse is occupied by two helmeted soldiers standing and facing one another with spears in their outer hands and shields in their inner hands.[90] These coins are extremely common throughout the eastern half of the Roman empire during the 4th c.

C1 (SID 94.C1, from the area north of Passes 1 and 2)
Diam. 1.1; th. 0.1
Bronze. Obverse: turreted draped female bust facing right, illegible inscription to the right. Reverse: two line inscription beginning with ΕΠ[........].
1st c. B.C.

C2 (SID 94.C2, Building 4)
Diam. 1.6; th. 0.1
Bronze. Obverse: draped and diademed bust of Constantine I facing right, CONSTAN[TINUS AUG]. Reverse: two soldiers standing opposite each other, unidentifiable object in between, [GLOR]IA EXERCI[TUS].
A.D. 330

---

[1] In total, 3506 sherds were collected: 371 fine wares, 1544 plain and cooking wares, and 1591 coarse wares (amphorae and pithoi).
[2] For Tarsus see Jones (1950). In the following catalogue the work is referred to as Tarsus, followed by the ceramic form number. For Antioch see Waagé (1948), referred to in the catalogue as Antioch, followed by the ceramic form number.
[3] For Anemurium see Williams (1989), referred to in the catalogue as Anemurium, followed by the ceramic form number. For Porsuk: Abadie-Reynal 1989.
[4] For Samaria see Kenyon (1957), referred to in the catalogue as Samaria, followed by the ceramic form number.
[5] For the positions of the passes and general methodology in collection, see Chapter 4.
[6] Hayes 1986, 9-13. Slane (1997, 272-74) suggests the sites of Tyre or Sidon as possible production centers for ESA. Using chemical analysis Gunneweg, Perlman and Yellin (1983, 11-14) proposed Cyprus as the source of production for ESA. These findings, however, have not been accepted by Slane or Hayes. A recent report (which has not been read firsthand by the present author) suggests that the Gulf of Issus may have been the source of production of ESA. For the citation see Hayes (2000, 286).
[7] According to Hayes (1986, 52) Eastern Sigillata B (ESB) is not commonly found in the east. It is very rare at Antioch, where it is called Samian Ware by Waagé (1948, 38) and at Tel Anafa, Slane (1997, 380). Similarly Çandarlı Ware, although created near Pergamon in Asia Minor does not appear commonly in the East (Hayes 1986, 72). Cypriot Sigillata, which was probably made on Cyprus, is also rare in Syria, although it is common in Cilicia Tracheia. See Hayes (1986, 80-81) and Williams (1989, 1-2), where it is the most common sigillata at Anemurium, followed by ESA. At Samaria ESA dominates (Kenyon 1957, 283-84) and at Porsuk ESA monopolizes the sigillata imports (Abadie-Reynal 1989, 223).

[8] All fabric measures will follow the Munsell color chart.

[9] Since no petrological study has been conducted on any pottery from Küçük Burnaz, the author is hesitant to identify the glittery gold substance securely as mica. Kenyon (1957, 284) reports the presence of mica in the second of the two ESA fabrics she identified at Samaria. The micaceous fabric was particularly common in hemispherical bowls. She dates this fabric after her Roman 1 phase. Slane (1997, 269) reports a pinkish fabric from Tel Anafa (7.5 YR 7/4) with "sparkling inclusions" which has an orange slip, which sounds similar to the Type 3 fabric from Küçük Burnaz.

[10] Kenyon 1957, 284, 471-77.

[11] Slane 1997, 270-71.

[12] Hayes 1986, 9-48.

[13] Waagé 1948, 22-60.

[14] Williams (1989, 137, fig. 9) publishes a bowl with coarse rouletting in her miscellaneous sigillata category. The rouletting is found on the broadest point of the vessel. She suggests that the decoration is related to ESA bowls with deep, carefully cut indentations, styled in imitation of cut-glass technique.

[15] Hayes 1972, 13. In the following catalogue entries referring to this work are cited as Hayes, followed by the ARS form number.

[16] Hayes 1972, 419.

[17] See plates XIIb, right, and XIIIa for a bowl with a similar stamped decoration. Hayes identifies the stamp type as his group A (ii).

[18] See Hayes (1972, pl. 40). This type of stamp is usually found on ARS Forms 69, 70, 75, 117.

[19] The profile of the foot is similar and the stamped decoration nearly identical: fringed circles between chevrons.

[20] Hayes 1972, 323-24.

[21] Hayes 1980, lix.

[22] Hayes 1972, 419.

[23] Ibid, 323.

[24] Hayes (1972, 333) mentions a Form 3 bowl from the Athenian Agora (Robinson 1959, P 27027) where the clay and slip are orange and rather soft fired. Caroline Williams (1989, 27, 52-53) identified a similar fabric at Anemurium, calling it Imitation Late Roman C Ware. She described the fabric as a soft, porous, orange clay, rather fine grained with white lime inclusions, silver mica and silica flakes. The slip is much darker than the fabric. The ware was common at Anemurium, with 33 examples, and Williams thought it may have been local, since a kiln site in the area has produced fragments of amphorae with a similar fabric.

[25] Hayes, 1972. In the following catalog entries referring to this work are cited as Hayes, followed by the LRC form number.

[26] Loffreda 1974, #5702, foto 17.8, fig 25.28. Unfortunately the sherd comes from an unstratified context.

[27] The figure can be compared to other Bacchic figures (Hayes 1972, fig. 77, #55). A stamped bowl fragment from Antioch depicts the lower portion of a striding figure similar to the Küçük Burnaz Bacchus (Antioch, Fig. 33, lower right).

[28] Spain: Mayet 1975; France: Grataloup 1988; Cosa: Moevs 1973; Ostia: Ricci 1973. See Ghini (1995, 112-120) for a table summarizing the forms, dates and production centers.

[29] Hayes 1997, 68-70.

[30] Ibid, 67.

[31] Waagé 1948, 42.

[32] Jones 1950, 190.

[33] Hayes (1997, 69-70, fig. 28.2, pl. 25, right) identifies the type as coming from either Thrace or the Dardanelles, and dates it from the 1st through the 3rd c. A.D. Slane (1990, #196) illustrates a collarino-type mug from the Sanctuary of Demeter and Kore from Corinth, and dates it to the 2nd c. A.D.

[34] See, however, Williams (1989, 61-90) and recently Evrin's study of cookware from Tarsus (2002). Useful studies from more distant regions include those from Tel Anafa, Berlin (1997), Knossos, Hayes (1983), Carthage, Fulford and Peacock (1984) and Berenice, Riley (1979).

[35] Evrin 2002, 65-66, 76. She describes this type of cooking vessel as having an everted half over-folded, flat rim with a sharp carination at the fold. The body is globular. Because the walls are thin and easily shattered, no complete profile has been recovered.

[36] Isler 1969, 210, abb. 18.

[37] Four toes were identified as well as 81 handle fragments, two of these had sections of rim attached.

[38] Rauh and Slane 2000, 328.

[39] Hayes (1983) reports two amphorae with this form from the Villa of Dionysus at Knossos. One (Type 17) with a smooth buff fabric comes from a mid-2nd c. A.D. context, and a second (Type 45) with a coarse red fabric, also coming from a mid-2nd c. A.D. context, which is similar to the Anemurium type. Examples also come from the Athenian Agora (Robinson 1959): G 199 (reddish clay with a white slip, early 2nd c. A.D. date), L 11 (soft reddish clay with grits and a white slip, second half of the 3rd c. A.D. date) and M 239 (dark reddish clay with a white slip, early 4th c. A.D. date). This amphora shape is the same as Zemer type 41. Zemer (1978, 52) describes an example taken from the sea at Atlit as having a gray fabric and dates it to the 2nd-3rd c. A.D. He suggests a North African origin. Alpözen, Berkay and Özdaş (1995, 75) illustrate an example in the Bodrum Museum, and follow Zemer for date and origin. At Berenice, Riley (1979, 186-87) found several examples of this amphora form, classifying it as his Mid-Roman Type 4 and dating it to the 2nd and 3rd c. At least two of his examples (D236 and D237) resemble the fabric from Anemurium. The most recent study of the type (Lund, forthcoming, quoted in Rauh and Slane, 2000, 328) compares a micaceous form from Rough Cilicia with a non-micaceous form from SW Cyprus, and concludes that the micaceous form circulated less widely. All the examples from Küçük Burnaz are micaceous.

[40] Other designations: Peacock and Williams (1986) Class 44; Lloris (1970) Form 82; Williams (1989) Amphora Type B; Zemer (1978) Types 63-64.

[41] Williams 1989, 95-96; Fulford and Peacock 1984, 119; Riley 1979, 212.

[42] Peacock and Williams 1986, 185-87, Class 44.

[43] Fulford and Peacock 1984, 20.

[44] Empereur and Picon 1989, 236-43. For a recent discussion of LR1 in Cilicia, see Elton (2003, 176-78).

[45] At Anemurium, Williams (1989, 95), describes the fabric of her LR1 amphorae as light brown or orange-brown (5 YR 6/6)

with a gritty surface texture. At Berenice, Riley (1979, 212) identifies two fabrics, one being buff to orange in color (5 YR 6/6) with gray grits and occasional quartz inclusions sometimes having a pinkish wash (7.5 YR 8/4) and the other a yellow cream color (2.5 Y 8/4) with gray grits. The examples from Carthage (Fulford and Peacock 1984, 20) are cream-buff in color (7.5 YR 7/4) with limestone grains, darker grains and some mica.

[46] The shape of the handle and its fabric resemble Hayes Type 26 (1983, 151, fig. 24.67) from the Villa of Dionysus at Knossos which he dates to the 3rd c. A.D.

[47] Williams 1989, 91.

[48] Empereur and Picon 1989, 231-32, figs. 5-8. Two ateliers were clustered on the western side of the Gulf of Issus, around Yumurtalık and a third was in the east at Seleucia Pieria.

[49] See Chapter 5, page 27.

[50] Mitchell 1980, 75.

[51] For Anemurium see Tömöry (1977, 30, n. 6) who also mentions examples from Mopsuestia and pieces in the Adana Museum. For Corycus see Volbach (1930) and for Tarsus see Day (1941).

[52] Antioch: Waagé 1948, 82-105; Al Mina: Lane 1938.

[53] Gates 1998, 1999; Redford *et al.* 2001.

[54] Mitchell 1980, 74-75.

[55] For an example of the shape see Dark (2001, color plate 58).

[56] Dark 2001, 73.

[57] Lane 1938, pl. XXI, fig. 7b and c.

[58] Redford has suggested that one fragment, **P132**, may be an import.

[59] Redford 1999, 110.

[60] Tömöry 1977, 30, n. 6.

[61] Gates 1999, 198-99, n. 30; Redford *et al.* 2001, 70-71.

[62] See Dark (2001, 74) for a discussion and fig. 34 for an illustration. Tripod separators were also found at Aşvan Kale, Mitchell (1980, fig. 105.1298a, 1299).

[63] Broneer 1930, 102-14.

[64] Waagé 1934, 65-66, pl. X. 1827; Waagé 1941, 66, nos. 147-49.

[65] See Baydur (1987, pl. 39) who illustrates three lamps with vine decoration on their rims.

[66] See Chapter 5, pages 51-52.

[67] Although the precise place and date of the invention of glass blowing is still not known, it apparently developed in the Levant during the 1st c. B.C. See Hayes (1975, 29), Harden (1969, 45-48) and most recently Stern (1999) for a full discussion of Roman glass blowing.

[68] For the following see Price and Cottam (1998, 14-16) and Harden (1969, 60-62).

[69] Schreurs and Brill 1984.

[70] Harden 1971, 80.

[71] Christopher Lightfoot, personal communication.

[72] For a general discussion of glass in Cilicia see Stern (1984)

and (1989b). Glass at Anemurium: Stern 1985. Glass in Smooth Cilicia: Stern 1989a.

[73] For an explanation of these techniques see Price and Cottam (1998, 25-29).

[74] The base is similar to a type of base with "pinched toes" found on flasks or beakers throughout the Eastern Mediterranean. Examples are known from Cyprus (Vessberg 1952, 123, pl. IV.12), Jalame (Israel) (Weinberg 1988, 59, no. 161, fig. 4-22, color pl. 4A), Karanis (Egypt) (Harden 1936, 219-20, nos. 678-85, class IX.c.iv., pl. XIX) and Dura Europos (Syria) (Clairmont 1963, 50-52, pl. V, 204, 207 and 208, and pl. VI. 211). The form can vary in terms of height and number of toes and ranges in date from the 2nd to the 4th c. A.D. Stern (1989a, 592) reports that bases with pinched toes are commonly found in Rough Cilicia but notes that none appear in the collection in the Adana Museum.

[75] Isings (1957, 139-140) Form 111. See Harden (1934, 167-73) for a discussion of "wine glasses" from Karanis, under his Class VII. Several examples are in olive-green glass. Examples are known from Samaria (Crowfoot 1957, 415-16) and Sardis (von Saldern 1980, 53-60). See also Hayes (1975, 84, fig. 11. 382-83).

[76] Stern 1985 44-46, fig. 3.

[77] Williams 1985, 53, fig. 10. 18-20.

[78] Erten 2003, 148, fig. 21.3.

[79] Stern 1989a, 592, fig. 18.2.

[80] So identified at Gerasa, Bauer 1938, 516-17. See Stern (2001, 261-63) for a recent discussion of these goblets. She suggests that the "wine-glasses" were used both for lighting and drinking.

[81] Stern 1985, 44; 1984, fig. 11.

[82] Price and Cottam 1998, 22.

[83] Ibid. 32.

[84] This technique was probably invented in Syria and is typical of the 4th and 5th c. A.D. A common motif is concentric circles. See Stern (2001, 27, 133-34) for a discussion of the technique and Cat. #155 for an example of an expanded mold blown bowl with concentric circles.

[85] Stern 2001, 30.

[86] Christopher Lighfoot identified this vessel as a lamp. See Crowfoot and Harden (1931) for a discussion of glass lamps.

[87] von Saldern 1980, 38-53, esp. 52-53. The lamp compares well with example no. 298, pl. 23.

[88] See Meyer (1999) for a discussion of the image of Tyche on Cilician coinage, especially 192, n. 25, for a list of cities who put busts of Tyche on their bronze coins.

[89] SNG Levante, pl. 122, 1807-8.

[90] RIC VII, 562-68. See no. 59 (p. 579) for this coin type, whose obverse bears two helmeted soldiers standing and facing one another with spears in their outer hands and shields in their inner hands; between them are two standards.

CONCLUSION

The History of Occupation of Küçük Burnaz

Although one of the coins found near the site dates back to the 2nd c. B.C., the earliest ceramic remains come from the mid-1st c. B.C. This likely marks the initial foundation of the settlement at Küçük Burnaz and can be connected to Pompey's reorganization of Cilicia and the region's integration into the Roman Empire. The newly won stability for the region included a rise in population, since the nearby city of Epiphaneia received an influx of pirates at that time. The settlement at Küçük Burnaz could have been founded in tandem with the renovation of that city, located only 12 km to the northeast. It is unlikely that any of the buildings visible at present at Küçük Burnaz were constructed at this time, however. Any architecture from this early period could still be hidden under the sand, or else may have been destroyed when Shapur I sacked the region of A.D. 260.

According to the ceramic evidence available at present, there was lively activity at the site through the first half of the 1st c. A.D. There is an apparent decline in the amount of artifacts identified from the later 1st -3rd c. A.D., although enough fragments of ceramics and glass survive to indicate that the site was not completely abandoned. The 4th and 5th c. A.D. saw a period of relative stability in Smooth Cilicia, as the region served as a mustering ground for armies sent to engage the Persians in the east. Judging from the ceramic remains this was a busy time for the site at Küçük Burnaz. Stylistically, much of the architecture appears to date to this period as well.

The 6th c. was a trouble-filled time for the region, witnessing plague, earthquake and invasion. The latest securely dated ceramic in the catalogue belongs to the end of the 6th c. A.D., possibly indicating that the site ceased to function after the Persian invasion of the late 6th c. Certainly the ultimate abandonment of the region in the 630's, to create a buffer zone between the Byzantine and Islamic Empires, marked the final demise of Roman activity at Küçük Burnaz. Thereafter the site was not occupied until the 13th c. A.D. when the Smaller Baths (Building 2) was briefly inhabited when the region was under Armenian rule.

The function and possible identity of the ruins at Küçük Burnaz

As mentioned above, the findings of the 1991 geologic survey indicated that originally the site at Küçük Burnaz stood on the seashore. Özgen and Gates concluded that the site probably served as a port in antiquity, and this appears to be likely. Its location, at the northernmost end of the Gulf of Issus, would have made it convenient to sailing vessels, since the prevailing sea breezes blow from the southwest into the gulf.[1] In a paper delivered at a conference on ancient Mediterranean harbors, Geoffrey Rickman, drawing on comparisons with modern port design, presented a useful definition for a port. It should possess a sheltered harbor, preferably along a small river that would also provide fresh water, and marine facilities (wharves, storage areas and warehouses). It should also connect to a roadway, or inland waterway, in order to be linked to the interior.[2] In the same conference, Yehuda Karmon stressed the importance of this last criterion, noting the symbiotic relationship between the port and the hinterland it served. The hinterland, connected to the port by means of inland communication, provided the port with exports, such as raw materials, agricultural produce and industrial goods. In turn the hinterland received imports from the port.[3] The situation at Küçük Burnaz, positioned on a small stream and along a major highway, meets with Rickman's criteria. As a port located on a major highway and close to two other lesser roads, it could easily connect to its hinterland, the city of Epiphaneia and the rich farmlands and settlements in northern Plain of Issus.[4]

The buildings found on the site, namely baths (Buildings 1 and 2) and facilities for water storage (Buildings 3 and 11), are elements one would expect to find in a harbor town. It is also possible that some of the structures possessing long and narrow dimensions (Buildings 7, 8 and 12) could have served as storage facilities, although their poor state of preservation makes this suggestion difficult to prove.

It is possible that the architectural enhancement of the port in the 4th and 5th c. not only served the communities in the Plain of Issus, but was designed to help with the supplying and movement of troops traveling east to face the Persians. It may have occurred under Imperial authority, with the army responsible for some of the construction. This scenario could explain the dominance of western building techniques found throughout the site. However, certain elements that appear to be eastern, such as the use of pitched brick, may reflect local involvement. The combination of military and civilian forces in the same construction project is not unusual in the Roman world.[5]

There is evidence to suggest Küçük Burnaz' ancient identity as well as other possible functions for the site in antiquity. Ancient testimonia refer to a site on the Gulf of Issus called Catabolos (sometimes referred to as Catabolo or Catavolo), located somewhere between Issus and Aegeae. The name first appears in the *Itinerarium Antonini Augusti*, a document probably compiled initially during the reign of Caracalla, but amended under Diocletian.[6] The itinerary seems to have been based on an edict sent by Caracalla to prepare regions for his imperial visit as he journeyed east for the Parthian War (A.D. 214-215).[7] The reference to Catabolos is found in the section of the itinerary recording the route from Rome to Egypt via Asia Minor. The itinerary records halting places (*stationes* and *mansiones*) and their distances from one another. Accordingly, Catabolos is listed as being 24 Roman miles after Aegeae and 16 Roman miles before Baeae, thus somewhere along the road near the northern tip of the Gulf of Issus.[8]

A later reference to Catabolos is found in the *Res Gestae Divi Sapporis*, a trilingual inscription in Middle Persian, Parthian and Greek from Naqs-i Rustam near Persepolis. The inscription records details of the campaigns of Shapur I against the Romans, naming the regions he and his troops invaded and the cities they destroyed. In the section concerning his third campaign of A.D. 260, Shapur boasts of the Cilician cities he laid waste: Alexandria, Catabolos, Aegeae and Mopsuestia.[9] Honigmann and Maricq, publishers of the inscription, suggested that Catabolos was a coastal village located at the northern edge of the Gulf of Issus, near the Burnaz Cayı.[10]

Less than a century after Shapur's attack, Catabolos is mentioned again, in the *Itinerarium Burdigalense*, an itinerary recording an anonymous pilgrim's journey from Bordeaux to Jerusalem in A.D. 333. In this fascinating document the Bordeaux Pilgrim, as he is called today, chronicles his journey, listing the places he stopped en route and their distances from one another. He records three types of accommodations, a city or *civitas*, a place with a bed for the night or *mansio*, and a place to change horses or *mutatio*. After entering Cilicia he stopped at Adana (which he called a *civitas*) and then rested at the *civitas* of Mansista (Mopsuestia). From there he paused at the *mutatio* of Tardequeia, which has been identified as Kurt Kulagı, located 24 km east of Mopsuestia (maps 1-3).[11] Although the antiquities from this site consist of only a few marble column fragments, an impressive 17th c. caravansary reflects the long tradition of hospitality the location afforded. From Tardequeia the pilgrim traveled 16 Roman miles to the *mansio* of Catavolo, and from there 17 Roman miles to the *mansio* of Baeae.[12]

A late literary reference to Catabolos is found in the *Ravenna Cosmography*, a work compiled in the 11th c. A.D. from documents dating back to the 5th c. A.D.[13] Although errors have crept into their names, the work provides a recognizable collection of Cilician toponyms: Adanon (Adana), Momsuestia (Mopsuestia), Epiphania, Isson (Issus), Catavolon (Catabolos), Aedis (Aegeae), Malion (Mallus). Distances between the places are not given, but it seems to reiterate the general location of Catabolos mentioned in the earlier references.[14]

In addition to the literary testimonia, the Peutinger Map presents a graphic account of the location of Catabolos. This map, discovered at the end of the 15th c. A.D., is a medieval copy of an ancient map whose origins may reach as far back as the 1st c. B.C.[15] In addition to some medieval additions, the map appears to have undergone alterations at the beginning of the 3rd c. A.D. as well as at the end of the 4th - beginning of the 5th c. A.D.[16] On the plan, Catavolo is located along the main coastal road between Aegeae and Issus, as well as along a secondary route leading from Mopsuestia.[17]

The testimonia thus place Catabolos on the coast, east of Aegeae and west of Issus/Baeae/Alexandria ad Issum. The earliest reference could possibly date to the late 1st c. B.C. and the latest could belong to the medieval period but by and large the references seem to describe the ancient world of the

3rd - 5th c. A.D.[18]

The name Catabolos probably described the function of the site. It appears to be related to the Greek word κατάβολος, found in a scholiast of Thucydides 1.30, used to explain the word ἐπίνειον, a seaport or naval station. It also appears in a medieval etymology (*Etymologicum Magnum*, 336.21) to define the term ἐμπορεῖον, a trading post.[19] Thus a site named Catabolos could reflect the settlement's function as either a naval station or trade center, or both.

It has long been suggested, and recently championed by Hild and Hellenkemper, that Catabolos is to be identified with Muttalip Hüyük.[20] The location of the mound is appropriate, positioned on the sea and at the confluence of two roadways, one leading up from Aegeae and one from Mopsuestia. Muttalip Hüyük most likely had a harbor, perhaps represented by the ancient remains at the south end of the mound. It must be remembered, however, that at least in the 5th c. A.D. Muttalip Hüyük probably bore the name of Mutlubakke, a name which may be of Luwian origin and thus may have been the name for the settlement since the 2nd millennium. The mound's later Arabic and Turkish names appear to be variations of the name Mutlubakke, indicating a firm connection between name and place. The association of Muttalip Hüyük with Catabolos was particularly appealing when there were no other ruins known along the north end of the Gulf of Issus. With the discovery of the remains at Küçük Burnaz, however, the possibility that they represent Catabolos needs to be addressed.

Since the location and the character of the remains at Küçük Burnaz are in keeping with a port, the name Catabolos is immediately suitable. Its precise position on the Gulf of Issus also fits well with the ancient testimonia. The Antonine Itinerary, the Bordeaux Pilgrim and the Peutinger Map give distances in Roman miles (one Roman mile = 1.48 km[21]), and although the distances of these itineraries can be problematical it may be instructive to look at some distances and compare them to the actual positions of Küçük Burnaz and Muttalip Hüyük. The Antonine Itinerary gives the distance between Catabolos and Baeae as 16 Roman miles (24 km), while the Bordeaux Pilgrim lists the distance as 17 Roman miles or 25 km. In reality the distance to Muttalip Hüyük is 29 km, while the distance to Küçük Burnaz is 25 km. Similarly, the distance between Mopsuestia and Catabolos on the Peutinger Table is 24 Roman miles or 35 km, while the actual distance from Mopsuestia to Muttalip Hüyük is 31 km, but to Küçük Burnaz is 35 km.[22] Based on these measurements, the position of Küçük Burnaz seems to fit that of Catabolos more closely than does Muttalip Hüyük.

Although it may never be possible to determine whether Catabolos was located at Küçük Burnaz or at Muttalip Hüyük, it is likely that the two settlements, located only 4 km apart, worked closely together. It is even possible that the port at Küçük Burnaz was created either to supplement whatever harbor facilities existed at Muttalip Hüyük or even to replace them in order to better accommodate the settlements of the plain. In the early 19th c. when Ainsworth was examining the ancient remains in the Plain of Issus, he suggested that the black gate at Karanlıkkapı and the gate he saw to the east in the sand (Küçük Burnaz's Eastern Gate, Building 6) functioned together. He thought both served as entryways for a large city at whose heart lay the mound of Muttalip Hüyük. This intriguing possibility could help to explain Shapur's claim of seizing the city of Catabolos and its environs. Shapur does not mention Mutlubakke, but may have referred to both settlements as Catabolos.

Catabolos is also referred to as a *mansio*, specifically by the Bordeaux Pilgrim, and implicitly in the Antonine Itinerary. *Mansiones* initially were road stations equipped to handle an Imperial party.[23] Typical road stops ought to have an inn and a bath to accommodate guests as well as facilities for horses, grooms and vehicles. Carpenters, blacksmiths and veterinarians might also be available to handle roadside emergencies.[24] The few *mansiones* that have been excavated are located mainly in Western Europe. Two well-known examples of Augustan date, from Styria, Austria and the Little Saint Bernard Pass in Switzerland, have stables and rooms arranged around a central court.[25] Recent excavations of the *mansio* of Vacanas on the via Cassia in Italy, however, have yielded a different plan, with the *mansio* consisting of an inn, other unidentified buildings and a bath, lined up along the roadway.[26] It is possible that some of the ruins at Küçük Burnaz represent the *mansio* at Catabolos, perhaps the Smaller Baths (Building 2) together with Building 4, which, equipped with marble revetment, painted plaster, and window glass, could have been an inn.

It is also possible that the *mansio* at Catabolos may have had an expanded function in the 4th and 5th c. A.D. Van Berchem suggested that *mansiones* began being equipped with storage facilities during the reign of Septimius Severus in order to serve as collecting points for the *annona militaris*, the tax imposed on provincials to help supply the army.[27] Many scholars have accepted this proposition,[28] although Rickman makes a compelling argument that the *annona militaris* did not become systematized as a regular tax until the time of Diocletian.[29] Such *mansiones* would have served as rear supply bases, equipped with warehouses and other storage facilities to hold grain and other commodities needed by the troops.[30] Certainly the situation at Küçük Burnaz could have fulfilled this specific function, although at present this cannot be proved.

In any case, the ancient port at Küçük Burnaz, along a major roadsystem and within a fertile plain would have been instrumental in the shipping of grain and other goods by sea, in or out of the region during all periods of its existence. In addition, during periods of conflict in the east, the port would have been an ideal place to land troops.

Whatever the function and identity of the ruins at Küçük Burnaz this study has provided valuable information on Black Cilicia, a little-known corner of the Roman world. It is hoped that this work will encourage further research in this interesting region.

[1] Murray 1995, 39-40, fig. 4.

[2] Rickman 1985, 105-13.

[3] Karmon 1985, 1-6.

[4] Karmon (1985) suggests that a small port would serve a surrounding hinterland of 20-30 km.

[5] MacMullen (1959, 214-17) discusses the role of the army in provincial building, particularly prevalent during the later empire, a topic further discussed by Mitchell (1987, 336-42) who notes that in constructions devoted to local security and defense, there is often an ambiguity between military and civilian participation.

[6] Chevallier 1976, 34.

[7] As proposed first by van Berchem (1937, 1973) and seconded with some reservations by Rickman (1971, 279). For possible epigraphic and numismatic evidence for Caracalla's journey through Asia Minor see Levick (1969, 426-46), whose findings are revised by Johnston (1983, 58-76).

[8] *Itinerarium Antonini Augusti* 146.

[9] Maricq 1958, 295-360, esp. 313, line 27 of the Greek text.

[10] Honigmann and Maricq 1953, 159.

[11] For Tardequeia see Hild and Hellenkemper (1990, 427).

[12] *Itin. Burdigalense* 580 (Geyer 1898, 17).

[13] Chevallier 1976, 38-39.

[14] *Ravennas Anonymus Cosmographia*, 16.5.

[15] Hild 1991, 309.

[16] Chevallier 1976, 28-34.

[17] Stretch 92 (Constantinople to Antioch) section X.4. According to Konrad Miller (1962) the line recording the secondary route between Mopsuestia and Catabolos, a major roadway in antiquity, has been lost in a copying error. The Roman numerals that relate the distance between the two places survive, however.

[18] There has long been confusion between Catabolos and a similarly named place, Castabalum. According to Curtius (3.7.5), Alexander the Great, while marching towards Issus in 333 B.C., stopped in Mallus and then after a day's march reached a place called Castabalum where he met up with his general Parmenio. The next day he marched to Issus. Some scholars (Levick, 1969, 445) have thought that Alexander must have marched to Castabala (later known as Castabala Hierapolis) located *c.* 80 km north of Mallus in the foothills of the Taurus Mountains. Other scholars (Bauer 1899, 124; Hammond 1980, 93), recognizing that the distance between Mallus and Castabala Hierapolis was impossibly great for the march described by Curtius, have suggested that Castabalum was the same place as Catabolos. Certainly the position along the ancient road leading to Issus is appropriate, but in fact Catabolos and Castabalum although similar, are two different names. A possible solution lies in the introduction of yet another similarly named site: Kastanbul Harabe (which translates as "the ruins of Kastanbul") located on the west coast of the Gulf of Issus, 15 km from Aegeae. In Roman times (and undoubtedly earlier) it was positioned along a road that ran east from Mallus to the Gulf of Issus and then north along the coast. The site of Kastanbul occupies a hill *c.* 1.30 km from the present shoreline. On the hill was found a Roman tomb, while on the neighboring hill to the east can be seen tile and Roman ceramics (Hellenkemper and Hild 1986, 295-96).

Obviously the Turkish name Kastanbul bears a close resemblance to Castabalum, and it may have been there that Alexander stopped before pressing on to Issus.

[19] Αμαντο (1933, 149-50) discusses the etymology of this word, noting that even today, harbor towns on the Greek islands of Andros and Patmos preserve the name Κατάβολον.

[20] Hild and Hellenkemper 1990, 362.

[21] Chevallier 1976, 39.

[22] The distances between Mopsuestia and Catabolos given by the Bordeaux Pilgrim are problematical, since he records 15 Roman miles to Tardequeia and another 16 Roman miles from Tardequeia to Catabolos, thus adding up to 31 Roman miles or 46 km, a distance too great for either Muttalip Hüyük or Küçük Burnaz.

[23] Chevallier 1976, 34-37; Rickman 1971, 279; van Berchem 1973.

[24] Chevallier 1976, 187; Casson 1994, 184.

[25] Casson 1994, 201-202, Chevallier 1976, 187.

[26] Gazzetti 1986, 157-161, fig. 3.

[27] van Berchem 1937, 1973.

[28] Pekary 1968, 166; Kubitschek RE XIV, 1231-52; Chevallier 1976, 184-85.

[29] Rickman 1971, 278-90.

[30] Ibid, 289.

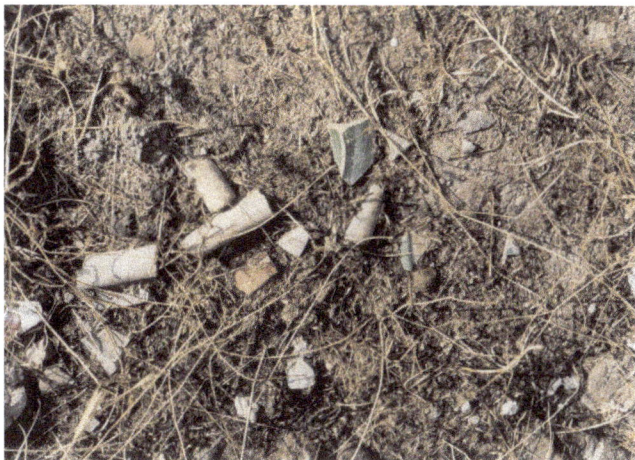

Color Plate 1. Pottery scatter, Epiphaneia

Color Plate 2. Building 2, Room A, west wall, painted plaster

Color Plate 3. Building 5, pediment block

Color Plate 4. Building 9, column drum with painted plaster

Color Plate 5. Building 9, column drum with painted plaster, detail

Color Plate 6. Window glass

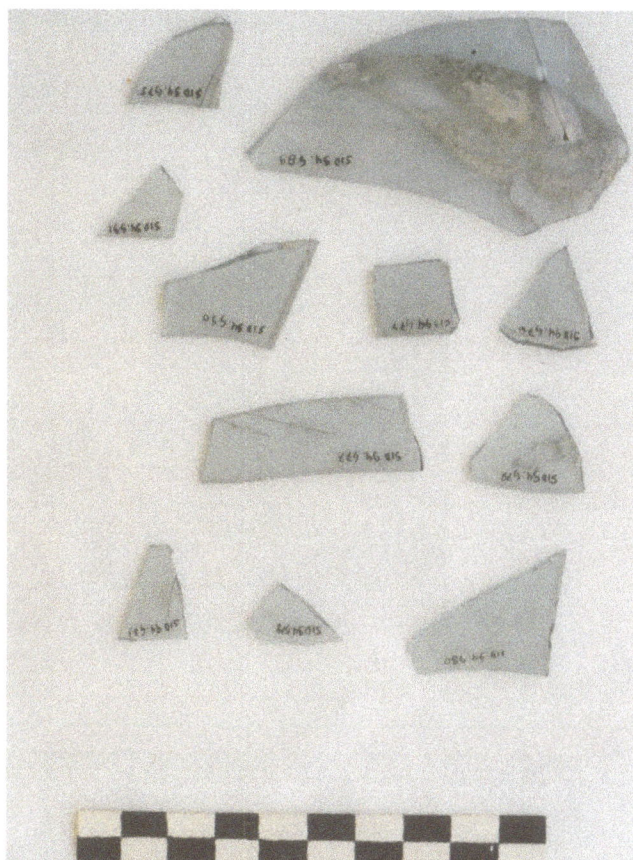

Color Plate 7. Window glass

Color Plate 8. Examples of Plain Ware Type 1

Color Plate 9. Examples of Plain Ware Type 2

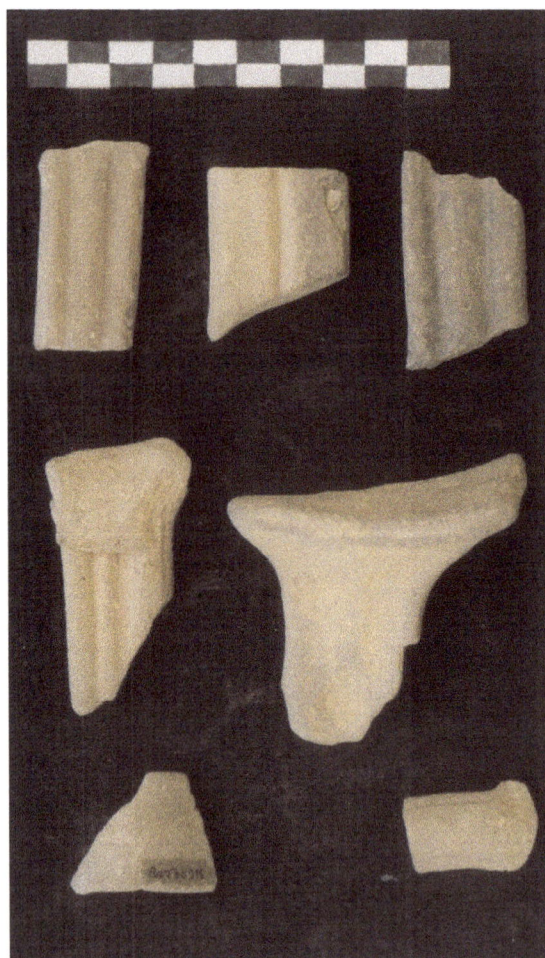

Color Plate 10. Examples of Plain Ware Type 3

Color Plate 11. Examples of Sgraffiato Ware

Color Plate 12. Examples of glass vessels

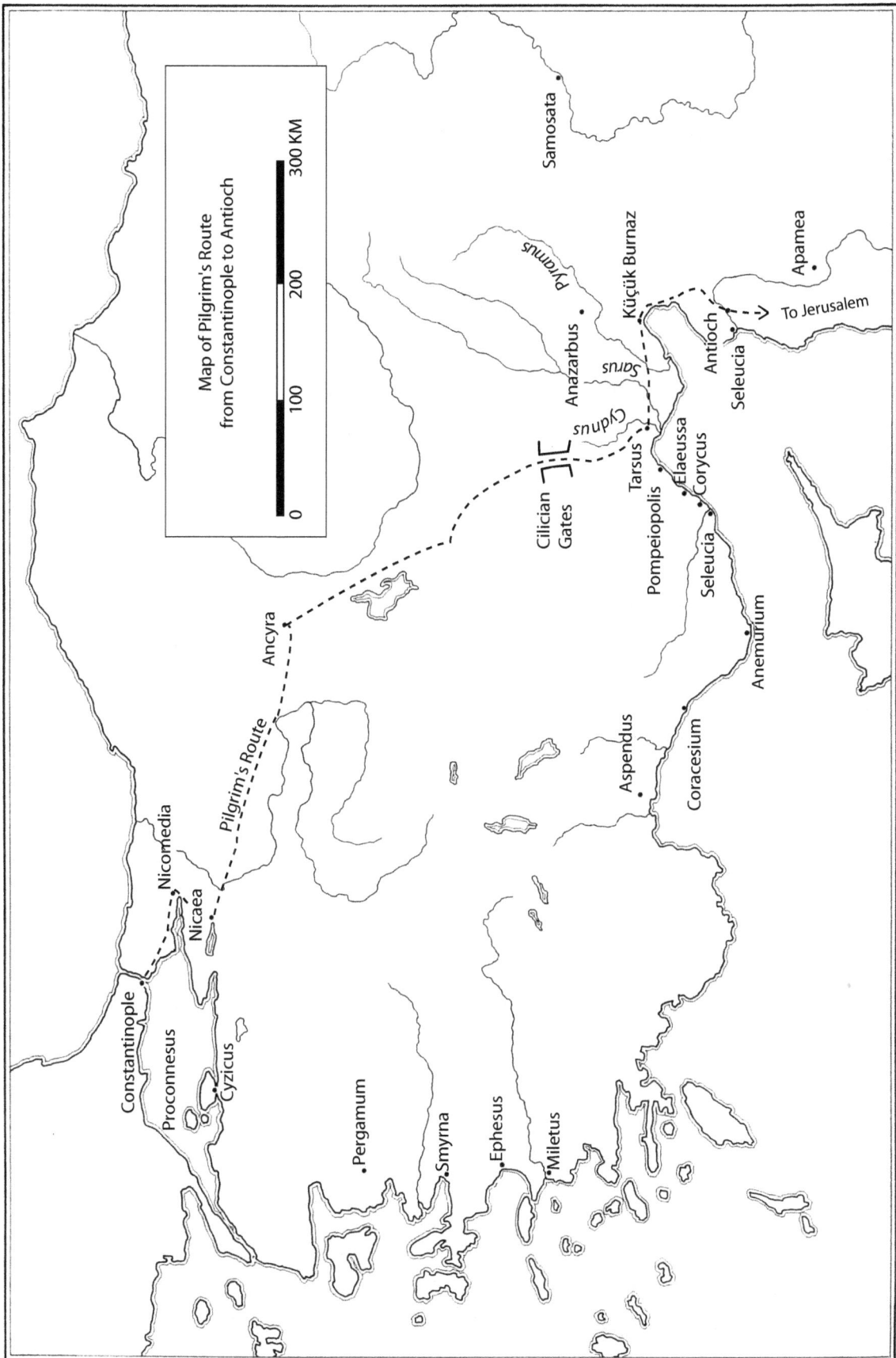

Map 1. Map of the Pilgrim's Route from Constantinople to Antioch

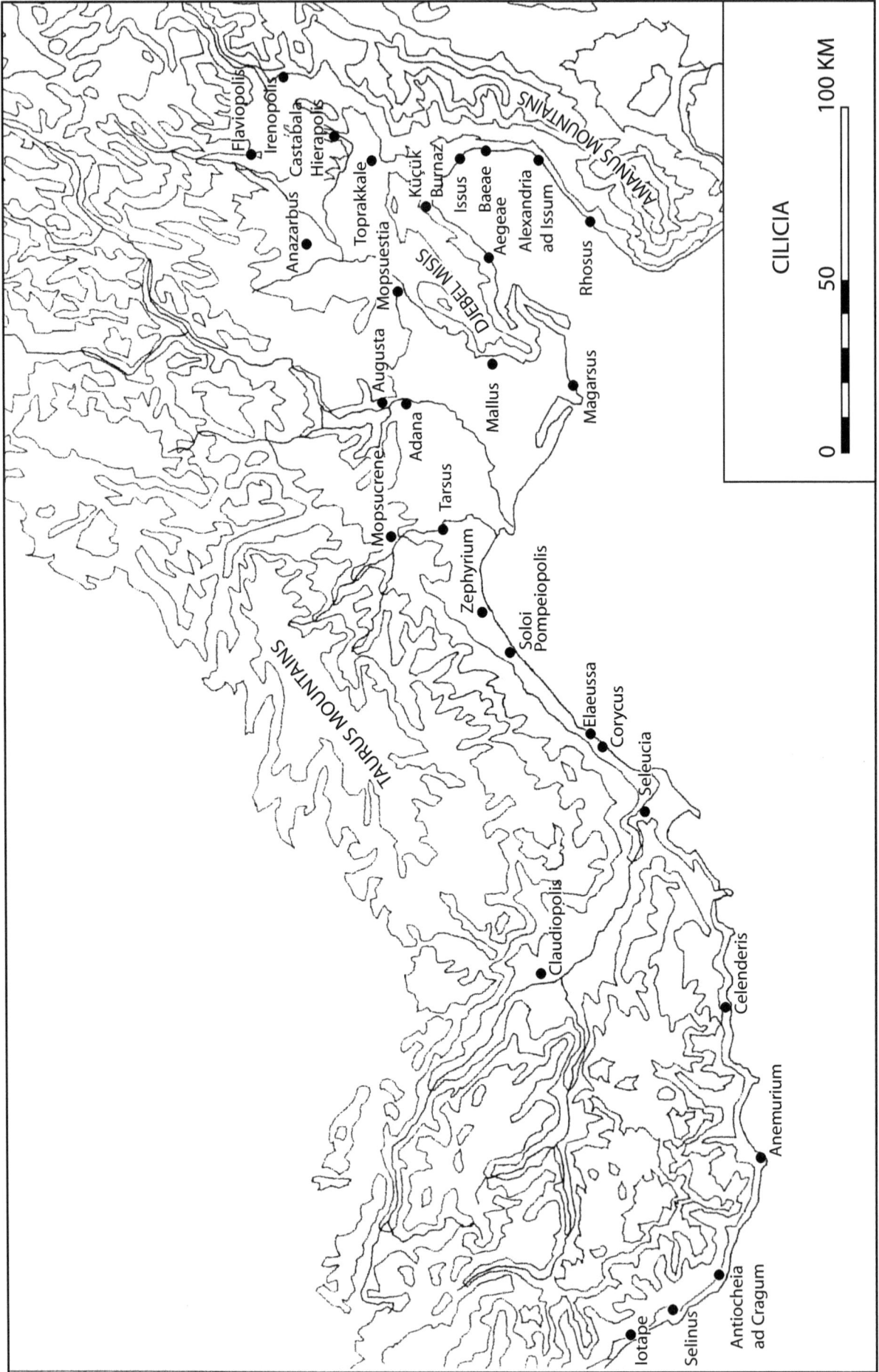

Map 2. Map of Cilicia

Aqueduct

GÖZENE
(EPIPHANEIA)

KARAHÜYÜK

Modern Road

TURUNÇLU

Aqueduct

KÜÇÜK-
BURNAZ

MUTTALIP HÜYÜK

Modern Road

SARIMAZIKÖYÜ

KARANLIKKAPI

Aqueduct

İNCIRLI

KURTPINAR

KURTKULAĞI

GULF OF ISKENDERUN

0   5KM

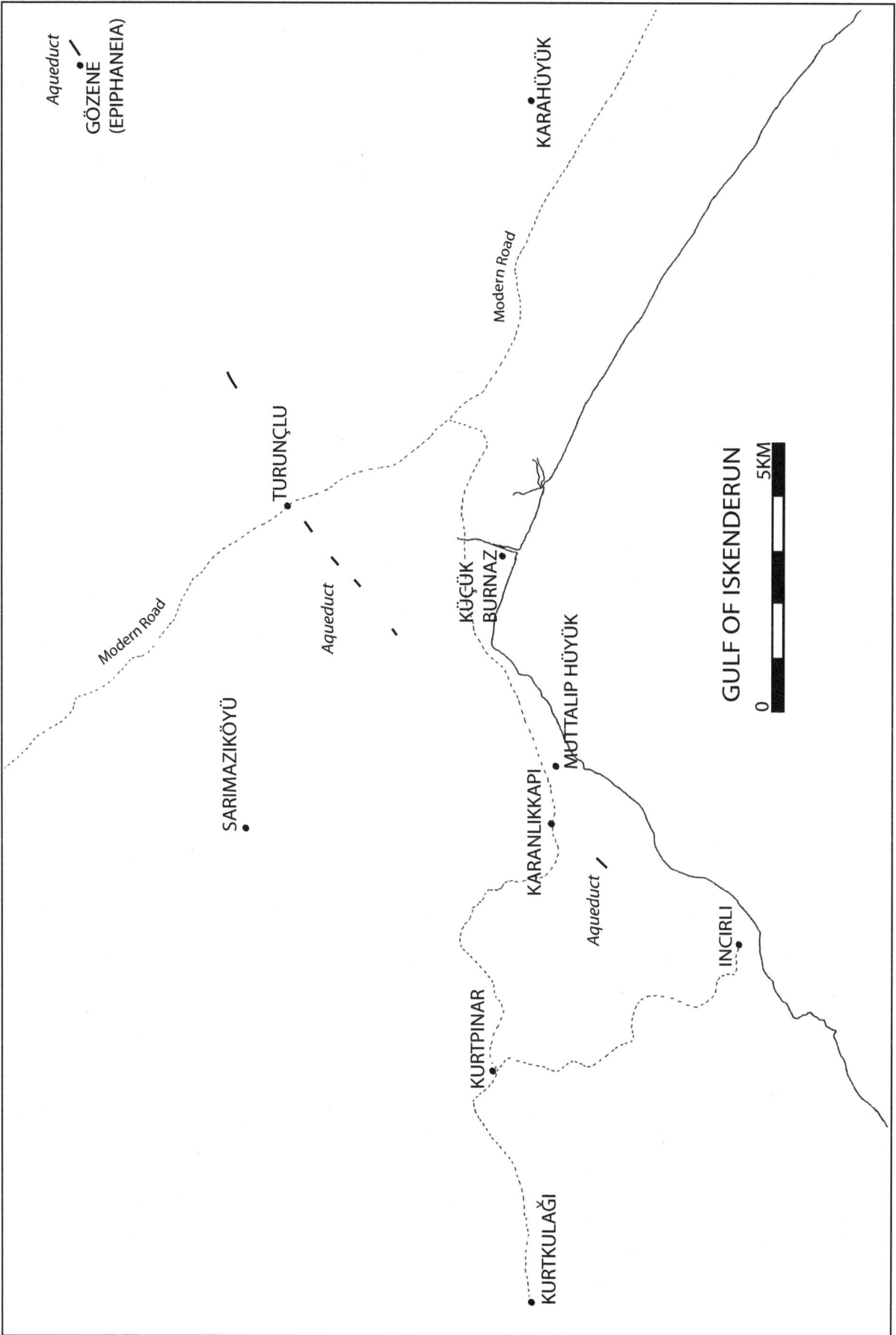

Map 3. Map of the Northern Plain of Issus

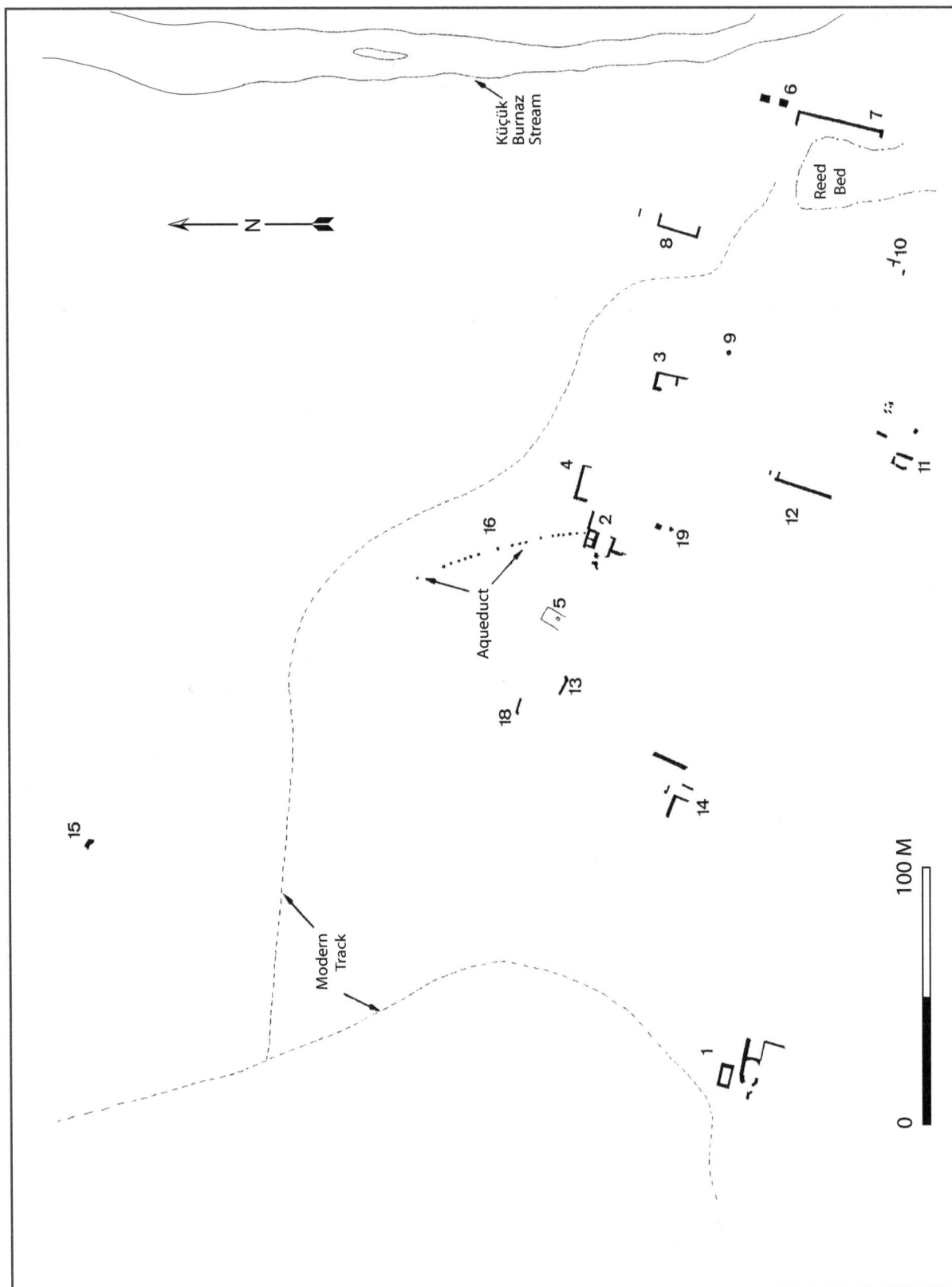

Küçük Burnaz Stream

Reed Bed

N

Aqueduct

Modern Track

8

6

7

10

3

9

11

4

2

16

19

12

5

13

18

14

1

15

0

100 M

Map 4. Plan of Küçük Burnaz

ABBREVIATIONS

AJA	American Journal of Archaeology
AnatSt	Anatolian Studies
AncW	The Ancient World
AntJ	The Antiquaries Journal
AST	Araştırma Sonuçları Toplantası
ArchJ	Archaeological Journal
AthMitt	Mitteilungen des Deutschen Archäologischen Instituts, Athenische Abteilung
BSA	Annual of the British School at Athens
BSR	Papers of the British School at Rome
BCH	Bulletin de correspondance hellénique
CahArch	Cahiers archéologiques
CRAI	Comptes Rendus des séances de l'Académie des inscriptions et belles-lettres
HSCP	Harvard Studies in Classical Philology
JRA	Journal of Roman Archaeology
JAS	Journal of Archaeological Science
JESHO	Journal of the Economic and Social History of the Orient
JEA	Journal of Egyptian Archaeology
JdI	Jahrbuch des Deutschen Archäologischen Instituts
JGS	Journal of Glass Studies
JHS	Journal of Hellenic Studies
JRS	Journal of Roman Studies
KölnJb	Kölner Jahrbuch für Vor-und Frühgeschichte
KST	Kazı Sonuçları Toplantısı
MAMA	Monumenta Asiae Minoris Antiqua
OJA	Oxford Journal of Archaeology
ÖJhBeibl	Jahresheft des Österreichischen Archäologischen Instituts
OpArch	Opuscula Archaeologica
ProcBritAc	Proceedings of the British Academy
RA	Revue archéologique
RömMitt	Mitteilungen des Deutschen Archäologischen Instituts, Römische Abteilung
TürkArkDerg	Türk Arkeoloji Dergisi

BIBLIOGRAPHY

Abadie-Reynal, C. 1989. "La Céramique romaine de Porsuk," *KST* 11, 221-28.

Adam, J.-P. 1994. *Roman building: Materials and techniques* (Bloomington and Indianapolis).

Ainsworth, W.F. 1838. "Notes upon the comparative geography of the Cilician and Syrian Gates," *Journal of the Royal Geographic Society* 8, 185-95.
_____ 1842. *Travels and researches in Asia Minor* vol. 2 (London).

Akok, M. 1957. "Augusta şehri harabesi," *TürkArkDerg* 7.2, 17-20.

Alishan, P.L.M. 1899. *Sissoùan ou l'Arméno-Cilicie* (Vienna).

Alpözen, T.O. 1975. "Bodrum Müzesi ticarı amphoraları," *TürkArkDerg* 22, 5-32.

Alpözen, T.O., B. Berkaya and A.H. Özdaş 1995. *Commercial amphoras of the Bodrum Museum of Underwater Archaeology* (Bodrum).

Αμαντο, K. 1933. "Συμμεικτα," *Ελλενικα* 6, 149-50.

Badian, E. 1964. "Sulla's Cilicia command," *Studies in Greek and Roman History*, 157-78.

Ballance, M.H. 1964. "Derbe and Faustinopolis," *AnatSt* 14, 139-45.

Barker, W. B. 1853. *Lares and Penates: or, Cilicia and its governors* (London).

Barnes, T.D. 1982. *The new empire of Diocletian and Constantine* (Cambridge, MA).

Bauer, A. 1899. "Die Schlacht bei Issos," *ÖJhBeibl* 2, 105-28.

Bauer, P.V.C. 1938. "Glassware," in C.H. Kraeling (ed), *Gerasa, city of the Decapolis* (New Haven) 505-46.

Baydur, N. 1987. "Tarsus-Dönüktaş kazısı 1985," *KST* 8.2, 13-37.

Belon du Mans, P. 1554. *Les observations de plusieurs singularitez et choses memorables* (Paris).

Bell, G. 1906. "Notes on a journey through Cilicia and Lycaonia," *RA* 7, 1-29.

Bent, J.T. 1890. "Recent discoveries in Eastern Cilicia," *JHS* 11, 231-35.

Berlin, A. 1997. "The plain wares," in S. Herbert (ed) *Tel Anafa II, i. The Hellenistic and Roman pottery, JRA Supplementary Series* no. 10 (Ann Arbor) 1-248.

Bingöl, E. 1985. Turkey Geology. *Tübinger Atlas des Vor-deren Orients* AII4 (Wiesbaden).

Birley, A.R. 1999. *The African Emperor. Septimius Severus* (London).

Boase, T.S.R. 1978. *The Cilician Kingdom of Armenia* (New York).

Bodribb, G. 1987. *Roman brick and tile* (Gloucester).

Boon, B.C. 1966. "Roman window glass from Wales," *JGS* 8, 41-45.

Borgia, E. 2003. "Archaeology in Cilicia in the ancient traveller's notes," *Olba* 7, 41-77.

Bowersock, G.W., P. Brown and O. Grabar 1999. *Late Antiquity: A guide to the postclassical world* (Cambridge and London).

Boyce, A. 1969. "The foundation year of Pompeiopolis in Cilicia," in *Hommage à Marcel Renard* vol. 3 (Brussels) 87-103.

Braund, D.C. 1989. *Rome and the friendly king: The character of client kingship* (London).

Brinkmann, R. 1976. *Geology of Turkey* (Stuttgart).

Broneer, O. 1930. *Corinth IV.II: Terracotta Lamps* (Cambridge).
_____ 1977. *Isthmia III: Terracotta Lamps* (Princeton).

Broughton, T.R.S. 1938. "Roman Asia," in T. Frank (ed) *An economic survey of ancient Rome* vol. IV (London) 499-916.

Brown, F.E. 1936. "The Roman Baths," in M.I. Rostovtzeff *et al.* (edd) *The excavations at Dura Europos. Preliminary report of the 6th season* (New Haven) 84-105.

Cahen, C. 1968. *Pre-Ottoman Turkey* (London).

Calder, W.M. 1912. "Colonia Caesareia Antiocheia," *JRS* 2, 78-109.

Cameron, A. 1993. *The Mediterranean world in late antiquity. AD 395-600* (London).

Casabonne, O. 1999. "Local powers and Persian model in Achaemenid Cilicia: A reassessment," *Olba* 2, 57-66.

Casson, L. 1994. *Travel in the ancient world* (Baltimore and London).

Chevallier, R. 1976. *Roman roads* (London).

Clairmont, C.W. 1963. *The excavations at Dura-Europos. Final report IV.V: The glass vessels* (New Haven).

Cohen, G. 1995. *The Hellenistic settlements in Europe, the Islands and Asia Minor* (Berkeley).

Cox, D.H. 1949. *The Excavations at Dura-Europos. Final report IV.I.2: The Greek and Roman pottery* (New Haven).

Creswell, K.A.C. 1932. *Early Muslim architecture vol. I: Umayyads,*

A.D. 622-750 (Oxford).

Crowfoot, G.M. 1957. "Glass," in J.W. Crowfoot, G.M. Crowfoot and K.M. Kenyon, *Samaria-Sebaste III. The objects from Samaria* (London) 403-422.

Crowfoot, G.M. and D.B. Harden 1931. "Early Byzantine and later glass lamps," *JEA* 17, 196-208.

Crowfoot, J.W., G.M. Crowfoot and K.M. Kenyon 1957. *Samaria-Sebaste III. The objects from Samaria* (London).

Cuinet, V. 1891. *La Turquie d'Asie* vol. 2 (Paris).

Dagron, G. 1980. "Two documents concerning mid-sixth-century Mopsuestia," in *Charanis Studies. Essays in honor of Peter Charanis* (New Brunswick, NJ) 19-30.

Dagron, G. and D. Feissel 1987. *Inscriptions de Cilicie* (Travaux et memoires du centre de Recherche d'Histoire et Civilization de Byzance. College de France: Monograph BD 4).

Dark, K. 2001. *Byzantine pottery* (Charleston).

Davies, J.G. 1953. *The origin and development of early Christian church architecture* (New York).

Day, F.F. 1941. "The Islamic finds at Tarsus," *Asia* 41, 143-48.

de Boor, C. (ed) 1883-5. *Theophanis Chronographia* (Leipzig)

Deichmann, F.W. 1979. "Westliche Bautechnik in römischen und römaischen Osten," *RömMitt* 86, 473-527.

Delvoye, C. 1976. "Sur le passage des voutes et des coupoles in briques de l'Anatolie à la péninsule balkanique," *BCH* 100, 235-238.

Desideri, P. 1991a. "Cilicia ellenistica,"*Quaderni Storici* 76, 141-65.
_____ 1991b. "Scambi e identità culturale: la Cilicia," *Quaderni Storici* 76, 5-16.
_____ 1991c. "Strabo's Cilicians," *De Anatolia Antiqua* 1, 299-304.
_____ 2001. "The cities of Pedias in the Roman period," in É. Jean, A.M. Dinçol and S. Durugönül (edd) *La Cilicie: espaces et pouvoirs locaux (2e millénaire av. J.-C. - 4e siécle ap. J.-C.). Actes de la table ronde internationale d'Istanbul. 2-5 novembre 1999* (Paris) 411-15.

Desideri, P. and A.M. Jasink. 1990. *Cilicia. Dall'età di Kizzuwatna alla conquista macedone* (Turin).

Dewdney, J.C. 1971. *Turkey, an introductory geography* (New York and Washington).

Doblhofer, E. 1961-1963. "Mopsus. Arzt der Menschen. Mit einem Anhang: Eine Ehreninschrift aus Erzin," *ÖJhBeibl* 46, 5-18

Dodge, H. 1987. "Brick construction in Roman Greece and Asia Minor," in S. Macready and F.H. Thompson (edd) *Roman architec-*ture in the Greek world* (London) 106-116.
_____ 1988a. "Palmyra and the marble trade: Evidence from the Baths of Diocletian," *Levant* 20, 215-30.
_____ 1988b. "Decorative stones for architecture in the Roman Empire," *OJA* 7, 65-80.
_____ 1990. "The architectural impact of Rome in the East," in M. Henig (ed) *Architecture and architectural sculpture in the Roman Empire* (Oxford) 108-20.
_____ 1992. "Main quarries and decorative stones of the Roman World," in H. Dodge, and B. Ward-Perkins (edd) *Marble in antiquity. Collected papers of J.B. Ward-Perkins. Archaeological monographs of the British School at Rome,* 6 (London) 153-59.

Dodge, H. and B. Ward-Perkins (edd) 1992. *Marble in antiquity. Collected papers of J.B. Ward-Perkins. Archaeological monographs of the British School at Rome,* 6 (London).

Downey, G. 1961. *A history of Antioch in Syria from Seleucus to the Arab conquest* (Princeton).

Dreizehnter, A. 1975. "Pompeius als Städtgründer," *Chiron* 5, 213-45.

Dupont-Sommer, A. and L. Robert 1964. *La déesse de Hiérapolis Castabala (Cilicie)* (Paris).

Edwards, R.W. 1987. *The fortifications of Armenian Cilicia* (Washington, D.C.).

Elderkin, G.W. (ed) 1934. *Antioch on-the-Orontes I: The excavations of 1932* (Princeton).

Elton, H. 2003. "The economy of Cilicia in Late Antiquity," *Olba* 8, 173-81.

Empereur, J.-Y. and M. Picon 1989. "Les régions de production d'amphores impériales en Méditerraneé orientale," in M. Lenoir, D. Manacorda and D. Panella (edd) *Amphores romaines et histoire économique. Actes du colloque de Sienne. 22-24 mai 1986* (Rome) 223-48.

Equini Schneider, E. 1999. *Elaiussa Sebaste I: Campagne di scavo 1995-1997* (Rome).

Erim, K. and J. Reynolds 1970. "The copy of Diocletian's edict on maximum prices from Aphrodisias in Caria," *JRS* 60, 120-41.

Erten, E. 2003. "Glass finds from Olba Survey - 2001," *Olba* 7, 145-54.

Evrin, Ç.T. 2000. *Tarsus Republic Square Late Roman cooking wares* (MA thesis, Bilkent University).

Eyice, S. 1954. "Deux anciennes églises Byzantines de la Citadelle d'Amasra (Paphlagonie)," *CahArch* 7, 97-105.

Fant, J.C. 1993. "Ideology, gift and trade: A distribution model for the Roman Imperial Marbles," *JRA Supplementary Series* no. 6, 145-70.

Farrington, A. 1987. "Imperial bath building in south-west Asia Minor," in S. Macready and F.H. Thompson (edd) *Roman architecture in the Greek world* (London) 50-59.

_____ 1995. *Roman baths of Lycia, an architectural study* (Ankara).

Fisher, C.S. 1934. "The tower area, Bath A, Bath B, House A, the Roman Villa and Bath C," in G. W. Elderkin (ed) *Antioch on-the-Orontes I: The excavations of 1932* (Princeton) 1-31.

_____ 1938. "Description of the site," in C.H Kraeling (ed) *Gerasa, city of the Decapolis* (New Haven) 11-25.

Freely, J. 1998. *The eastern Mediterranean coast of Turkey* (Istanbul).

Freeman, P. 1986. "The Province of Cilicia and its origins," in P. Freeman and D. Kennedy (edd) *The defence of the Roman and Byzantine East. Proceedings of a colloquium at the University of Sheffield, April.* British Institute of Archaeology at Ankara, Monograph 8 (BAR international series 297) 253-75.

French, D. 1981. *Roman roads and milestones in Asia Minor* Fasc. 1: *The pilgrim's road*, Fasc. 2: *An interim catalogue of milestones* (2 vols.). British Institute of Archaeology at Ankara, Monograph 3, 9 (BAR international series 15, 392, Oxford).

Freu, J. 2001. "De l'indépendance à l'annexion: Le Kizzuwatna et Le Hatti aux XVIe et XVe siècles avant notre ère," in É. Jean, A.M. Dinçol and S. Durugönül (edd) *La Cilicie: Espaces et pouvoirs locaux (2e millénaire av. J.-C. - 4e siècle ap. J.-C.). Actes de la table ronde internationale d'Istanbul. 2-5 novembre 1999* (Paris) 13-36.

Fulford, M.G., and D.P.S. Peacock 1984. *Excavations at Carthage: The British Museum. Vol. I. 2: The Avenue du President Habib Bourguiba, Salammbo. The pottery and other objects from the site* (Huddersfield).

Garstang, J. and O.R. Gurney 1959. *The geography of the Hittite Empire* (London).

Gates, M.-H. 1994a. "The 1992 Excavations at Kinet Hüyük (Dörtyol/Hatay)," *KST* 15.1, 193-200.

_____ 1994b. "Archaeology in Turkey," *AJA* 98, 261.

_____ 1995. "Archaeology in Turkey," *AJA* 99, 227.

_____ 1996. "Archaeology in Turkey," *AJA* 100, 293-94.

_____ 1997. "Archaeology in Turkey," *AJA* 101, 253-54.

_____ 1999. "1997 archaeological excavations at Kinet Höyük (Yeşil-Dörtyol, Hatay)," *KST* 20.1, 259-81.

_____ 2000. "1998 excavations at Kinet Höyük (Yeşil-Dörtyol, Hatay)," *KST* 21.1, 193-208.

_____ 2001. "1999 excavations at Kinet Höyük (Yeşil-Dörtyol, Hatay)," *KST* 22.1, 203-22.

_____ 2002. "Kinet Höyük 2000 (Yeşil-Dörtyol, Hatay)," *KST* 23.2, 55-62.

_____ 2003. "2001 season at Kinet Höyük (Yeşil-Dörtyol, Hatay)," *KST* 24.1, 283-298.

Gazzetti, G. 1986. "La 'Mansio' di Vacanas al XXI miglio della via Cassia," *Archeologia nella Tuscia II: atti degli incontri di studio organazzati a Viterbo, 1984* (Rome) 155-65.

Geyer, P. (ed) 1898. *Itineraria Hierosolymitana*. Saeculi III-VIII (Vienna).

Ghazarian, J.G. 2000. *The Armenian Kingdom in Cilicia during the Crusades* (Richmond).

Ghini, G. 1995. "Ceramica a pareti sottili, " in M. Balzano and A. Camilli (edd) *Ceramica Romana, guida allo studio* vol II (Rome) 99-157.

Ginouves, R. 1972. *Le theatron à gradins droits et l'Odeon d'Argos* (Etudes péloponnésiennes 6, Paris)

Goldman, H. 1950. *Excavations at Gözlü Kule, Tarsus. 1: The Hellenistic and Roman periods* (Princeton).

Gough, Mary 1954. *Travel into yesterday. An account of archaeological journeying through the plain and rough places of the Roman province of Cilicia, in southern Turkey* (New York).

Gough, Michael. 1952. "Anazarbus," *AnatSt* 2, 85-150.

_____ 1955. "Early churches in Cilicia," *Byzan-tinoslavica* 16, 201-11.

_____ 1956. "Augusta Ciliciae," *AnatSt* 6, 165-77.

_____ 1976. "Epiphaneia," in R. Stillwell (ed) *The Princeton Encyclopedia of Classical Sites* (Princeton) 315.

Grataloup, C. 1988. *Les céramiques à parois fines. Rue des Farges à Lyon* (Oxford).

Greenhalgh, P. 1980. *Pompey, the Roman Alexander* (Columbia, MO).

Gregory, T. 1985. "An early Byzantine complex at Akra Sophia near Corinth," *Hesperia* 54, 411-28.

Gunneweg, J., I. Perlman, and J. Yellin. 1983. *The provenience, typology and chronology of Eastern Terra Sigillata* (Qedem. Monographs of the Hebrew University of Jerusalem 17, Jerusalem).

Gurney, O.R. 1990. *The Hittites* (London).

Halfmann, H. 1986. *Itinera principum* (Stuttgart).

Hammond, N.G.L. 1980. *Alexander the Great. King, commander and statesman* (Park Ridge, NJ).

_____ 1994. "One or two passes at the Cilician-Syrian border?" *AncW* 25.1, 15-26.

Harden, D.B. 1936. *Roman glass from Karanis* (Ann Arbor).

_____ 1961. "Domestic window glass: Roman, Saxon and Medieval," in *Studies in building history: Essays in recognition of the work of B.H. St. J. O'Neil* (London) 39-62.

_____ 1968. "Ancient glass I: Pre-Roman," *ArchJ* 125, 46-72.

_____ 1969. "Ancient glass II: Roman," *ArchJ* 126, 44-77.

_____ 1971. "Ancient glass III: Post-Roman," *ArchJ* 128, 78-117.

_____ 1974. "Window glass from the Roman-British bath-house at Garden Hill, Hartfield, Sussex," *AntJ* 54, 280-82.

Hayes, J.W. 1967. "North Syrian mortaria," *Hesperia* 36, 337-47.
_____ 1972. *Late Roman pottery* (London).
_____ 1973. "Roman pottery from the South Stoa at Corinth," *Hesperia* 42, 416-70.
_____ 1975. *Roman and Pre-Roman glass in the Royal Ontario Museum* (Toronto).
_____ 1980. *A supplement to Late Roman pottery* (London).
_____ 1983. "The Villa Dionysos excavations, Knossos: The pottery," *BSA* 78, 97-169.
_____ 1986 "Sigillate Orientali," in *Enciclopedia dell'arte antica classica e orientale. Atlante delle forme ceramiche II.Ceramica fine Romana nel bacino Mediter-raneo (Tardo Ellenismo e Primo Impero)* 3-96.
_____ 1991. *Paphos III. The Hellenistic and Roman pottery* (Nicosia).
_____ 1992. *Excavations at Saraçhane in Istanbul II. The pottery* (Princeton)
_____ 1997. *Handbook of Mediterranean Roman pottery* (Norman).
_____ 2000. "From Rome to Beirut and beyond: Asia Minor and Eastern Mediterranean trade connections," *Rei Cretariae Romanae Fautorum*, Acta 36, 285-97.

Heberdey, R. and A. Wilhelm 1896. *Reisen in Kilikien*, Österreichis-chen Akademie der Wissenschaften Philosophisch-Historische Klasse Denkschriften 44/6 (Vienna).

Hellenkemper, H. 1984. "Das wiedergefundene Issos," in J. Özels and V. Thewalt (edd) *Aus dem Östen des Alexanderreiches* (Cologne).

Hellenkemper, H. and F. Hild 1986. *Neue Forschungen in Kilikien, Österreichischen Akademie der Wissenschaften Philosophisch-Historische Klasse Denkschriften* 186 (Vienna).

Hicks, E.L. 1890. "Inscriptions from eastern Cilicia, " *JHS* 11, 236-54.

Hild, F. 1991. "Die Route der Tabula Peutingeriana (Tab. Peut.) von Iconium über ad fines und tetrapyrgia nach Pompeiopolis in Kilikien," *De Anatolia Antiqua* I, 309-16.
_____ 1993. "Eirenupolis in der Kilikia Pedias," in G. Dobesch and G. Rehrenböck (edd) *Die epigraphische und altertumskundliche Erforschung Kleinasiens. Hundert Jahre Kleinasiatische Kommission der Österreichischen Akademie der Wissenschaften: Akten des symposium von 23. bis 25. Oktober 1990* (Österreichis-chen Akademie der Wissenschaften Philosophisch-Historische Klasse Denkschriften 236) 221-26.

Hild, F. and H. Hellenkemper 1984. "Kommagene - Kilikien - Isaurien," in K. Wessel and M. Restle (edd) *Reallexikon zur byzantinische Kunst* 3, 161-320.
_____ 1990. *Kilikien und Isaurien*, Österre-ichischen Akademie der Wissenschaften Philosophisch-Historische Klasse Denkschriften 215. Tabula Imperii Byzantini Band 5 (Vienna).

Hoben, W. 1969.*Untersuchen zur Stellung kleinasiatischer Dynasten in den Machtkämpfen der ausgehenden römischen Republik* (Mainz).

Hodge, A.T. 1992. *Roman aqueducts and water supply* (London).

Hoffmann, A. 1989. "Zum 'Bedesten' in Amastris. Ein römischer Marktbau?" in *Festschrift für W. Müller-Wiener. Istanbuler Mitteilungen* 39, 197-210.

Honigmann, E. 1950. "Neronias - Irenopolis in Eastern Cilicia," *Byzantion* 20, 39-61.
_____ 1987. "Missis," in M.Th. Houtsma, A.J. Wensinck, E. Lévi-Provençal, H.A.R. Gibb and W. Heffening (edd) *First encyclo-pedia of Islam*, 1913-1936, Vol. V (Leiden) 521-27.

Honigmann, E. and A. Maricq 1953. *Recherches sur les Res Gestae Divi Saporis* (Brussels).

Huber, G. 1969. "Die Restaurierung der Therme II 7A in Anamur," *TürkArkDerg* 18, 47-58.

Houwink ten Cate, P.H.J. 1961. *The Luwian population groups in Lycia and Cilicia Aspera during the Hellenistic period* (Leiden).

Hunt, E.D. 1982. *Holy Land pilgrimage in the Later Roman Empire A.D. 312-460* (Oxford).

Isings, C. 1957. *Roman glass from dated finds* (Groningen).

Isler, H.P. 1969. "Heriaon von Samos: Eine frühbyzantinische Zisterne," *AthMitt* 84, 202-30.

Janke, A. 1904. *Auf Alexanders des Grossen Pfaden. Eine Reise durch Kleinasien* (Berlin).

Jasink, A.M. 1991. "Hittite and Assyrian routes to Cilicia," *De Anatolia Antiqua* 1, 253-59.
_____ 1995. *Gli Stati Neo-Ittiti. Analisi delle Fonti Scritte ed Sintesi Storica* (Pavia).

Jean, É. 1999."The 'Greeks' in Cilicia at the end of the 2nd milleni-um B.C.: Classical sources and archaeological evidence," *Olba* 2, 27-39.

Johnston, A. 1983. "Caracalla's path: The numismatic evidence," *Historia* 32, 58-76.

Jones, A.H.M. 1964. *The later Roman empire: 284-602* (Norman).
_____ 1983. *The Cities of the Eastern Roman Provinces* (repr. of 1937 edn., Oxford).

Jones, F.F. 1950. "The pottery," in H. Goldman (ed) *Excavations at Gözlü Kule, Tarsus. 1: The Hellenistic and Roman periods* (Princeton) 149-296.

Kaegi, W. 1992. *Byzantium and the Early Islamic conquests* (Cambridge).

Karmon, Y. 1985. "Geographical components in the study of ancient

Mediterranean ports," in A. Raban (ed) *Harbour archaeology: Proceedings of the first international workshop on ancient Mediterranean harbours, Caesarea Maritima 24-28.6.83.* BAR International Series 257 (Oxford) 1-6.

Kenyon, K.M. 1957. "Terra Sigillata, stratified groups," in J.W. Crowfoot, G.M. Crowfoot and K.M. Kenyon, *Samaria-Sebaste III. The objects from Samaria* (London) 281-305.

Kettenhofen, E. 1982. *Die römisch-persischen Kriege des 3. Jahrhunderts n. Chr.* (Wiesbaden).

Kinneir, J.M. 1818. *Journey through Asia Minor, Armenia and Koordistan, in the years 1813 and 1814* (London).

Kiray, M.K. 1974. "Social change in Çukurova: A comparison of 4 villages," in P. Benedict, E. Tümertekin and F. Mansur (edd) *Turkey. Geographic and social perspectives* (Leiden) 179-203.

Konrad, M. 1999. "Amphorae (East)," in G.W. Bowersock, P. Brown and O. Grabar (edd) *Late Antiquity: A guide to the postclassical world* (Cambridge and London) 294.

Kraeling, C.H. (ed) 1938. *Gerasa, city of the Decapolis* (New Haven).

Krautheimer, R. 1967. *Early Christian and Byzantine architecture* (Baltimore).

Krinzinger, F. and W. Reiter 1993. "Archäologische Forschungen in Hierapolis-Kastabala," in G. Dobesch and G. Rehrenböck (edd) *Die epigraphische und altertumskundliche Erforschung Kleinasiens. Hundert Jahre Kleinasiatische Kommission der Österreichischen Akademie der Wissen-schaften: Akten des symposium von 23. bis 25. Oktober 1990* (Österreichischen Akademie der Wissenschaften Philosophisch-Historische Klasse Denkschriften 236) 269-81.

Lane, A. 1938. "Medieval finds at Al Mina," *Archaeologia* 87, 19-78.

Langlois, V. 1861. *Voyage dans la Cilicia* (Paris).

Lassus, J. 1938. "Une villa de plaìsance à Daphné-Yakto," in R. Stillwell (ed) *Antioch on-the-Orontes II. The excavations. 1933-1936* (Princeton) 95-147.

Leach, J. 1978. *Pompey the Great* (London).

Levick, B. 1967. *Roman colonies in southern Asia Minor* (Oxford).
———— 1969. "Caracalla's path," in *Hommage à Marcel Renard,* vol. 2 (Brussels) 426-46.

Liebmann-Frankfort, T. 1969. "La provincia Cilicia et son intégration dans l'empire romain," in *Hommage à Marcel Renard,* vol. 2 (Brussels) 447-57.

Lightfoot, C.S. 1989. *A catalogue of glass vessels in the Afyon Museum,* BAR International Series 530 (Oxford).

Lloris, M.B. 1970. *Las anforas Romanas en España* (Zaragoza).

Loffreda, L. 1974. *Cafarnao II: La ceramica* (Jerusalem).

Lucas, P. 1714. *Voyage du sieur Paul Lucas* (Paris).

MacMullen, R. 1959. "Roman imperial building in the provinces," *HSCP* 64, 207-35.

Magie, D. 1950. *Roman rule in Asia Minor* (Princeton).

Mango, C. 1980. *Byzantium. The empire of New Rome* (New York).
———— 1985. *Byzantine architecture* (New York).

Maraval, P. 1985. *Lieux saints et pèlerinages d'Orient* (Paris).

Maricq, A. 1958. "Classica et Orientalia. Res Gestae Divi Saporis," *Syria* 35, 295-360.

Marmier, G. 1884. "Les routes de l'Amanus," *Gazette archéologique* 9, 43-50.

Matthers, J. (ed) 1981. *River Qoueiq, northern Syria and its catchment. Studies arising from the Tell Rifa'at Survey 1977-1979*, BAR International Series 598 (Oxford).

Mayet, F. 1975. *Les céramiques à parois fines dans la péninsula ibérique* (Paris).
———— 1980. "Les céramiques à parois fines: état de la question." in P. Léveque and J.-P. Morel (edd) *Céramiques hellénistiques et romaines* (Paris) 201-29.

Meyer, M. 1999. "Die sog. Tyche von Antiocheia als Münzmotiv in Kilikien," *Olba* 2, 185-94.
———— 2001. "Cilicia as part of the Seleucid Empire: The beginning of municipal coinage," in É. Jean, A.M. Dinçol and S. Durugönül (edd) *La Cilicie: Espaces et pouvoirs locaux (2e millénaire av. J.-C. - 4e siècle ap. J.-C.). Actes de la table ronde internationale d'Istanbul. 2-5 novembre 1999* (Paris) 505-14.

Miller, K. 1916. *Itineraria Romana. Römische Reisewege an der Hand der Tabula Peutingeria* (Stuttgart).
———— 1962. *Die Peutingersche Tafel* (Stuttgart).

Mitchell, S. 1980. *Aşvan Kale: Keban rescue excavations, Eastern Anatolia*. British Institute of Archaeology at Ankara, Monograph 1 (Oxford).
———— 1987. "Imperial building in the Eastern Roman provinces," *HSCP* 91, 333-65.

Moevs, M.T. 1973. *The Roman thin walled pottery from Cosa (1948-1954)* (Rome).

Mørkholm, O. 1966. *Antiochus IV of Syria* (Copenhagen).

Murray, W. 1995. "Ancient sailing winds in the eastern Mediterranean: The case for Cyprus," in V. Karageorghis and D. Michaelides (edd) *Proceedings of the international symposium on Cyprus and the sea* (Nicosia) 33-43.

Mutafian, C. 1988. *La Cilicie au carrefour des empires* (Paris).

Olmstead, A.T. 1948. *History of the Persian empire* (Chicago and London).

Onurkan, S. 1967. "Observations on two types of buildings," in E. Rosenbaum, G. Huber and S. Onurkan, *A survey of coastal cities in western Cilicia* (Ankara) 69-85.

Ostrogorsky, G. 1980. *History of the Byzantine state* (Oxford).

Ozaner, F.S. and A. Çalık 1995. "New thoughts on the battlefield of Issus," *Arkeometri Sonuçları Toplantası* 10, 153-75.

Ozaner, F.S., M.-H. Gates and I. Özgen 1993. "Dating the coastal dunes of Karabasamak District (Iskenderun Bay) by geomorphological and archaeological methods," *Arkeometri Sonuçları Toplantası* 8, 357-67.

Özgen I. and M.-H. Gates. 1992a. "Report on the Bilkent University archaeological survey in Cilicia and the northern Hatay: August 1991," *AST* 10, 387-94.
_____ 1992b. Unpublished report to the Turkish Ministry of Culture on the Bilkent University archaeological survey in Cilicia and the northern Hatay: August 1991, 1-12.

Parker, A.J. 1992. *Ancient shipwrecks of the Mediterranean and the Roman provinces*, BAR international Series 80 (Oxford).

Peacock, D.P.S. and D.F. Williams 1986. *Amphorae and the Roman economy: An introductory guide* (London).

Pekary, T. 1968. *Untersuchen zu den römischen Reich-strassen* (Bonn).

Pococke, R. 1745. *A description of the East,* vol. 2 (London).

Price, J. and S. Cottam. 1998. *Roman-British glass vessels: A handbook* (York).

Rauh, N. K. and K.W. Slane 2000, "Possible amphora kiln sites in W Rough Cilicia," *JRA* 13, 317-28.

Redford, S. 1998. *The archaeology of the frontier in the medieval Near East: Excavations at Gritille, Turkey* (Philadelphia).

Redford, S., S. Ikram, E.M. Parr, and T. Beach 2001. "Excavations at medieval Kinet, Turkey: A preliminary report," *Ancient Near Eastern Studies* 38, 58-138.

RIC 1966. *The Roman Imperial Coinage, Volume VII. Constantine and Licinius.* AD 313-337 (London).

Ricci, A. 1973. "Ceramica a pareti sottili," in A. Carandini and C. Panella (edd) *Ostia* III (*Studi Misc.* 21) 341-63.

Rickman, G.E. 1971. *Roman granaries and store buildings* (Cambridge).
_____ 1985. "Towards a study of Roman ports, in A.

Raban (ed) *Harbour archaeology: Proceedings of the first international workshop on ancient Mediterranean harbours, Caesarea Maritima 24-28.6.83.* BAR International Series 257 (Oxford) 105-13.

Riley, J.A. 1979. *Excavations at Sidi Khrebish Benghazi (Berenice) II: Coarse pottery* (Tripoli).

Rivoira, G.T. 1925. *Roman architecture and its principles of construction under the empire* (New York).

Robinson, H.S. 1959. *The Athenian Agora V: Pottery of the Roman period* (Princeton).

Röder, J. 1981. "Marmer Phrygium. Die antiken Marmor-bruche von Iscehisar in Westanatolien," *JDAI* 86, 253-312.

Rook, T. 1978. "The development and operation of Roman hypocausted baths," *JAS* 5, 269-82.
_____ 1979a. "Tiled roofs," in A. McWhirr (ed) *Roman brick and tile: Studies in manufacture, distribution, and use in the Western Empire,* BAR International Series 68 (Oxford) 295-301.
_____ 1979b. "The effect of the evolution of flues upon the development of architecture," in A. McWhirr (ed) *Roman brick and tile: Studies in manufacture, distribution, and use in the Western Empire,* BAR International Series 68 (Oxford) 303-308.

Rosenbaum, E., G. Huber and S. Onurkan 1967. *A survey of coastal cities in western Cilicia* (Ankara).

Russell, J. 1991. "Cilicia - Nutrix Virorum: Cilicians abroad in peace and war during Hellenistic and Roman times," *De Anatolia Antiqua* 1, 283-97.

Sayar, M.H. 1993. "Epigraphische forschungen in Ostkilikien 1990," in G. Dobesch and G. Rehrenböck (edd) *Die epigraphische und altertumskundliche Erforschung Kleinasiens. Hundert Jahre Kleinasiatische Kommission der Österreichischen Akademie der Wissenschaften: Akten des symposium von 23. bis 25. Oktober 1990* (Österreichischen Akademie der Wissenschaften Philosophisch-Historische Klasse Denk-schriften 236) 319-27.
_____ 2000. *Die Inschriften von Anazarbos und Umgebung (Bonn).*
_____ 2001. "Tarkondimotos. Seine Dynastie, seine Politik und seine Reich," in É. Jean, A.M. Dinçol and S. Durugönül (edd) *La Cilicie: Espaces et pouvoirs locaux (2e millénaire av. J.-C. - 4e siècle ap. J.-C.). Actes de la table ronde internationale d'Istanbul. 2-5 novembre 1999* (Paris) 373-80.
_____ 2002. "Antike Strassenverbindungen Kilikiens in der römischen Kaiserzeit," in E. Olshausen and H. Sonnabend (edd) *Stuttgarter Kolloquium zur historischen Geographie des Altertums 7. 1999. Zu Wasser und zu Land. Verkehrswege in der antiken Welt.* (Stuttgart) 452-73.

Sayar, M., Siewert, P. and H. Taeuber 1989. *Inschriften aus Hierapolis-Kastabala. Bericht über eine reise nach Ost-kilikien.* Österreichischen Akademie der Wissenschaften Philosophisch-Historische Klasse Denkschriften 547 (Vienna).

Schneider, A.M. and W. Karnapp 1938. *Die Stadtmauer von Iznik (Nicaea)* (Berlin).

Schreurs, J. and R. Brill 1984. "Iron and sulfur related colors in ancient glasses," *Archaeometry* 26, 199-209.

Seager, R. 1979. *Pompey: A political biography* (Oxford).

Seeck, O. (ed) 1876. *Notitia Dignitatum* (Berlin).

Seton-Williams, M.V. 1954. "Cilician survey," *AnatSt* 4, 121-74.

Shaw, B.D. 1990. "Bandit highlands and lowland peace: The mountains of Isauria-Cilicia," *JESHO* 33, 199-233, 237-70.

Sherwin-White, A.N. 1976. "Rome, Pamphylia and Cilicia," *JRS* 66, 1-14.
_____ 1984. *Roman foreign policy in the East. 168 B.C. to A.D. 1* (Norman).

Sinclair, T.A. 1990. *Eastern Turkey: An architectural and archaeological survey,* vol. 4 (London).

Slane, K. 1990. *Corinth XVIII. II. The Sanctuary of Demeter and Kore. The Roman pottery and lamps* (Princeton).
_____ 1997. "The fine wares," in S. Herbert (ed) *Tel Anafa II, i. The Hellenistic and Roman pottery*, *JRA Supplementary Series* no. 10 (Ann Arbor) 249-406.

Spanu, M. 1999. "Prime note su cisterne e terme della città," in E. Equini Schneider, *Elaiussa Sebaste I: Campagne de scavo 1995-1997* (Rome) 83-114.
_____ 2001. "Teatri ed edifici da spettacolo in Cilicia," in É. Jean, A.M. Dinçol and S. Durugönül (edd)*La Cilicie: Espaces et pouvoirs locaux (2e millénaire av. J.-C. - 4e siècle ap. J.-C.). Actes de la table ronde internationale d'Istanbul. 2-5 novembre 1999* (Paris) 445-77.
_____ 2003. "Roman influence in Cilicia through architecture," *Olba* 8, 1-38.

Stark, F. 1958. *Alexander's path from Caria to Cilicia* (London).

Stern, E.M. 1984. "Antikes Glas in der Südtürkei," *Glastechnische Berichte* 57.5, 132-39.
_____ 1985. "Ancient and Medieval glass from the Necropolis Church of Anemurium," *Annales du 9o congrès internationale d'étude historique du verre, Nancy, 22-28 mai* (Liege) 35-63.
_____ 1989a. "Glass vessels exhibited in the Bölge Museum, Adana," *Belleten* 53, 583-93.
_____ 1989b. "The production of glass vessels in Roman Cilicia," *KölnJb* 22, 121-28.
_____ 1999. "Roman glass blowing in a cultural context," *AJA* 103, 441-84.
_____ 2001. *Roman, Byzantine, and early Medieval glass: 10 B.C.E.-700 C.E. Ernesto Wolf Collection* (Ostfildern-Ruit).

Stillwell, R. (ed) 1938. *Antioch on-the-Orontes II. The excavations. 1933-1936* (Princeton).
_____ 1941. *Antioch on-the-Orontes III. The excavations.*

1937-1939 (Princeton).

SNG 1986. *Sylloge Nummorum Graecorum.* Switzerland I. Levante-Cilicia (Berne).
Sullivan, R.D. 1990. *Near Eastern royalty and Rome. 100-30 B.C.* (Toronto).

Syme, R. 1939. "Observations on the province of Cilicia," in W.M. Calder and J. Keil (edd) *Anatolian studies presented to William Hepburn Buckler* (Manchester) 299-332.
_____ 1995. *Anatolica. Studies in Strabo* (Oxford).

Taeuber, H. 1991."Die syrisch-kilikische Grenze während der Prinzipatszeit," *Tyche* 6, 201-10.

Tırpan, A. 1989. "Roman masonry techniques at the capital of the Commogenian Kingdom," in D.H. French and C.S. Lightfoot (edd), *The Eastern Frontier of the Roman Empire* vol II. British Institute of Archaeology at Ankara, Monograph 11 (BAR International series Ser 553, Oxford) 519-36.

Tobin, J. 1995. "The city in the sand dunes: A survey of a Roman port facility in Cilicia," *AST* 13.2, 151-64.
_____ 1999. "Küçük Burnaz: A Late Roman *Mansio* in Smooth Cilicia," *Olba* 2, 221-26.
_____ 2001. "The Tarcontimotid dynasty in Smooth Cilicia," in É. Jean, A.M. Dinçol and S. Durugönül (edd) *La Cilicie: Espaces et pouvoirs locaux (2e millénaire av. J.-C. - 4e siècle ap. J.-C.). Actes de la table ronde internationale d'Istanbul. 2-5 novembre 1999* (Paris) 381-87.

Tomaschek, W. 1891. "Zur historischen Topographie von Kleinasien im Mittelalter," *Sitzungsberichte der kaiserlichen Akademie der Wissenschaften Philosophisch-Historische Klasse Denkschriften* (Vienna) 124, 57-75.

Tömöry, T. 1977. "Medieval sgraffiato ware from Anemurium in Cilicia," *Belleten* 161, 557-81.

Trémouille, M.-C. 2001. "Kizzuwatna, terre de frontière," in É. Jean, A.M. Dinçol and S. Durugönül (edd) *La Cilicie: Espaces et pouvoirs locaux (2e millénaire av. J.-C. - 4e siècle ap. J.-C.). Actes de la table ronde internationale d'Istanbul. 2-5 novembre 1999* (Paris) 57-78.

van Berchem, D. 1937. *L'annone militaire dans l'empire romain au 3e siècle* (Paris).
_____ 1973. "L'itineraire Antonin et le voyage en orient de Caracalla," *CRAI*, 123-26.

van Deman, E. 1912. "Methods of determining the date of Roman concrete monuments," *AJA* 16, 230-51.

Vann, R.L. 1995. "Survey of ancient harbors in Turkey: The 1993 season at Pompeiopolis," *AST* 5, 29-34.

Verzone, P. 1957. "Città ellenistiche e romane dell'Asia Minore," *Palladio* n. s. 7, 9-25, 54-68.

Vessberg, O. 1952. "Roman glass in Cyprus," *OpArch* 7, 109-65.

Volbach, W.F. 1930. "Byzantische Keramik aus Kilikien," in *MAMA* II. Meriamlik und Korykos, 197-201.

von Saldern, A. 1980. *Ancient and Byzantine glass from Sardis* (Cambridge).

Waagé, F. 1934. "Lamps," in G.W. Elderkin (ed) *Antioch on-the-Orontes I: The excavations of 1932* (Princeton) 58-67.
_____ 1941. "Lamps," in R. Stillwell (ed) *Antioch on-the-Orontes III. The excavations. 1937-1939* (Princeton) 55-82
_____ 1948. *Antioch-on-the-Orontes, Vol IV Part 1: Ceramics and the Islamic coins* (Princeton).

Waelkens, M. 1987. "The adoption of Roman building techniques in the architecture of Asia Minor," in S. Macready and F.H. Thompson (edd) *Roman architecture in the Greek world* (London) 94-105.

Ward-Perkins, J.B. 1947. "The Italian element in Late Roman and Early Medieval architecture," *ProcBritAc* 33, 163-94.
_____ 1955. "The Aqueduct at Aspendos," *BSR* 23, 115-23.
_____ 1958. "Notes on the structure and building methods of early Byzantine architecture," in D. Talbot-Rice (ed) *The Great Palace of the Byzantine Emperors, 2nd Report* (Edinburgh) 52-104.
_____ 1978. "The architecture of Roman Anatolia: The Roman contribution," *The Proceedings of the Xth International Congress of Classical Archaeology. Ankara-Izmir, 23-30/ix/1973* (Ankara) 881-91.
_____ 1981. *Roman imperial architecture* (Harmondsworth).

Weinberg, G.D. 1988. *Excavations at Jalame. Site of a glass factory in Late Roman Palestine* (Columbia).

Weiss, P. 1982. "Ein Altar für Gordian III, die ältern Gordiane und die Severer aus Aigeae (Kilikien)," *Chiron* 12, 190-205.

Wilkinson, J. 1981. *Egeria's travels to the Holy Land* (Jerusalem and Warminster).

Williams, C. 1977. "A Byzantine well-deposit from Anemurium (Rough Cilicia)," *AnatSt* 27, 175-90.
_____ 1985. "The pottery and glass at Alahan," in M. Gough (ed) *Alahan, an early Christian monastery in Southern Turkey* (Toronto) 35-61.
_____ 1989. *Anemurium, the Roman and early Byzantine pottery* (Toronto)

Williams, H. 1981. *Kenchreai. Eastern port of Corinth. Vol V. The lamps* (Leiden).

Yakar, J. 2001. "The socio-economic organization of the rural sector in Kizzuwatna. An archaeological assessment," in É. Jean, A.M. Dinçol and S. Durugönül (edd) *La Cilicie: Espaces et pouvoirs locaux (2e millénaire av. J.-C. - 4e siècle ap. J.-C.). Actes de la table ronde internationale d'Istanbul. 2-5 novembre 1999* (Paris) 37-46.

Yegül, F. 1986. *The Bath-Gymnasium Complex at Sardis* (Cambridge).
_____ 1992. *Baths and bathing in Classical Antiquity* (New York).
_____ 2003. "Cilicia at the crossroads: Transformations of baths and bathing culture in the Roman East," *Olba* 8, 55-72.

Zemer, A. 1978. *Storage jars in ancient sea trade* (Haifa).

Ziegler, R. 1993. "Ären kilikischen Städte und Politik des Pompeius in Südostkleinasien," *Tyche* 8, 203-19.

INDEX

www.ingramcontent.com/pod-product-compliance
Lightning Source LLC
Chambersburg PA
CBHW061003030426
42334CB00033B/3341